Slumlord
MILLIONAIRE

Roland "Spanky" Macher

Slumlord Millionaire

Copyright © 2016 by Roland "Spanky" Macher

All rights reserved. No part of this book may be reproduced or transmitted in any form or by any means without written permission of the author.

978-0-9988090-0-7

Published by:
Slumlord Millionaire LLC

To Roland, Lauren and Patrick with love

Special thanks to JJ, Dallas, Julie and Jeff

"Be more concerned with your
character than your reputation,
because your character
is what you really are,
while your reputation is
merely what others think you are"

John Wooden

Contents

Preface 1
Introduction. 3

Part I Foundation 9
    Chapter 1   Do You Have What It Takes? 13
    Chapter 2   Getting Started. 25
    Chapter 3   Setting Goals 37
    Chapter 4   Risk. 51
    Chapter 5   Establishing a Blueprint and Mission Statement. 59
    Chapter 6   Budget. 75
    Chapter 7   Funding 81
    Chapter 8   Assembling Your Team 87

Part II Market 99
    Chapter 9   Prospecting. 103
    Chapter 10   Finding the Deals. 113
    Chapter 11   Valuation 127
    Chapter 12   Negotiating. 141
    Chapter 13   The Purchase 157
    Chapter 14   Financing the Deal 163
    Chapter 15   Venues for Financing Your Deal. 177

Part III The Property 187
    Chapter 16   Renovation to Hold or to Flip 189
    Chapter 17   The Renovation 195
    Chapter 18   Managing Projects 211
    Chapter 19   Landlording 223
    Chapter 20   Marketing Your House, Either for Flipping or Renting . .231
    Chapter 21   Leasing 255
    Chapter 22   Land Trusts 271
    Chapter 23   Insurance 275
    Chapter 24   Recordkeeping 277

Part IV Evaluation 279

Part V The Emotion 289

Part VI Four Case Studies. 307

    Glossary 317

    Appendices. 333

Preface

I AM ABOUT TO CHANGE YOUR LIFE FOREVER. After you read this book you will have the tools and the knowledge to fulfill your dreams of entering the real-estate business. It will be up to you to buy your properties right, to renovate them properly, and then, if you elect, to hold them and manage them properly.

Be careful of knowing just a little too much; that type of information can be dangerous, and it could be your downfall. Every bit of knowledge that you gain from this book and others will be part of the process of building your portfolio.

I sure don't have all the answers, probably only some of them. I will provide you a guideline, direction, a blueprint that will enable you to move positively and carefully toward success. Nothing is better than good judgment, doing your due diligence, and just being smart about what you want to do for yourself. Trust yourself and your instincts, and you will be fine.

There are some advantages to going out on your own and starting your own portfolio, the first of which is that it gives you independence and freedom. You are building equity and your own personal wealth. You won't be renting anymore: you are working towards fulfilling your plan to reach and be a part of the American Dream.

You are about to enter a new phase of your career, and it is going to be great. Let's face it: you probably are not doing this for fun. You want to make a profit, you want to enrich yourself and maybe become a millionaire. Isn't that your goal by starting this new endeavor?

Take seriously the decisions that you make today in building your blueprint. You have yourself and your family to think about. This is not a gift; it is not easy, nor is it roll-the-dice and winner-take-all. We will give you the tools to succeed, but you must make it happen.

Introduction

MANY PEOPLE ARE JUST AS HAPPY as they can be driving a cab: working for someone else, satisfied with the day-to-day responsibility of that job, and going home and forgetting about its pressures. You know, that's great and it works. There are those, on the other hand, who don't want to drive the cab but own their own car. This brings an entirely new level of responsibility, but it is the basis of the American Dream: to work for yourself and to have an income that is commensurate with your success, which really could be unlimited. Many people have made a lot of money with their entrepreneurial idea. Facebook is a good example; Mark Zuckerberg realized his dream with a pretty cool idea.

No one said it was easy to own your own car, but think of the independence you felt when you bought your first car. Mine was a 1967 blue Volkswagen bug. I paid twelve hundred dollars for it in 1972, and what a car it was. I drove it all during college until I opened up Spanky's, my first restaurant, and bought a van. I have savored that independence ever since, and I have never been satisfied to work for the man. This is the particular ethic that leads to success in a small business like income property. It begins as a dream, something in your mind that you think of often, and it becomes something you spend a good part of your life building and building, learning, doing what is necessary to live that dream.

Zero to Millions in Three to Five Years

I don't like these claims. Don't confuse them with hard work, proper planning, and a solid business plan. Think about it for a moment: If this were true; if it were that easy, why isn't everyone in the field; why are there not so many millionaires? Because it is hard, and get-rich-quick is a scheme to heighten your unrealistic expectations. It is hard; you have to use caution to see your blueprint through; you need to run your investments as a business. I will show you how to do this with an air of caution and a safety net to provide good, steady growth to success.

I tried a get-rich-quick scheme once. A friend of mine was buying condos in Vegas. This was a Turnberry project that had just moved into Vegas during the early 2000s, before the bubble. Property and deals were hot. This was at the beginning when resort areas were selling high-end condos, many of them in a presale form. My friend, I, and some other friends along with us then purchased two places preconstruction.

They sold out; he sold the contract on one unit which paid the deposit on the other unit, plus extra. My eyes were wide open when he shared this with me. I thought I would be a millionaire in three years. I could do this. Phase Two came about in this Turnberry project; there were only a few places left for sale. So sure, I plopped down $50,000 and did a presale condo. Six months later we were set to close at about the same time the bubble burst. The value of the property dropped 20%. They were selling for less than my contract.

What a mistake—but truly who knew? There is no crystal ball here giving you all the answers. The bottom line to this get-rich-quick scheme was simple: we could not read the market trends and the economy. There was no cash reserve to sustain the property through the bubble. Las Vegas was one of the

INTRODUCTION

hardest hit areas in the country. You do have to be careful in your real-estate investments. Remember to follow your plan and try not to deviate from it.

A lot of people have the misconception that you can get rich quick in real estate. There are a lot of people who have written books, given lectures, and advised people that it is possible. I have not seen that to date. Nothing replaces honesty, integrity, and hard work in any field or any investment. You have to work hard; that is the key ingredient. You can make money in real estate, and if done wisely and with a plan, with a purposeful mission statement, you can make a lot of money. You can set yourself up for life. Many people do, but even more try and fail.

The purpose of this book is to provide a road map of success, a plan, which may take you in a different direction. Once you decide to move forward, I will lay out the tools to your success.

> The purpose of this book is to provide a road map of success, a plan, which may take you in a different direction. Once you decide to move forward, I will lay out the tools to your success.

In today's uncertain economy, the real-estate market has made investors rich and made some broke. I will discuss these thoughts and try to give you the guidance to be successful. Not since the depression has the housing market been so bad. Over the last 15 years homeowners and investors invested in newer, bigger homes. They speculated and then they over-speculated. Some saw the bubble coming; many did not. I invested heavily on the trend in various aspects of real estate. I was seeking a big payoff and saw a big opportunity. I worked hard on the plan but did not have liquid depth, which you need for sustainability. It is simply not true that all real estate will necessarily increase in value, that everything is a good deal, that you cannot lose.

I like the low-end properties—the true rehabs. In this market they are very difficult to sell through conventional means. There are truly some creative ways to sell these properties; however you are usually dealing with a different clientele with less disposable money and a credit score that may prevent you from borrowing money. A scrupulous investor can make a greater return on these types of properties than the other route of merely flipping. You take a greater risk and usually have a lower initial investment and have to wait for your return.

Remember if you have enough of these types of properties you can create a greater, more consistent cash flow over a longer period of time. And who doesn't want that? With greater assets and lower liabilities you can go to banks or other lenders for larger loans for larger projects. Remember, it's wise to take baby steps; this is not a get-rich-quick scheme. It's long term.

For years on end when I got started I made small deposits and had small closing costs and would borrow the money needed to purchase my real-estate investments. I stair-stepped the mortgages—none over 10 years. It hurt the cash flow, but truly I did not want to pay on a 30-year mortgage. The money I saved by not paying all that interest was college for the kids and retirement for me. What a great plan; it provided both cash for the children and long-term needs for myself.

Later on after a few crises I decided no more mortgages, that I was going to be a bottom feeder and pay cash for everything, even repairs. This past year I

There are a lot of real-estate enthusiasts that will make you believe that making millions with no money in real estate is as easy as 1-2-3. It is not. Beware of those infomercials, books, and reality shows that want you to believe that anyone can do it and it is easy. I want to stress that it does take hard work and a good plan—a little cash will also help. Just don't listen to the get-rich schemes that may lure you into buying a video, a book, or something that is not real. I will share with you

INTRODUCTION

purchased a great many properties. I had too many projects and overspent my cash flow. This is easy to do. It's the old problem of robbing Peter to pay Paul. It does work for a short time but you do have to pay Peter back. It usually is easier since you may have more properties to pay from.

I have been from rags to riches several times and have done it different ways. In the past it was a hobby and always a fulfilling passion. Now I am doing it for what I hope is the last time and have secured it by putting it in an LLC owned and operated by my children. I just need enough to get by for retirement but have amassed a fortune for them. With the stock market so volatile and our economy in gloom, the dollar becoming worthless, China on the verge of bubbling or taking over in world financial domination, my children will have lots of paid-off property for security. All they have to do is maintain and manage them. They will all be taken care of. In 20 years all the property will be worth the bank.

But as you know even if you own the car, it does not mean that you know how to drive it. To learn how to drive this car, to achieve this financial security, read on.

---

the facts, stories, and the how-to take yourself from rags to riches. It is a conservative approach with information that you can digest. Something you can hang your hat on to be successful. I don't have all the answers, but I do have a lot of them. Certainly there are many different ways to get from point A to point B. I know from experience what has worked for me, and my goal is to present a practical approach to real-estate success. How you execute your plan is important. Do it legally; be courteous and professional at all times.

PART 1

Foundation

YOU HATE YOUR JOB. You're working late into the evenings, weekends, all the time. You are starting to feel distant from your family, and now it is taking a toll on your health. You have a choice: do you want the fame and the fortune, and a coffin; or do you want to make some sacrifices and work for yourself, along with your health and peace of mind? You must decide. Maybe today is the day you have the courage to say, "Enough is enough. I quit. I am done; I want to go home." You can make that decision to change. It's always best if you have the support of your loved ones.

Step outside the box and take a look at where you are and where you are going. The day you change your direction could very well be the first day of the rest of your life. Nothing will get better unless you decide that it's going to get better.

Your destiny is in your own hands. You can complain all you want, and you may find an audience. Your spouse, your parents or children, or even your boss may have suggestions for you. It's up to you to filter their comments and suggestions, good and bad, and use whichever ones work for you to become successful. They may have a suggestion that can turn you around.

You control your destiny. No one has the ability to think for you. Your thoughts, your decisions, are all yours. You may be influenced, maybe persuaded, coerced, but ultimately you decide what direction you will take. How many decisions have I made that were wrong, that I knew were wrong but made anyway. There was the decision to expand the restaurants to be a powerhouse, to be able to make enough money to meet all the business and personal obligations. Sounded easy enough, sure. The roll-the-dice, winner-take-all method just did not work. I wanted it to, but it did not, and there were consequences that I had to accept. Sure I had to take responsibility. I could have said *Stop* or *No*; I should have said them more often. Being conservative is not a bad way to go sometimes. I have not always taken risks. Now is time to step back, look at the big picture, and be a little more conservative.

George Washington Carver once wrote, "Ninety-nine percent of all failures come from people who have a habit of making excuses." There are no more excuses; take control of your life and your destiny. I have made a lot of excuses in my life, but I have taken full responsibility for what I have done. And this is the bottom line: take responsibility for your actions and their consequences.

"Ninety-nine percent of all failures come from people who have a habit of making excuses."

GEORGE WASHINGTON CARVER

We strive for happiness, which becomes the force behind the pressure to succeed; however I am not convinced that we have a scale or a ruler that measures happiness. How many miserable people have you met in your life? They just don't seem to be happy; even if it hit them right in their nose, they wouldn't be happy. Some people are able to understand happiness and get everything they can get out of life every day. These are the truly happy, because they are truly grateful for all they have. When does excess take over and we lose all understanding of what happiness is and what it can do for us as persons?

All the money in the world cannot buy you happiness. Bear this in mind as you work towards your new career. Don't have a take-no-prisoner philosophy.

Does it make you happy? Really? You must find balance in your life, so you can reach optimal happiness.

It is important to have family and friends, to be connected to your loved ones. In all our roads to success we will all take different paths. We will all encounter speed bumps that we will have to endure to succeed. Some of them may even hurt us. It is important no matter what we have to endure, what struggles we may have, that we take full responsibility for our actions. You become the driver of your own success or failure.

Ultimately you are the one responsible for your actions; no one else can be. At any time I could have left the situation that I was in early on: I had little ownership, felt tied down with no escape, and was suffering abuse. Even still, I could have made other choices. Good or bad, I elected to stay where I was and make the best of it, to build yet another empire. Beware the ego as an impediment to change! It has a way of getting involved in the decisions that we make. You think the decision that you are making is a good decision. It may be at the time, but in the long run it just may not. You took a chance and it was wrong; responsibility comes with the territory.

Many people including myself want to blame others for the mistakes, the errors of judgment for unhappiness. It's so much better to take full responsibility and then make the necessary changes. You will feel better when it is over, and you can move on. It's easy to blame others for something, anything. It does not work that way. It's up to you to steer your course.

CHAPTER 1

Do You Have What It Takes?

Do you have what it takes to be a success in business? A lot of people have the dream but are never able to fulfill it. It takes a person with an intense level of ambition to take the leap of faith and start a business, to become an entrepreneur: someone who wants to grow professionally, to become more independent and hopefully see great rewards. It does require a leap of faith that could ultimately bring you greater success.

Are you up for the challenge? You must understand at the outset that it will take time, energy, education, and enthusiasm to make your business successful. It will take hard work. You don't want to start this and then quit. When you are in, you are in; be committed. Even one property is a business. It may be frustrating at times. If you have worked for someone else for a long time, you may not have had many challenges, causing you to have missed opportunities that could have afforded you greater security, maybe greater financial gain. You must ask yourself if you can handle it—the risk, the adventure of the hunt, the art of the deal.

There will be times of adversity; you must have the ability to evaluate the deals, to look at the pros and the cons, and make an intelligent decision. Are you the risk taker that you think you are? Are you able to handle a negative answer or rejection when you banked on being right? That may happen all the time. You want to be right more than you are wrong, but when you are wrong and headed in the wrong direction, are you able to take a left turn, to make a quick decision to turn that negative into a positive? Not everyone can without running the gamut of negative feelings, including self-pity. The challenge is to make your business successful; this is your goal. Remember, Rome was not built overnight. You must have patience; let your investment work for you so that what you have today you can build on tomorrow and in the future.

Self-satisfaction is powerful. If you have no interest in being a rocket scientist, then really why bother? It's best to do something that you will enjoy. Real estate can be done on a part-time basis, maybe only nights and weekends, using your full-time job as your cornerstone of economic stability. It's hard to jump right out there and start a new business. Sometimes given the nature of real estate you can start small and on your own terms, that is, how much money and time you want to put into it. A slow pace allows your time and cash to be budgeted properly. If you are new to the business it will allow you time to learn it. You can make mistakes without worrying about your financial security. You may get really good at it and eventually have to hire people and quit your day job.

One day I asked my friend who was struggling in his job, "How about real estate?" He told me, "Sure, that would be great." He asked me how to get started, and I told him start by mowing yards and cleaning up after people's messes. He told me that he could not do that, that he was worth more than $7.00 an hour. This business is not for ninnies. Start small.

Not everyone is cut out for running a business. It takes a special person with entrepreneurial characteristics: do you have an idea that may work? Commitment? In any new venture it will take

> You want to be right more than you are wrong, but when you are wrong and headed in the wrong direction, are you able to take a left turn, to make a quick decision to turn that negative into a positive?

some courage; you are putting yourself out there. You are making a commitment. If it was easy, everyone would do it, and there wouldn't be room for you to succeed. Although with the economy so bad today, the door is wide open. You will have some ups and downs; not everything is going to work the way you want it to; you may get frustrated. Train yourself to conquer your fears. Be able to put them in prospective. Make a list. Today the list has ten things that bother you—so you do what you can. Tomorrow there is a new list of ten things that you need to do; yesterday's ten items don't seem to be as important today.

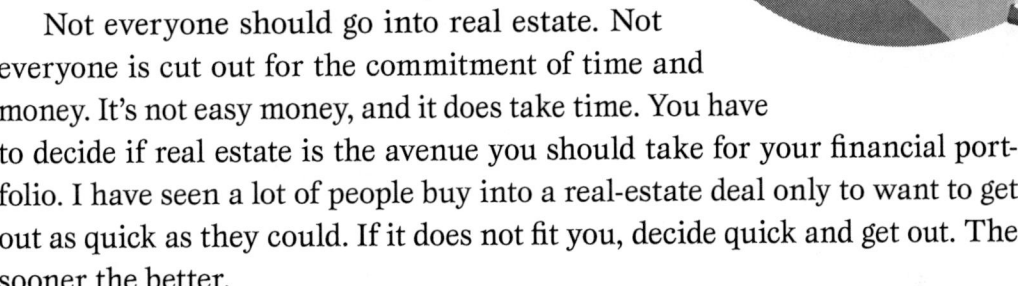

Not everyone should go into real estate. Not everyone is cut out for the commitment of time and money. It's not easy money, and it does take time. You have to decide if real estate is the avenue you should take for your financial portfolio. I have seen a lot of people buy into a real-estate deal only to want to get out as quick as they could. If it does not fit you, decide quick and get out. The sooner the better.

Don't be foolish in any of your predictions or your assumptions that this process is easy and that it can be done overnight. It will take time to make money. You have to be diligent and aggressive in all aspects. Here are some key elements to consider when evaluating whether you should get into real estate:

- ▶ Do you have the time to commit to the work: prospecting, financing, property maintenance, and property management? It does take time like any business opportunity.
- ▶ Can you do this type of work? I have seen people try to follow in my footsteps and fail.
- ▶ You may become a slave to your business; you will get calls at times when you least expect them. Some investors work their property

during the day and do office work or prospecting at night. You will always have those renters calling you on weekends or nights, as well as the annoying repair. Decide how you plan to manage your time here. You can make it easy or hard; you decide.
- Be sure that you have a sincere interest in being a property owner; that a mortgage does not bother you; that you can handle the work, the headaches, and all the ups and downs of owning property. A lot of people don't even like owning their own home, or owning their own home is more than enough and owning any more property would be way too much. If so, it's a good idea to partner with someone who can lead you through your first deal. This is a great way to learn the business.

I have offered many people at different times the opportunity to learn the business by being an apprentice. They shadow you for about a year, participating in all the work, renting, prospecting, maintenance, flipping, to a point where they feel comfortable. They work for a reasonably cheap wage to learn the work. If they succeed, you can help them with their first property to get them started. I have offered this to several folks and to date none have stepped up to do it. It sounds good until they realize that they have to work. There are those who want to do something; they talk about their dreams but do not take that leap of faith to make it happen. It's a job, it's real, and if you work hard you can be successful.

They say the devil is in the details. I try to emphasize the details so that everything else falls into place. What's important here is to figure out what you are strong at and what you are weak at—use your strengths and get help with your weaknesses. Are you determined to be successful? No one will do it for you, and only you will be motivated to get the job done. It's not easy, and as I have said it is not for everyone. You need to have the fortitude to succeed. Again, if it were easy everyone would do it and be successful.

Here are a few things to consider during a self-assessment:

CHAPTER 1: DO YOU HAVE WHAT IT TAKES?

- ▶ Do you spend half the day in bed? Ten or more hours per day is way too much.
- ▶ Can you start on time, keeping a schedule or routine that people can count on?
- ▶ Do you waste a lot of time doing nothing? How about watching TV or playing video games? Are you consumed with these activities?
- ▶ Do you take care of your health and allow time to keep yourself in good shape? If you are sickly or don't take care of yourself, you won't last long. It is important to have a balance: health, family, business, yourself.
- ▶ Be honest with yourself and consider whether you can do this type of work. Are you ready to start? Are you determined to succeed?
- ▶ How well do you interact with people? Can you hire, fire, or direct employees and subcontractors to do what you need done? Not everyone is a good manager. Just because at one time you were an outstanding employee does not automatically make you a good manager. Likewise managers require a skill-set to manage people and situations.
- ▶ Can you handle the daily highs and lows of business? Sure it's great when things are running smoothly, and there are no problems. Usually that does not last forever. There will be times when you are going to have problems and you are going to have to deal with them. In crises, you will be evaluated on how well you were able to solve the problems at hand. Are you a problem solver, and can you do so without having to upset the apple cart? Some people can and some people will just fall apart. The issues related to this are time and money: you must balance them so it all works out. Success is your ultimate goal, by being able to solve each problem that you are confronted with.

As you will hear me say over and over again, what matter are your ability, talent, and interest to undertake this challenge.

Ask yourself a few of these questions:

1. Are you a handyman? Determine what you can do and cannot do. A lot of people say they can paint but really cannot paint. I am an average handyman, but I always try to get a little help when it comes to the detail items (for example, plumbing, electrical, and sheetrock), and I try to do the labor-intense things that no one wants to do. How much you sub out will depend largely on your available cash and expertise on the project—and how quick you want to get it done. The nice thing about being a handyman, the more you do the better you will get; read books, check the internet, learn from others, watch a professional—but just start practicing.

2. Are you organized in all areas? From the office (keeping financial records, preparing specific jobs for your employees, being sure you can return phone calls and keep a calendar) to prospecting and making time for your family. You don't have to be an expert in all the areas, but it is important to have some knowledge so that you don't get swallowed up. Think beyond tomorrow; have a plan—both short term and long term—that falls within your mission statement and one that follows the path of your blueprint.

3. Can you handle success and failure? If you fail or are rejected will you be able to get up and get going again, not allowing rejection to deter you from succeeding? You will make mistakes, and you will be rejected. It's difficult to look at that as a learning experience and to pick up the pieces to move forward in a positive light.

    There will be rejection; try to use it in a positive way—like when you put in offers on properties, your low-ball offers, most of which will get rejected. Can't let it bother you; that's the name of the game. Have grit to accept it and move on to the next best deal. Because the next deal *is* out there; all you have to do is find it. Sooner or later someone will accept your deal.

There are many other ways that you will be rejected and may feel discouraged. That's all part of the process. Like anything else, you have to take the good with the bad. When you get rejected, take it as motivation to re-invent the situation and turn it into a positive. You don't want your associates or family to feel that disappointment; remain steadfast and positive. When you are with your family you may want to emphasize some of these areas:

- You are committed to your spouse and the family's financial security.
- You always want to spend quality time with your family; once the time is gone you cannot get it back. Live with them, get them to endorse your mission and encourage your hard work and success.
- Stay emotionally connected to their needs. Don't put yourself first. Put them first.
- Stay positive, project a positive attitude, Try not to be negative even when you may be. They don't have to know.
- Smile; say thank you; be considerate and passionate.
- Share with your family your short- and long-term goals, so they feel connected to your mission of success.

4. Are you willing to put the time in? If you are a zero-cash player all you have is time. So you will have to do the work yourself. It does take longer and does require a greater commitment.

5. Do you have the cash? Always be aware of what cash you will have available for the project. Do you plan to work at a job full time and use your disposable dollars for this project? That's fine and works;

just keep on track with your budget. If you plan another route—investors or bank loans—that will change the way you manage your project.

6. Do you have the time? Nothing is built overnight, not even Rome. So prepare yourself to make the commitment of time and energy. It truly is a part-time job like punching a time clock at a department store. What sometimes is frustrating is that you may not see the immediate reward. To get some satisfaction, I like doing some show and tell; after a day's or a week's work I can look back and say, "Great job. I accomplished something that I am proud of." If you don't have the time, then be prepared to bring in someone to help you. You will need cash flow to pay the person. I also felt like I needed to see progress and was always in a rush to get things done. Painting the outside of a house on a pretty day is a good example; I would bring in a whole crew. Remember it takes time to set up the equipment, get drinks and lunch, and have cash ready at the end of the day, so you've got to think ahead. What's great is looking back at the day's work.

7. Are you committed to obtaining your goals? As a prospector, I have found many opportunities for flip and investment properties where people run out of money on a half-done property. One I purchased was a huge 4 bedroom, 3 bath house. It took me 9 months to finish it, but it was great. All the hard work was done. Many materials were in the property to work with. The price I paid for the house was close to the value of the materials in the property. But don't be fooled: it cost a great deal more to finish what I had to do. But I did it. The costs that I figured were double what I put in it. The rent originally was to be $600-$700; however today I am renting it for $800 with a good tenant. That's a home run. So stay focused stay committed until the job is done. You cannot rent or sell the property if it is not completed.

So you have to want to do something. You've got to have heart and some common sense. You cannot be afraid of taking on the task. If you are, then you really should not do it. So many people think someone else's job is so easy. Like the Sunday afternoon quarterback who can coach the team better from his couch at home than the coach can.

Do you have the grit to be a flipper? Flipping looks easy: the promise of making a lot of money with no money. You see people doing it all around you, and you wonder, "Hey, if they can do it, why can't I? It can't be that hard." So many people have the misconception that it's easy, but make no mistake: the commitment that it will require of you will be stressful. Whether you have the money to make it happen or not, you need determination, desire, fortitude, drive, skills, and true grit to succeed.

It's best, like any new endeavor, to do a self-assessment of your abilities before you get started. Don't waste your time and energy trying to succeed at something you aren't good at.

If you decide to build your fortune in real estate part time, assuming you will work on this nights and weekends, it will take longer, but that is fine. It can turn into a lucrative hobby. If you plan to do it part time, there are some factors to consider:

- ▶ Do you have the time to put into it? If you work an 8-to-5 day job, you will have nights and weekends. Some people have second and third shift jobs, which allow them to work during the day. Our schedules are all different, but you should be able to develop a part-time flipping schedule around your job. I would say that with each situation there will be good and bad. You just have to find your niche and work it to the best of your ability. You can do it.
- ▶ The seasons of the year may play a role in your scheduling. During daylight saving time you can work late into the evenings—after your day job; plus the weather is usually pretty good for working.
- ▶ A day job will also give you financial income, the stability to get a loan from an institution if you choose to. You won't have to worry about your monthly mortgage or your utilities. That's important.

When the time comes to think about working full time, then you can put together a budget to see if it makes any sense.

Remember that when you flip part time, it truly is part time; with your other responsibilities, your time devoted to it may be limited. You may feel like you just can't get anything done—that once you get started on something, it's time to go back to your full-time job. It may drive you crazy, but stick with it: you will get that project done.

You will know when and if you are ready to do property full time, if that is your goal. It is not for everyone, and over a period of time you will know. If indeed it is in your DNA to move forward, then do so cautiously. Be sure you have your ducks in a row so you can go at it 100%. Here are a few things to consider:

- Don't quit a job where you may be close to any type of retirement benefits.
- Be sure to have some cash reserves both for your personal expenses as well as for the maintenance of the properties.
- When you go into flipping and rehabbing full time you will face different problems and concerns.
- Your style of living may need to change for awhile, as you build up your new business.
- Have dependable people around to help you in a pinch.
- Have a list of subcontractors (like a plumber or electrician) in case you have some specialized work.
- Have deals in the pipeline ready to go as well as some serious sources of financing so you can close on the properties.
- Have your sources of supplies—materials all set up so you can move quickly.
- Know who your advisors are, your experts, and have them ready to go with internal systems in place.
- Develop a stream of potential buyers for properties and a list of the properties they're looking for.
- Know what your first move will be, and go ahead and make it.

I can give you a detailed lesson on managerial skills and there are lots of books and classes you can take advantage of to advance yourself in your weak areas.

It is not easy to develop a portfolio worth quitting your job for, thinking you are going to get a six-figure income. There is more to it than meets the eye. So with no illusions you need to truly evaluate your commitment and exactly what you are willing to put into it, especially in terms of money and time and results. It will help to write your mission statement.

Keep your eyes open; be aware of the commitment you are about to make.

Remember if all you had to do was read a book with no additional effort and make millions, why isn't everyone doing it and succeeding?

Always err on the side of caution and not greed.

Understand yourself and the commitment you can make based on your life. Marriage, girlfriend, job, kids, home—these things and others will play a vital role in your success.

SUCCESS

If you are in a hole in your current career and cannot get out, what are you going to do? How about climbing out and filling up the hole? Put a permanent fix on the problem. If you want change in your life, then you have to decide to change. Sure it takes courage to make that first move; it won't be easy. You've got to recognize your tragic flaw, your shortcomings, and then find your strengths, so you can expand upon them to find greater success. You can do it; you owe it to yourself. Make solid decisions in your life to move it forward in a positive direction.

You know, if you don't like the bread talk to the baker not the candlestick maker. Find the right person to complain to and be sure that he can solve your complaint. Don't waste your time; instead, seek a long-term resolution to the problem, one that will fit both your short- and long-term goals, one that helps you reach your mission. Take action; don't sit there and wallow in your own misery. There is a solution; just find it and stop complaining.

Don't be a product, a victim of your own environment. If you are unhappy with the direction you are taking, well then change it for the better. Staying the course is not the solution; all you are doing is making yourself more miserable. Why bother? Life is too short; we must find not only success but also happiness, to enjoy all that we are doing day in and day out.

CHAPTER 2

Getting Started

PEOPLE NEED A PLACE TO LIVE; they need shelter, whether it's to rent an apartment or a house or to buy a home; there is a need. All types of people of all walks of life need this shelter, although their needs will all be different, depending on economic and social status. Will they want to live in the rich suburbs or will they live in the city? Over the years I have seen in cities like Chicago people migrating to the suburbs, and then with redevelopment people have been enticed to move back into the cities—a reverse migration. Demand for different housing is based also on need. An empty nester or a retiree won't be interested in buying in a young neighborhood with a cul-de-sac, whereas a young family man is going to want the house in the suburbs with the cul-de-sac. When you decide on your plan and start to purchase properties, then you can market your property for sale or rent. This is a strategy in itself as poorer people tend not to use internet for searching for property to rent or buy.

Whether you are thinking a change in career or a supplemental income, it's best to start small. So you can learn the business and apply the techniques I will teach you. In your mission statement and your business plan, you will identify a time frame for entering the game and ending the game. Most people start working in real estate on a small level—one they can manage easily to learn the business.

The easiest place to start is purchasing your own home. You face the same type of expenses as you will with a rental property, without a rental income: the utilities have to be paid, the mortgage, as well as repairs and maintenance. Once you have made that first step, you are on your way. That is a huge step to make, especially if you have a mortgage and are committing to thirty years of payments. In order to qualify for a loan, you need to make sure you have a reliable, good job with proper income.

Young couples may buy a starter home and later on at some point buy a larger home to accommodate a family. If the income justifies another loan, then they can sometimes keep the first home and use it as a rental property. Others expand by buying a vacation home. In order to buy a home at the beach, you need a nice size income as well as a good credit score. This is the period of time when you may decide that you like real estate and buy other properties to rent out. What begins as a hobby or a secondary source of income may turn into a business of its own.

Buying a vacation home as a second home or an investment property requires a serious commitment, different from the normal home purchase. Investment should not be your main focus when buying a vacation home. There is usually a large cash outlay with monthly expenses and little income. Some people buy in areas that are attractive to renters and rent weeks out during peak season. This requires a higher kind of management and owners tend to use property specialists to help them with this type of unique property management. Sometimes you can rent a property enough times in the summer to cover the mortgage for the year, which is the ideal situation, but if you can't you could have a serious negative cash flow. Also, you are

CHAPTER 2: GETTING STARTED

There are advantages to buying your first home. If it is a stair-stepper home, this is a good potential for rental property in the future. You should be able to cover your mortgage on the house, plus a little extra. If it is a large home, maybe cutting it close to your financial means, it could be a little harder for you to put it in a rental portfolio. This could also make it more difficult to upgrade to a different house. Each circumstance and situation is different because your current income and credit score will weigh heavily. Having your first home gives you the ability to build equity. This equity can be used now to expand your portfolio or as retirement money down the road.

People have said that a home is not an investment. This is not true; a home is an investment in both long term and short term—as long as you do not get caught in a bubble like the one that burst in the late 2000s, where properties were over-the-top in price. A lot of people lost a lot of money on both personal properties and investment properties. You would have needed a lot of money to carry you through that crisis. Many people did not have that kind of money.

very limited in putting in your personal items, so it can be user-friendly for the tenants. There tends to be more chances of damage to the property, which requires someone really to have an eye on the renters. You are still required to have considerable insurance on the property. You pay for utilities, repairs, as well as replacement for items in use at the home. You need to be sure you are getting a respectable price from the rental.

Be sure you pick an area that you don't mind going to, one that you will enjoy for a long time. There are some great tax advantages as well. Consult your accountant or financial advisor with your plan. It's always good to get some advice.

If you have lived in your personal home for a good amount of time and have a good deal of equity, you could sell the home and buy some rental property.

Like other ventures with potential rewards, flipping is easier said than done. It takes knowledge to do it correctly and make a profit. Anyone can buy a home but not everyone can buy a home and fix it up, market the property, and finally organize the sale of the property. If it was that easy everyone would do it and everyone would make money. That's just not the case. It can improve your lifestyle, but each flip will be different and will continue to develop your knowledge and make you better at doing this type of work. This book will provide the insight, knowledge, and technique to be successful.

When you start flipping it is the beginning of your real-estate career. You don't have to be a real-estate agent to be a flipper. You can buy and sell properties as an individual owner. You will have many additional responsibilities, like paying all expenses, finding insurance, collecting income, and handling repairs and maintenance—but don't be intimidated.

Your due diligence is important; that's why I suggest staying in your geographical area to start so you can learn the business, without having also to learn the lay of the land. Once you feel good enough, knowledgeable enough, you can branch out.

> It is important to learn all the techniques of successful flipping. Remember to build relationships on trust, integrity, honesty, and hard work.

It is important to learn all the techniques of successful flipping. Remember to build relationships on trust, integrity, honesty, and hard work. If you say you will do something, then do it. Back it up. If you present a plan for success, then work toward that success. Admit your mistakes and losses. Recognize them as a learning tool to do better on the next project. Remember to network with as many people as you can in an effort to have a steady flow of information. You will always need leads, sources of supplies, and professionals who can help you succeed. Flipping properties is a great way to develop your financial situation. Especially when you have nothing and you start part time and develop into a full-time thriving business.

Read resource books carefully and develop your mission statement with a solid blueprint. Take your time during the process of learning this new trade. Start with an easy house so that if it does not work out, you won't take a beating. Most real-estate fortunes that have been built by beginners are in older, low-down-payment buildings, ones with moderate rents and without a lot of repairs and maintenance. If you don't like it for whatever reason, you can unload the property and move on. It certainly is better than over-committing to a long-term lease on a brick and mortar retail store that you cannot get out of.

Like any new job or experience you can easily become overwhelmed. Best to take on only what you can handle. Start small and work up to the larger projects. Be careful about overextending yourself—it's easy to do. I have done it, and in most cases I was able to catch up. You must catch up; you can't continue to overextend yourself; at some point you need to get your legs under you and give yourself a solid base to move forward again. Developing a forward-thinking business plan is important, so is being able to maneuver that plan as required for success. People tend to take more risks when they are over-confident, but when the confidence is not based on real numbers, we can become overextended. That's a stressful situation to be in and could work against you as a double negative, especially if you don't have a fall-back position. Cash may be the answer, and it just may be the thing that you don't have. So be careful not to be overzealous. There is another deal around the corner; be patient.

Time is money and you want to make the best use of your time. As well as your expertise. Decide when it is time for you to hire help or a subcontractor. There will be a time during your growth that you will want to obtain outside help; just know when. You don't want to spend all your profit on help or contractors especially if you can do some of it yourself. Don't be disappointed to know that the world is full of dishonest people, that

your trust in someone may backfire; that a contractor may take your deposit and never do the work and now cannot be found, or an employee who steals your tools or does such a bad job on a project that it has to be redone. Welcome to the day-to-day grind of entrepreneurship. It's your first day towards success.

Just remember that it takes time to make money; don't think that you are going to make a million dollars overnight. A good investment will yield a nice return. Learn to be patient, and all good things will happen. Start slow and work yourself up to bigger deals. You may go for awhile wondering what next and when, feeling frustrated that it is not going quick enough, and then one day you will be in the zone. Great deals come your way, and your portfolio allows you to borrow what you need to buy the property.

The Move

Some investors will buy a fixer-upper in a neighborhood that they like and move into the property for a couple of years. Then do another after that and follow the same routine. I do not like the moving. I am a nester, personally. This is a good plan only for people who do not mind moving. These people are called nomadic flippers: they live in a property while they renovate it or until they sell it. There are different levels of this type of flipper. Some people will just rehab a bathroom and bedroom and live in the property while they are fixing up the rest of it; others will renovate the entire property and then move in.

It is easier to get a mortgage in these cases since the home will be your primary residence. You are able to maximize all of the tax advantages

CHAPTER 2: GETTING STARTED

The point is that if you can handle only one property per year or maybe two, then you should beware of buying five. Do what you think you can handle. Build a strong base to grow from. Just remember if you come across a good deal it may be tough to pass up, and you will want to take advantage of the deal. I would not pass it up. Even if you have to scale down your lifestyle for a short period in order to make it happen, I would do it. It may put you behind the money eight ball for awhile, but I tell you I would not think twice about it. But I am a little more aggressive than most in buying properties. I want it all today.

Manage your time. Make a schedule that works for you, so your time is not wasted.

> Just remember that it takes time to make money; don't think that you are going to make a million dollars overnight.

---

by doing this. The first couple of years you will be able to depreciate all of the interest. This is primarily all that you will pay. You will not have to live through the remodeling or the construction of this project. Move in when the house is completely done. Remember though, you must pull a building permit to do the work and have it approved. You do not usually have to have code enforcement inspect it since you are moving in the property yourself. But down the road you may, if you decide to turn it into rental property.

Living in the house will inspire you to have it decorated nicely. It will be easier to sell in this condition. This is what a lot of investors do. Give yourself some time to relocate. It may be quick, so you should have a good and reliable plan to begin your next project and be able to see a completion date. A lot of new

continued on page 32

Try to buy your property as low as you can and then sell it for as much as you can. In today's market it is a little different in that we now talk wholesale as being another sales level. A true retail is a rare value, especially since the real-estate bust.

Develop a positive reputation. Do deals fairly. There are enough dishonest investors out there that you do not have to be one of them. Conduct business in a proper way. Cross your t's and dot your i's. Treat others as you want to be treated. There are vampires out there—don't be one of them.

Be sure you run your business ethically, morally, and legally. Be sure you are not too quick to judge others. Be fair to the desperate homeowner whose house you are going to try to buy at the lowest price to "help" them.

---

construction builders do this type of investing for the tax advantages. If you do not feel comfortable moving every couple of years, this is not a good option for you. And there are always other considerations: location, value, schools, towns, crime rate. Each time you move, there is the cost of moving, decorating, landscaping, and your personal time. Be sure you have made enough on the sale to justify the move.

SUCCESS

I have always had many ideas throughout my business life. Some of them have become a reality and some haven't. When I was building the restaurants, I thought outside the box and built some beautiful places. They were great ideas that came to life, which was very satisfying to me for years. Along the way I have had many other ideas that I have played with; some I lived, others lay dormant waiting for the dust to be blown off. Even those are great opportunities waiting for development.

Don't be held back by any fears that you may have; turn them into strengths, and they will provide you with opportunity and growth. Always try to maintain a positive and productive attitude. Negativity just won't get you anywhere; going into a project with a negative attitude will indeed spell failure. With a positive attitude in mind, you can succeed in all that you set out to accomplish.

Never take no for an answer. Be calm, don't panic, and have all your ducks in a row. Having done your due diligence, you are ready to succeed.

Being an entrepreneur is not easy. If it were, everyone would do it and everyone would be successful. Being an entrepreneur will take from you all that you've got. You know your breaking point: take on only what you can handle, and ask for help when you need it.

Don't let your fears get the best of you. If you are not sure, fake it. People don't have to know how you feel even though you may be nervous and not truly comfortable with the task. Sometimes just going for it will net you great results. Be committed to and confident in your task, your idea, your plan. If you want success bad enough, then you will succeed in all that you set out to accomplish. Your fear may actually be helpful in turning negatives into positives. Let it point out to you the most daunting tasks, so you know what to attack at the beginning of each day. If you feel fear, then there are obstacles ahead of you. Channel your fear in this way, and it can become your friend.

Slaying the fire-breathing dragon is much easier if you are prepared and know what you are up against. Dealing with the unexpected is much more difficult and can be a severe detriment to accomplishing your goals.

Out-of-control fear may cripple your motivation and desire to succeed, which is why it is best to put it in perspective and keep it there. There is an old German saying "Fear makes the wolf bigger than he is." How many times have you been confronted with fear and allowed it to overpower you? Master fear; make it work for you.

Those fears may arise from problems, distractions, competition, issues along the road. Much fear can arise from conducting illegal or shady business; always keep your business within the limits of the law. If you are a bank robber and get away with the first few jobs, you will always have a fear of getting caught.

Too many people today have made a living preying on businesses and families. They want money, and they try to get it illegally. Be aware of what many of these people are capable of doing to you and your business. Sure the people that are breaking the law fear that they could get caught—and rightfully so. We encourage those men to conduct their business with integrity.

Be wary of a Ponzi scheme, investment people who dazzle you with some money, convincing you of a wise investment that is very unwise.

Some people may view fear as a symbol or a sign of failure. However, if you want to climb that ladder of success to accomplish and reach your goals, you must turn fear to your advantage.

Overcoming obstacles, coming up with solutions for your fears, and avoiding those speed bumps will strengthen your objectives toward success. No one will do it for you. You must put the effort into your plan to make it work.

I personally have seen and been a part of many successes, enjoying all that it brought to my family and me. But I have also experienced many defeats, losses, some that left me broke. I was never afraid that I couldn't turn a negative situation into a positive. I worked hard to have no fear of failure, no fear of humiliation or defeat. I was driven by the strength to get up the next day and work a little harder and smarter to climb out of the hole I was in.

You must be motivated with ambition and courage, knowing you must not fear but knowing also when you need a ladder to climb out of a hole you're in, and then fill that hole, today, so you never fall into it again.

We all learn by our experiences—some good and some not so good. If we travel down the road that once failed us, we must be fully aware of the pros and cons of that path, so that we won't have any surprises this time around.

Eliminate fear as much as you can in your business, personal, and family life. Think ahead when you do your due diligence, so you can try to anticipate the unexpected. Indeed when something does come up, you will be both physically and emotionally prepared. You cannot be held at fault for being honest and doing your very best. You must continue to take great pride in all your accomplishments in life no matter large or small. You will succeed.

CHAPTER 3

Setting Goals

WHAT IS HUGELY IMPORTANT IS A VISION. Can you see the improvements that need to be made on a flipped house? Can you see where your business needs to be in the next year, in the next five years? Not everyone can see an end product. Here are a few goals to consider setting:

- ▶ Personal wealth. Long- and short-term cash flow equals wealth. If you need to produce a personal income you may have to go big at first. There's not much income in one property per year whether or not you pay cash for it. Everyone's needs will be different; evaluate what you want out of it. Be conservative; don't build a house of cards that may collapse. It is important to plan.
- ▶ Tax difference appreciation. Initially you can get some tax benefits from properties with the depreciation, especially if you are financing the property and the rehab of the project. This can continue through a depreciation schedule on your taxes, five to seven years. There may be a time to sell the property, capture the appreciation of it, and carefully move upward toward a larger project, and then do it again. Best to consult your accountant to set up a financial growth plan. Your accountant will give you good advice.

- ▶ Long-term wealth. For years I purchased property with the idea of having money for my children's education. It was a great plan, and it worked. The property has also provided a savings for retirement as well. You may not get the cash flow out of your properties today if you are looking for long-term growth. Sometimes you can get the best of both worlds; if it comes, great, but don't push it. Work towards it.
- ▶ Homeruns. You will get some homeruns if you work hard and stay in the business long enough. Personally, I worked every deal like I wanted to hit a homerun, sometimes I got a grand slam, sometimes just a single. You got to take it all. But at least when you get that great deal you will have established a blueprint to follow to do it again and again. The first one is the best, and it becomes the model to follow.

At many different times in your life you will set goals, both long-term and short-term goals. The short-term goals are goals that you can reach easily; the long-term goals are a collection of all the short-term goals that you've built up over time: reaching the top of the ladder. Climbing the ladder is always important.

SHORT TERM. The flip is an effective way of making a quick return on your investment. You are in the business of buying and selling, either at retail or wholesale. The more you can do, the more money you will make. When you stop buying, you won't have inventory to sell, and your income will stop. You are in and out, and to continue to make money you have to keep buying; it is never ending. If you are fortunate to get some big deals you may be able to enjoy a nice lifestyle and sit back some. If your margins are low, it may be a different story.

> **LONG TERM.** If you are planning to hold on to your investments for a long time you will have to have a plan. Most people have a portfolio of rental property, and they write off their expenses, including depreciation of the property. You can keep it as long as you want for whatever purpose you want. Some people get tired of the same old thing—non-paying tenants, mowing the yards, the constant repairs and maintenance—and may just decide to sell the property. I have always recommended to a young couple with children to buy investment property as a vehicle to later educate your children. You can hold on to a property for 15-18 years and when your children start college sell a property that may be paid off by then and pay for their college education. What a great way to plan for the future. There are other ways to do it as well; this is only one suggestion.

When you decide to sell, especially to liquidate a portfolio to meet your needs as they come up in your plan, there are many ways to cash out. Here are a few ideas:

- You can sell outright to get all the cash that you can. Remember to consult a tax accountant so you know the tax implications of your capital gain exposure. This may be a good option for you.
- You might sell the property through a lease purchase arrangement.
- Consider selling your property with a contract of deed.
- If the property is paid for, you can sell it and finance it. You become the bank, and payments to you will be deferred over time. Your income is amortized, therein allowing you to take the tax hit over a period of time.

A few reminders about speculation, which is a totally different game of real estate. You must have substantial cash reserves to get you through. Today if I were to buy raw land again, I would want to pay cash for it or borrow so little for it that the payments would be small, with little to no risk. Do not start with raw land as part of your portfolio. Maybe work up to it. Remember:

- You do not have an income on raw land.
- You will have expenses. There is usually some maintenance and always taxes.
- It can go down in value.
- It also tends to be slow to appreciate in value, unless you can pre-sell some parts of it—usually a corner or some portion of your road frontage.

You can offset some of the pit falls of raw land:

- renting to seasonal hunters;
- holding flea markets or seasonal retail sales;
- offering it for camping, parking areas, or recreation.

None of these will really pay dividends to you today; all it will do is sustain your investment. No-debt inventory is expensive to maintain. Be careful.

In this particular market, your strategies will change due to the short and long term. In the short term investors are buying foreclosures. These folks are following properties and usually buying on the courthouse steps. It used to be that this type of flipper could sell these properties retail. Not today; today they have had to carve out a wholesale niche. Remember that 80% of the people in today's market cannot borrow money; the credit crunch and debt crisis have made it very difficult. So the available buyers' market comprises the remaining 20%—usually folks with a good income and a good to excellent credit score. You are not buying lower-end homes at foreclosure to flip; you need to buy homes that are in desirable areas. These are important factors in your marketing strategy.

When you prepare your business plan, your blueprint, you will put together many ideas and thoughts to give you direction as you develop your real-estate fortune. It is important to identify your mission and plan appropriately. Many investors will use real estate as a main source of income, some as a long-term investment and some as a part-time job to supplement their income.

It is important, therefore, to identify your goals and, through your business plan, to outline how you will achieve those goals. I have always believed that no idea should be discredited. Put all of your ideas down on paper so you can analyze what is best for you. Here are some key considerations:

1. What kind of property do you want to invest in? Will it be high-, medium-, or low-end properties? Land, condos, lake property? Vacation rentals, time-share condos?

2. Figure out the money issue. How much will you invest? How much can you obtain? Where will the money come from?

3. What will be your commitment to this new endeavor? This is an important question.

4. Where do you want to invest? What will be your strategy? You can invest in neighborhoods, towns, states, areas. This will be key to your business plan. As well as the value of properties that you can afford. Personally I buy rundown slum houses in depressed neighborhoods in the city. I pay cash for them as well and try to keep the rehab costs at a minimum. This fits my blueprint.

5. Credit: This is an important element, which you have to look at if you plan to borrow money to build your portfolio. There is an entire process to improve your credit. You may have to explore this at some point.

6. Time management. You will have constraints on your time. Think about what you have time for and what you do not. Allow for flexibility of time so you can do it right.

7   Expertise is something we don't talk enough about. It is important. What can you do? Trade skills will help you financially; however you will have greater time constraints. If you have to hire people to work—labor or skilled trades—then that's going to require more cash out of your project. In putting together your plan, it is important to put a value on these items.

8   Time may or may not be on your side. If for instance you borrow money and are making payments on a loan, you should move the project along quickly. The faster you get it done, the quicker you can rent it and start paying your obligations. However, if you pay cash for a property and have time for renovation since you are not strapped to meet any loan obligations, you may be able to drag out this project. This is a great way to go if you are working this property part time, have a full-time job, and are under little pressure. I prefer this method for the novice who is just getting started.

9   Set your sights on what you want to do. Put your marketing plan in place. Set something up as a marketing vehicle that will bring leads to you continually, so that you can practice your prospecting techniques. More on this later.

10 Set up your vehicle of success: how you plan to operate. No matter how you plan to move forward, setting up your business legally is vital. Putting together an accounting system so that you can track income and expenses. You will need this for tax purposes. But also this is a way to calculate your success. The more you make in profit, the higher the grade; you want an A. It is necessary to track your results; use one of the many different computer programs that are available.

11 Start today rather than tomorrow. I always have a project in the "hopper" as I am working on one. That way I stay ahead of the wave.

12 Expand your holdings. Plan your next move. You will have setbacks: delinquent tenants, unforeseen expenses. Plan for the unexpected. Don't get upset—just do your best with it, so you will succeed.

13 Evaluation. This process is never ending. You will find yourself in a constant evaluation of your success—from the remodeling of a property and the completion of a project to reviewing your financial holdings. When you need to take a new direction, don't be afraid to do so.

14 Your niche. This is part of your blueprint of success. Decide early, when you are developing your mission statement, what's going to work for you. What you want to do initially may not be what you end up doing. In time you will develop a niche. This niche will evolve around your strategy. What do you feel comfortable doing? What do you like? I like the low-end properties since most people don't like them. Because they can be costly, they take a certain strategy to succeed in. It is a niche market. Flipping is hard in areas other than wholesale, and being a landlord can be frustrating. You will become an expert in your area.

What Type of Property do You Want to Get Into?

This is all part of your business strategy, your mission statement. As discussed, there will be many variables that direct you to make the ultimate decision. Let's look at a few:

Single-Family Homes

Single-family houses are somewhat easier to manage. Tenants put utilities in their names; they mow their yards and are supposed to take care of basic maintenance, whereas in multiunits the owner is generally responsible for all these items. There aren't many disadvantages to buying single-family homes, but the advantages are many.

- Tend to be easier to purchase and easier to find. Often you can get them with no cash down.
- Lower repair and maintenance costs if you write the lease properly.
- Fewer tenant issues. Ideal if you can get your tenant to take on a degree of ownership in the property.
- All utilities are paid by the tenant, so if there are leaky toilets you won't get surprised with a huge bill.
- Taxes will be proportionate to the building value, which tends to be lower.
- Renovation costs can be considerably less.
- You lease to one person instead of many different people.

- Your net return is usually equal to or better than multiunit per capita investment. Remember the bottom line.
- Your ability to refinance or take out a second mortgage to develop a portfolio is much better.
- Single-family homes are the stepping stones to a diverse portfolio.

New Single-Family Houses, New Constructions, Foreclosures, Usually Middle to Upper End.

These types of properties are for those who want lower maintenance costs and fewer renovation costs. You can usually flip these types of properties easier. You may want to flip the property at a wholesale price and never have to deal with tenants. Many investors make a good living doing this. These types of investors generally refuse to have tenants and boast that they are not landlords; however, with nicer properties you will generally get a better tenant, one that pays quicker than someone who is poorer.

You will have lower rehab or building costs on a newer property, which is why you paid more for the property initially. However the tenant or buyer will want something nicer as well; you may not be able to get by with the old carpet or poor paint job. On a rehab condemned property your building costs will be higher; however your purchase cost will be lower. Be sure that you work the formula to ensure the right returns. Then try not to deviate from the formula.

You may experience lower taxes on a rehab property especially if your area qualifies for any tax incentives, rebates, tax freezes—any type of programs that may be available in your area. Medium priced single family homes are an attractive way to go.

Old Single-Family Houses.

These are what I specialize in, usually found in a part of town that may be undesirable, one that most investors won't go into. But use it as an opportunity. There are some great deals in these neighborhoods, but they are not without some pitfalls. These older homes are a little harder to flip because most potential buyers suffer from bad credit or few financial resources.

Land contracts or rent-to-own opportunities are a way a lower-income person can get into one of these old single-family homes. They easily can put down a down payment especially around tax time or they can just pay a little more each month on what you may consider a rent or mortgage payment. Either way this is a good route to go when you are an owner of one of these properties. Maybe not so good if you are a buyer. You must be careful.

The renovation costs tend to be higher on an old single-family home. Do your homework on these types of properties and be sure you have accurate numbers to protect yourself. Use the investment formula that will provide you a benchmark of how much you should allow yourself to spend.

Honestly, if you rent one of these houses you will be amazed how much rent you may be able to get. If you watch what you spend on the renovation you could come out with a nice cash flow. In building your portfolio you will also be able to leverage the equity to borrow more money to buy other properties. Especially if you are in a position to use existing cash or sweat equity for the renovation or purchase of these properties. Personally I like this approach; however there are investors that prefer to use other people's money to build their portfolio.

Target Market for Single-Family Homes both Older and New Homes.

Different types of properties showing different values, locations, as well as price will attract different people all with different circumstances. You just have to find the round peg for the round hole. When you are thinking of your market then you target the folks you want; young married people, hippies and singles, empty nesters and retired people, single parents—each of these groups looks for different attributes in a dwelling.

When you are dealing with rental property there are some key issues that stand out for you to consider:

- Rental properties are generally safe investments.
- It takes less time to manage single-family houses or apartments.
- You can generate a positive cash flow. If the property is financed, remember you are paying off a mortgage every month you make a monthly payment. So you truly are building up some equity.
- There are more deals today than ever on zero down investments. Just remember the less you put down usually the smaller the positive cash flow. If you are able to put some money down, your equity will grow quicker. Your payments will be lower, cash flow better. But it does tie up funds for other projects.

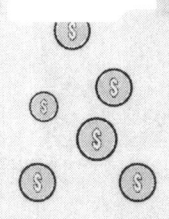

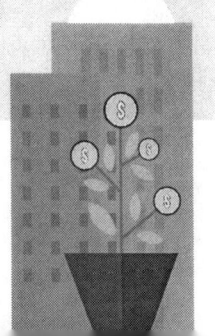

Remember to be patient; your portfolio will change over the years as you add properties and do more deals, whether they are flips or rentals. Keep your eyes open for bigger and better opportunities.

New Multiple Family Buildings

These are a little harder in today's economy, since new home builders in 2012 took a beating and predictions are that it will not get better for a few years to come. Your exposure will be greater with new multifamily dwellings. You may with good credit get a zero-based loan for the purchase and closing costs of a property. You would need to obtain a high appraisal which is harder to do today than it was years ago.

Credit restrictions today have made the field narrower for people to purchase new properties on credit. They just don't have the credit to do so. The banks have made it very difficult to do so. However, if you have good credit you may have an open field of opportunity to get some of these properties.

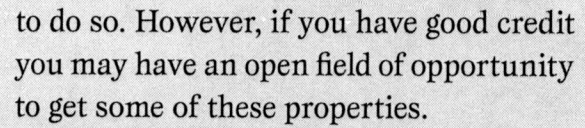

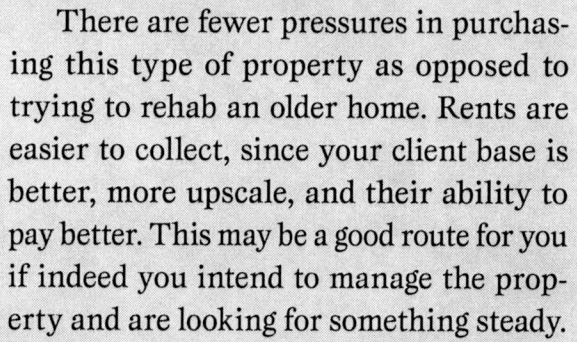

There are fewer pressures in purchasing this type of property as opposed to trying to rehab an older home. Rents are easier to collect, since your client base is better, more upscale, and their ability to pay better. This may be a good route for you if indeed you intend to manage the property and are looking for something steady.

CHAPTER 3: SETTING GOALS

There are different tax advantages and disadvantages to both schools of thought. Always look into what works for your personal situation and work towards a routine and result that will minimize your tax liability. I suggest you work closely with a tax accountant who has some experience in this area.

New multifamily properties will improve your overall portfolio. It should provide greater flexibility to borrow additional funds to grow into other projects. It may also improve your personal income as well.

The amount of time required to work may be less. There is no doubt that it is easier to do new properties than older properties. You won't be faced with the nagging repairs that you get with older properties. This is nice. But don't believe for a minute that you will get rich while you sleep. You will build up equity and value; like a lot of good things it will take time to mature.

SUCCESS

Matthew 16:26: What good is it to gain the whole world but lose your soul?

What a powerful statement. I feel that after all these years of coming in second, I have been constant and faithful to God. I have been put in situations that I did not like and all along, even though I truly knew I needed to be in a different place, the ties to my mother pulled me in the wrong direction; I could never bring myself to change because I knew she would feel betrayed or disappointed. I wasn't free. I struggled for years to blossom like a beautiful flower in an urban garden, but I never sold my soul during those years of heartache and grief.

CHAPTER 4

Risk

REAL ESTATE IS NOT FOR EVERYONE; like with any business venture, you have to fit the industry. You will know relatively quickly—nothing ventured, nothing gained. So if you have an inkling to try, then jump in. Start small and see how you do. You may enjoy the freedom to develop professionally and personally. But with the added responsibility, you really should have some idea of what you are getting into. If you are successful, which you should be, you will enjoy the success.

There is always a risk, and it's almost always tied to market conditions. It may not be as risky as the stock market, but it does have its level of volatility. As we saw in the late 2000s people were over leveraged. They paid too much for property and got caught; property values dropped over 50% in some areas, and people did lose a great deal of money. While others capitalizing on a bad market got into it at a discount rate. When the market returns—and at some point it will return—they will be in great shape. However you have to have staying power, cash reserves to hold on. That's when you consider the rental business. With so many foreclosures, people had to explore other options, like renting. If you were in the rental business, it was a good opportunity for you to make some money.

One of the problems with real estate is that there is little liquidity. You do get a monthly cash flow, but it's not like you can sell your investment tomorrow or today for instant cash to take care of an emergency. You must be cautious in your real-estate investments not to overextend yourself. You can become land rich and cash poor.

Protect your financial portfolio:

- Do not cosign notes for other people whether they are friends or relatives.
- If you are single manage your money wisely. If you are married, stay married. Be sure to have an open line of communication with your spouse.
- Do not ask for credit anywhere; you do not need any more credit cards or loans. Every time someone checks for credit it is a snag on your score; keep it clean.
- Avoid buying big ticket items like cars, electronics, etc.
- Pay your bills quickly, especially the revolving credit card balances.
- Do not move large amounts of money into your accounts at one time.
- Be able to handle the payment. You have to put the payment into your portfolio to see if it works for your cash flow.

Beware the domino effect: you build a nice portfolio on mortgaged, highly leveraged properties; maybe they are properties that you want to flip but no one is buying, or a portfolio on rental units; either way you have a serious mortgage payment. All it takes is one major problem: a series of evictions, non-paying tenants, a death, a repair or maintenance issue that exceeds your present cash flow—and you could lose it all. You don't have cash reserves, nothing to liquidate, and before you know it you are behind on the bills, mortgages, and lines of credit. It is essential to have a reserve, have some properties that are paid off in full, so you can use that rent money for expenses or reserve.

A good friend of mine invested in Myrtle Beach with a lot of low-end rental property—an area that is highly transitional and volatile. He was using his real-estate friend to help him manage the property. He had been making the mortgage and HOA payments from his regular job. He lost a few contracts in that business, and before he knew it he had to work extra just to keep up. Did I mention that he just had a baby and his wife was leaving him? Now that sounds like a domino effect disaster. He is struggling hard, and it is not easy: he is hanging on for dear life. Nothing is selling, and he even had to lower his rental rates.

It sounds like a house of cards may just have fallen. It hasn't fallen, but it could so easily. You have to have a solid foundation; go a little slower if you have to, just to be sure you don't have a budding nightmare on your hands—you don't want that. Especially since you worked so hard to build what you have.

Don't become greedy. You don't have to be the big man on campus. Who really needs bragging rights? It's not worth it to stick your neck out on the chopping block. Err on the side of caution: make reasonable, sound business decisions that will build a solid portfolio, not one that is all smoke and mirrors that may in the long run cost you a lot of money and reputation.

Like any business that you get into, investment property is not easy: there are ups and downs, which you have to learn to deal with. It's the unexpected that may surprise you. Can you operate on your feet so to speak? Have a fall-back position ready at hand? If you make a mistake—and you will—can you critically analyze the mistake, take corrective action, and move forward? You must be able to do that.

> If you make a mistake, you must be able to critically analyze the mistake, take corrective action, and move forward.

Many people don't realize how much risk there is in property management. There is risk, and you need to know that prior to just jumping into the game. Initially if you start with some low or medium residential properties, your risk will be less than if you are doing a large commercial building or land speculation. Start at a level that you can afford with little risk, work your way up to larger deals. If you are conservative and cautious, you may come out better in the long run.

Nothing worth having is not worth working for. You work hard, play by the rules, treat people fairly, and you would like to have a reward of some kind. What you don't want is someone to mismanage your business or take your money. Boy, have I had a time of this. That's why you want to put in the checks and balances that will make your business successful but really keep your people honest and therefore make sure that what you earned will be yours. What's yours is yours, of course, but what's theirs is theirs. Don't give them the temptation to steal. If they work, then they should be compensated, and truly when you have good people you want to do all that you can to take care of them. Respect them, teach them, give them an opportunity to grow and be successful.

Having gone through the restaurant business, I have learned that whenever you deal with cash you give someone a great opportunity to take what is not theirs. In the rental business a lot of your tenants will see the opportunity to take money. Embezzlement. It sounds harsh, but you see people doing it all the time. Just pick up your local paper. You may wonder where your rent money is. Your business will be successful when your people are making deposits.

You need a good recordkeeping system. You want to have the checks and balances in place so person A is not the only one checking on what they have done. You want Person B checking Person A, and Person C checking on A and B.

You need a good recordkeeping system.

Many people who do take money will start small and then take more as they gain confidence. After awhile, when they have become accustomed to taking money and improving their false lifestyle, they will become more brazen in their thefts and flashy with what they are doing with their money—your money. There are signs that you should look for in the work place when you think something like this is happening.

I remember the story when an IRS person was stopped at a light and up pulls a nice car, a Ferrari, and the IRS agent profiled this person, thinking to himself heck the way that man looks, with his dress and general appearance he cannot afford a car like that. So the IRS man wrote down the license plate number and did some research. You know after two years of a thorough investigation maybe a little intimidation and eventual humiliation the man in the Ferrari had to plea out a tax evasion charge and did 18 months in the Federal Prison in Beckley, West Virginia. Go figure.

The people that become guilty of embezzlement usually start to live beyond their means; they like the lavish lifestyles and they like to flaunt it. Over time it becomes more and more obvious of what they are doing. Many start to think that it is not stealing but owed to them by the company for the extra work they are putting in and how great of an employee they are.

You as the manager or the owner must try always to protect yourself and your company's reputation, your assets, your money, your tenants' interests, and the future of the good hard-working employees and owners.

When I went to prison for 22 months, my friend Ed was appointed to manage the properties that were in my children's name, maybe 25 of them. There were a few mortgages on them. It should have been easy. With no experience and knowledge of the real-estate business, he thought it would be a piece of cake to do and that he did not have to listen to anyone for advice or guidance. Well in only four months every house was boarded up for negligence by the city. No one was paying rent, all the stoves and refrigerators where stolen from the houses. All the heating systems were taken out; the grass was unmown, the trash piled up. It was a mess. He was interested in driving around town being a big shot, thinking he was in charge. Then he blamed me for the failures. When I got home my life was upside down: no tools, no vehicle, no credit cards (he did not pay them), and only 3 cents in two checking accounts—well, at least I had something to work with. Until two weeks later, when I got a notice from the bank that the accounts were closed and Ed had taken the 3 cents. Ha, what a day that was.

The point is, be careful whom you trust; be sure you manage everyone; don't assume a person knows what he is doing; teach and guide the people working for you, and again have a checks and balance system in place so you can be successful.

SUCCESS

Is now your time? Have you reached your pinnacle of success? When will it come? Many large companies over the years have failed, although they have been led by very smart and successful people—people who in their turn had to fail once or twice before they made a success out of themselves.

Milton Hershey was one great entrepreneur and philanthropist who failed a couple of times with his business. One included a candy store in Philadelphia, for which he borrowed and borrowed money from his rich aunt and some friends. It was not until later in his young life that he reinvented himself and struck gold. It could happen to you at a young age or when you are older.

Colonel Saunders of Kentucky Fried Chicken did not start his now successful franchise of chicken restaurants until he was in his early 60s. He never gave up, hoping that just around the corner was his success story. And it was. How many times did he have to reinvent himself before he hit it big?

Never give up working toward your dream.

Sometimes I think of people like my friend Ed, who at 18 joined the Marines and retired by 40. He then became a supervisor for the post office and after fifteen years of service with some crossover time and good timing, he retired again. Sure, the post office was having some financial problems and they were doing a major downsize, but what a deal for him. So now with passions for property management, music, restaurants, and clubs, he has been looking to reinvent himself again. He is an inspiration, having had two very successful careers and now taking some time to see what he really wants to do. To reinvent yourself, you generally draw on all your life experiences and try to assess what you liked and didn't like. It's not always easy; ask your spouse or trusted friend for advice.

The beauty of it all is that, if you're getting into income property as a second or third career, you already have a passion or two, and most important, stability. You may not have to take huge risks. It's not the game of winner-take-all, not at a later age. Maybe when you were younger you took greater risks, but now it really does not matter. You can approach each opportunity at an arm's length of caution.

Now if you don't have that luxury of a few retirements to fall back on, the desire to succeed may be greater, and you may find it in your heart to take greater risks, with of course the opportunity for greater payoff in the end. If you don't have years of experience and information at your disposal, you still have your ingenuity and entrepreneurial spirit to work for you. 🏠

CHAPTER 5

Establishing a Blueprint and Mission Statement

REMEMBER THAT WHEN YOU ARE WRITING YOUR BLUEPRINT, which will become your model of success, there are many factors that will play an important part.

- ▶ Do what you like to do. Be smart about it. If you don't like to manage properties then maybe you should consider a different type of property investment. Foreclosures or buying and selling property on the wholesale level may be an option for you.
- ▶ Cash. You will need a clear idea of your available cash, your creditworthiness, and your ability to borrow from third-party sources. This will have a strong effect on the route you may take. If you don't have access to $100,000 you may not build the new property, but $5,000 may buy you a fixer-upper to get started.
- ▶ Commitment. Decide what your commitment will be: Full time or part time. This will determine how fast you may buy and sell as well as how much cash you will need. One area plays an important role in another area. They are all comingled.

- ▶ Point of View: All people look at things differently and will tackle projects differently; it's most important that you have a point of view, a philosophy of how you want to tackle the development of your real-estate empire. You can do certain things, and you must recognize that there are things you cannot do. Understand your strengths and weaknesses. Rely on your strengths. Recognize your weaknesses and find ways to turn them into successes. It takes an astute business person to develop this line of thought.
- ▶ Work ethic: Either you have one or you don't. Can you stay focused on your goals?

Stay Close to Home

Think hard about your plan to invest when developing your blueprint; decide where you want to put your money. You may decide to invest locally or you may go out of town. There are advantages and disadvantages to both. Let's talk about them.

Out-of-town investments are difficult to manage. You may lose control of the property very easily. Repairs and maintenance will be difficult for you to do personally. It won't be like you can put a wrench in your car and fix a leak on the way to a movie.

I had some places out of state. Hilton Head was a fast-growing area, and I wanted to stay ahead of the curve, so I bought several patio homes in a gated community. At first I tried to manage the property myself and that was a disaster. The problem was that I did not realize the transient community, which causes a greater turnover than a higher-end area. Although Hilton Head was a hot area to buy in with terrific appreciation, the plan was to buy, hold, rent, and sell.

And that's what I did; I bought for $70,000, rented the property for

Mission Statement

Before you start your new adventure into real estate, it is important to decide what your purpose is—write it out so you have a focus. A complete mission statement should describe what the company will do for its customers, what it will do for its employees, and what it will provide for its owners.

Of course, not all companies, especially small ones or ones that will never have employees, need mission statements. However, a good mission statement will keep you focused on your overall objective and lay out the direction of development to follow your blueprint of success, which becomes part of your business plan.

a few years and sold it for $130,000 and almost doubled our money. It was a great investment.

I also realized that the rental market was transient and that I was better off using a local realtor on the island. As the rents increased each year so did the HOA fees; they continually took a bit out of our rent. After the management fees of 10%, the HOA, and the mortgage, there was no wiggle room for when money had to be put into the property, I had to invest in typical stuff, like paint, HVAC units, carpet, and plumbing. I watched this investment very carefully. You end up realizing that you cannot manage the property from afar. The laws are different from state to state, and that too makes it difficult to collect rents and damages and evict tenants.

continued on page 62

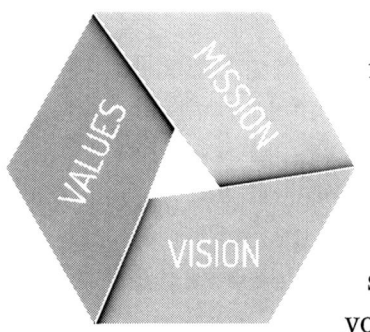

Sound confusing? Well, it's really not. It's simply a statement of what your objective is and how you are going to reach it. It communicates what the purpose of your organization will be. In a sense, it acts like a car: you are the driver; the road you drive on is the blueprint; how you get to your destination is the business plan. It is your mission statement that will give your employees, investors, and your business relationships an idea of what your goals are. Your mission statement should include certain key points.

- Key market: You must state clearly your key markets, your clientele, your customers, what price point you need to reach in order to provide your product or service.
- Contribution: This describes the product or service that you plan to provide to your customers.

So just be careful with out-of-state investments. It just seems more prudent to stay close to home. I started early in my prospecting decisions to control neighborhoods and streets. Remember how easy it is to control those areas. You can literally walk down the street to collect your rent or mow a yard.

It seems so easy to invest your hard earned money all over the world. Actually it is difficult, and you can lose control very easily. Even with hands-on management you can leave yourself wide open. Sure you can be successful, but if you can invest in your neighborhood, especially when you are starting out, you will be better off.

Out-of-state investments can easily and quickly go bad. One time, I took $50,000 and put in an option to purchase a condo in Vegas in Turnberry Towers. The idea was to

▶ Distinction. The mission statement should inform your customers exactly how your product or service is different from the others in the marketplace.

Again, it is your mission statement that will identify your business model and provide the vehicle for you and your customers to engage in profitable business. It must encompass all areas of your business—pricing, quality of product, service, your marketplace position, the goals you want to reach, your employee profile, as well as your relationship with customers, suppliers, competitors, investors, and the community.

Blueprint

Throughout this book, when I talk about blueprinting you must first understand what the word means, which is essential to your entry into the real-estate business, your path to success, as well as your eventual exit plan. Blueprinting

---

continue to ride the wave and then sell the contract. That would have been fine, except when the market crashed, I was not able to close and I lost my equity. At that time, Turnberry was appreciating 15-20% per year; if there were no crash, I could have been in and out with a nice profit.

Now is the time to buy in Vegas. Maybe not for resale today, but as a depressed market it is great for rental. In some of the research I have done, properties are selling for 80% of retail value. If you put the money with someone able to manage the property for at least 5 years, you may be ok.

> What is your ultimate goal—the place you want to be tomorrow, next year, and ten years from today.

in this sense is the direction that you will take in order to be successful. Consider it a road map to your success. It is individualized to both your short- and long-term goals and incorporates your financial and personal needs.

For each person the blueprint will be unique. You will take into consideration your ultimate goal, the place that you want to be tomorrow, next year, and ten years from today. You will have to evaluate your financial condition and all the factors relating to it, including credit, personal wealth, your talents, your expertise, your commitment of time, and other areas as well.

As you develop your blueprint you will better understand what you ultimately want to accomplish. And you must do this yourself; I cannot do it for you. As time goes on you will be able to follow this blueprint as a model to your success.

Let's talk about your plan and how you want to get started in real estate. Here are some options that you may have. You can take one, two, or an amalgamation of several; let's give it a look.

- **Wholesaling.** Wholesaling is selling a property, either rehabbed or "as is," below market price—at a price so low that the buyer can do what he wants to do with it. There is usually some room in that price for the buyer to sell it again at a market price and make some money.
- **Rehabbing** is fixing up a property you own and selling it at market price. You are then getting the ultimate return on your money by doing both things here: you are buying it right and then fixing it up and selling it at the right price.
- **Buy and Hold, Landlording.** On this path, you fix up the property that you purchase, rehabbing it to the point where you can rent it, and then rent it. This usually falls under the long-term plan because it involves a greater commitment and greater stability: from a good

CHAPTER 5: ESTABLISHING A BLUEPRINT AND MISSION STATEMENT

tenant, you will receive monthly rental payments that will service your debt, your expenses, and hopefully provide you with a profit.

▶ **Seller Financing and/or Contract of Deed.** You find a property that the seller is willing to finance for you. I have done many of these, and they are great. This approach does not have a negative effect on your credit and will help you expand fast. As either a flip property or a long-term rental, owner financing is great. Just be honest up front and communicate will with the seller. Be sure that you disclose all that you plan to do with the property with him. Be up front and honest; I know you will do that. If you have a property that has been paid for, you can act as the bank and hold the paper, or the mortgage of that house. This is a contract of deed. Basically when the property is paid for in full then you give the buyer the deed to the house. I love this when I am selling a property because I can now double dip on the property. I am getting market price for the property but also I am giving myself an income for a long period of time. I am also collecting income through the fair interest rate that I am charging as well. Additionally, I have put myself in a great tax situation: I am deferring my tax obligation by stretching it over the period of time that I have mortgage the property for. I have done many of these deals in Danville, Va, where I have taken a hard-working person and given him an opportunity to buy a house. They don't have to qualify for my contract of deed. I evaluate them on the

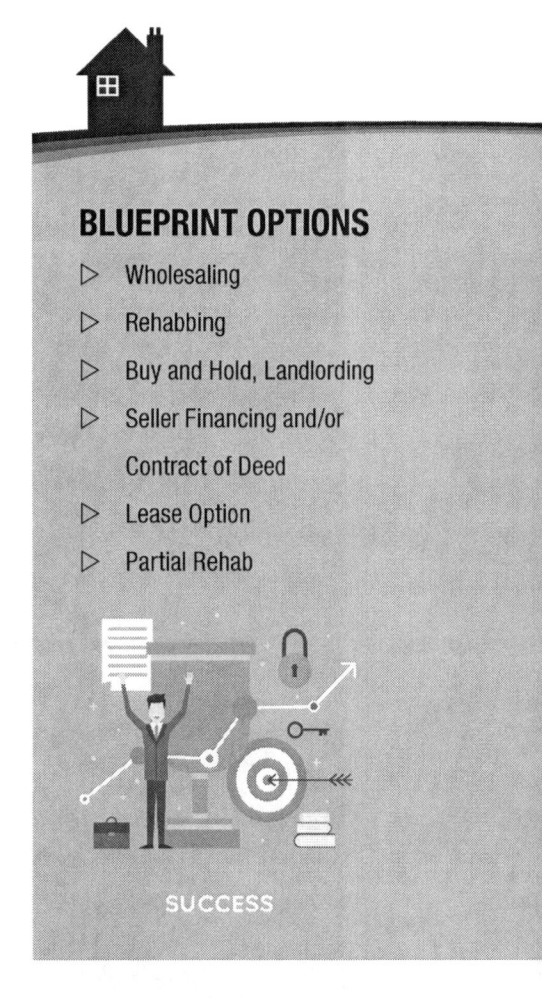

BLUEPRINT OPTIONS

▷ Wholesaling
▷ Rehabbing
▷ Buy and Hold, Landlording
▷ Seller Financing and/or Contract of Deed
▷ Lease Option
▷ Partial Rehab

SUCCESS

spot to see if they have the heart to make this kind of commitment. Ultimately, I am turning a person's dream into a reality.

- **Lease Option.** Of all the ways to do a deal, sellers like this and buyers should run the other way. Many sellers that I know want to do a lease option, especially around tax time when they get someone who just received a tax refund that he can use as a down payment. It might be only a few thousand dollars, but I know many sellers who would consider that a down payment. Understand for a moment that the seller knows that most of the buyers will default, so they want as big a down payment as they can. So the new buyer/tenant buys this property under the lease option, their rent payment is $500 but they pay $600. The $100 difference is to go into escrow until such

Supply and demand will play an important role in developing your strategy when developing your blueprint or model. I say that because if you want to flip in a certain neighborhood or dominate in that neighborhood and nothing is turning over for whatever reason, it is going to be difficult to buy there. Prices will tend to be higher, maybe closer to retail and not wholesale or below. The rental market in that area may be low as well. I don't want to push you to the low desirable areas, the low-income, distressed properties, but it is an option. What you will see there is usually more supply and less demand. There won't be a lot of people who have the ability to buy a home. So they are forced to rent. Flipping for cash becomes much more difficult; you may see more lease-to-own and contract sales there which again is a little different play. It will have a different turn on your cash flow as well.

I personally have done well in these neighborhoods due to the vast supply and the even greater demand to rent. A lot of investors do not like trying these neighborhoods, so the door is even wider for you to walk through. Just remember that the rental market is somewhat different

CHAPTER 5: ESTABLISHING A BLUEPRINT AND MISSION STATEMENT

point when enough is accumulated to be the total down payment as outlined by the agreement, whatever that amount would be. So if it is high enough the tenant may not be able ever to achieve that amount. All this money goes to the seller in a default status if the buyer cannot meet his obligation. I am not a fan of this, but if you think it works for you it is clearly an option.

- **Partial rehab.** This is when you buy a house right, but it turns out not to be right for your blueprint. You may want to put lipstick on this pig in order to wholesale it quick. Some people will do simple things, yard, roof, paint, just enough to sell it quicker than just leaving it alone. This is a solid mix of doing some work and selling it at a wholesale price.

---

as well. Your quality of tenant may not be what you bargained for. So look at that very carefully before you become overly excited about those opportunities.

You can profit from location, and once you plug the deal into your blueprint you will assess your location as an integral part of your decision. What may be valuable to one person may not have a value to someone else. The actual and perceived value of the location relating to the cost of the deal will determine your move. If you are a bottom feeder paying $5,000 for a condemned property, do you think it will be a desirable waterfront with a view, or a creek with skunks? If you buy a $200,000 property, the chances of getting that waterfront with a view is greater. You are paying up for that amenity. The question for you to decide is whether to do one deal at $200,000 or 10 deals at $20,000 each. You may not be able to double your money at $200,000 but you may be able to triple your money at a $20,000 investment; also with zero dollars you will have a harder time raising $200,000 than you will raising $20,000.

continued on page 68

So when you are building your own blueprint, take into account all the factors that influence your life; set your goals, write a mission statement that clearly states goals and timeline. Basically you want to have a plan for yourself. Then you can work backwards to see what you must do in order to reach that plan. It may take a little time to put together your strategic plan that will be a true blueprint of success.

When you develop your blueprint of success—something not everyone can do—an element of creativity comes into play. How are you going to formulate a plan that is better or as good as the next guy? If I have three people bidding on the same property why should I pick your deal over someone's deal?

When you are thinking about buying properties, be careful that you look at all areas of the purchase and how it will affect you today and tomorrow. Evaluate the negatives and positives of each deal individually. Do your due diligence on each deal: evaluate the outcome and how it will fit into your blueprint and your ultimate goals. It is imperative that you stay focused, that you stay on track, and that you have a plan that is achievable. You may not want

If you decide your blueprint is for higher-end properties, then water and views will be important. In my neighborhood, although there are no waterfront views, that $200,000 house is now a $50,000 house. I can flip that property wholesale for $125,000 and more than double my investment. Evaluate every deal as a stand-alone deal; let it stand for itself.

If my blueprint is low-end properties as a bottom feeder, I am thinking of location as it works for

to shoot for the moon on the first day, although that sure can be the ultimate goal. Put everything you do in perspective, so that it is achievable and realistic. Be able to walk away; don't get emotionally attached to anything that you may regret tomorrow. Remember you are in this business to make money and to be successful.

Pay attention to detail and don't ignore the negatives, which may bite you tomorrow. Be aware of whom you are you dealing with—it's not always the little old lady trying to sell her home. Be fair and equitable. Treat others how you want to be treated. The deal has to be good for you, but also fair for the other person. You will do just fine.

Business Plan

The plan you write does not have to be sophisticated, but you do need a blueprint of success. Your business plan is a formal statement of your business goals and how you will reasonably attain them. It can include background information about your organization. The business plan is the foundation of

---

my consistent offer of $5,000. I am not looking at views; I want value: value of purchase and value of rentability or resale.

The risk is greater as you move into higher-end locations and deals. As time moves on you may consider a specialization: waterfront, resorts, timeshares, condos, islands; there are all kinds of different opportunities for you to explore. There are a lot of locations.

If you wait for a transitional neighborhood to start you may be too late. Get in early if you can. Look for trends; be ahead of the curve.

your blueprint of success. Most importantly, the business plan will establish a forecast of both income and expenses, in the form of a budget; both operational expenses and raw materials, as well as all income from the goods and services that you sell, must be included in your budget, which will be the first way for you to establish profitability. Remember that the purpose of all of his is to enable you as an owner to have a definite picture of the outline of your potential costs and drawbacks that you may face.

You must decide what direction you want to go. A great deal of this decision will depend on you, your interest, your credit, your cash, your goals. A few thoughts:

- Decide what type of property you want to own. [See sidebar.]
- Calculate how much money you are willing to invest: available cash, second mortgages on home or other properties, lines of credit, 401Ks, lenders. [See chapter on funding.] Make a plan and execute it. You need to know if you are a zero-dollar player or a million-dollar player; you may start out today as a zero player, but it is my goal to get you to the million dollar mark. This will not happen overnight; you will have to work for it.
- Can you negotiate? Do you know how to make a deal? For years I have used the $5,000 rule. No matter the price of either wholesale or retail, I offer $5,000.
- Cash flow. Do you have cash reserves to do the repairs, make the improvements, and do what is necessary to the property? This is important. If you are just starting out and looking at your first house as a job to replace that $50,000 income, you might want to rethink your objective. However, if you have a job—any job, determine how much cash can be available for you to put into your investment and plan your renovation accordingly. You are the labor at first, and you don't get paid. Your pay day is later.

Focus

Stay focused on your mission; follow your blueprint. You may want to deviate from your plan, and that's fine as long as you are aware of the change of direction and understand the risk. Evaluate the pros and cons. Evaluate your success or failure afterward and get back on track.

Have a strategy. When you develop a mission statement and blueprint, you should be focused on your plan. It's best not to just run out there haphazardly and do whatever. You could get yourself upside down before you know it. You need a business plan or model, which will give you a rule to follow.

Tools of Success

- Answer all correspondence. Respond to e-mails and return all phone calls. You may want to get a separate cell phone for your properties.
- Touch your correspondence only once. Don't keep touching mail—move it or lose it.
- Do the most important things early—make a priority list day to day. Some items will fall off.
- Try to do all the hardest projects early; get them over with so no matter what happens the rest of the day, you've got a winner.
- Start early, work late—yes, a marathon day. You cannot get a lot of them in a week, but one or two will be make a huge difference when you sit down to review the week.
- Don't put off until tomorrow what you can finish today.
- I have found that when you work with someone you can accomplish 50% more. Two do the work of three people.
- Be ready for Monday. You get a jump on Monday by putting together a plan over the weekend or on Friday. If you can do a little work, do it. You will feel as though Monday is the best day of the week. The stage will have been set for the rest of the week and it will be big. Do multiple projects as you go along, like keeping files with prospective offers and rentals neat and organized so you don't have to rebuild an old memory.

- Stay organized and thorough. The better you can complete your files with current information, the better your outcome will be.
- Stay healthy and safe; don't get sick—dress properly.
- Keep a positive attitude—say hello with a smile.
- Swing for a home run, but singles are good.
- Don't give up. Keep it positive and real. Two steps forward and a step backwards are not great, but it's ok as long as you are moving forward.
- Put together a team—friends, contacts, maintenance people, family, real-estate agents, bankers. The stronger the team the better and greater your rewards will be.
- Develop strong relationships based on honesty, trust, and integrity.
- Stay on course. Follow your blue print of success, stick with it, go to work every day with a skip in your step.
- Be patient. All good things happen to people who work hard, are honest, and do the right thing. Don't let greed get the better part of you; it can and will bring you down. Avoid shortcuts that will cost you in the long run.

Copy cat. When you are working and developing your portfolio, look at what others are doing and evaluate how they operate. If they are doing something right and it fits your blueprint, it's ok to copy it. No one is going to criticize you for copying success; that's a way of learning; let someone else make a mistake. Someone is probably watching you as well, trying to learn about your operation and what is making you successful.

SUCCESS

Be ready for just about anything because you just don't know what will happen next. Like Murphy's Law: anything that can go wrong will go wrong. As a company and an individual are you prepared to handle the unexpected? In business, you can figure there will be shifts created by any number of factors; it could be the economy, a disaster, a loss of a key employee, a lawsuit—any number of things can occur that will require you to make a decision in order to protect your mission statement.

Think on your feet. Make decisions that arise from a sound and reasonable strategy for your company. Seize opportunities that present themselves. Think through the issues that will make you better. Grow as a company and individually. Become better each day. Learn how to gather all the information you need to make intelligent decisions. Assemble the facts, review the positives and negatives, make your plan, and evaluate the results.

CHAPTER 6

Budget

IF YOU HAVE DONE REPAIRS AND MAINTENANCE for awhile as either a job or a hobby you should have a good idea of what things will cost—whether it is a 2x4, a sheet of plywood, or even light bulbs, you can formulate a materials budget. At some point you may hire people; the quality of these workers will depend on the local unemployment level and on the wage you pay them (remember to account for experience and skill level when you choose a wage). It will be cheaper to hire someone directly than a subcontractor; however subcontractors are an option as well. After working with a few of them you should get a pretty good idea of how much things will cost. For instance upgrading electrical service for a home may cost $1000 each time you do the job. So you should be able to budget a flip or a rehab job with some level of accuracy. You can even have some of your tenants do some work.

You will know relatively quickly how your pro-forma or budget is developing with the renovation. List all the work that you plan to accomplish: everything that you can do, what your employees can do, as well as that work that will require a contractor. From that list, plug in the cost of each task. Obtain at least two, preferably three, quotes for the contracted work, and pick the best one. Just make sure you are evaluating apples to apples. The scope of the work should be the same for each contractor, so the quotes can be properly evaluated. This area may be the biggest part of your budget. It will give you a snap shot as to where you stand.

Prepare your to-do list ahead of time, but at the same time be ready to alter it based on your budgetary requirements, labor, and time constraints.

Try to do as much of the work as you and your crew can do. Do not forget to price out the materials. There are tricks to saving monies on materials to include the following:

- Habitat store
- close-out
- your salvage yard
- other contractors
- 2nd hand store
- damaged, recycled products

The Best

Continue to strive to be the best you can be. It is easy to compromise what you truly believe in and what is right. I have done it many times, and I am sure at the time it was for all the right reasons. It's hard now not to look back to second guess myself. Could have, should have, but did not. Most of the time you have a good reason to have done what you did—even if it was wrong. You have to live with the reward or the guilt that you made the right choice.

People that judge you will become so critical of those decisions, especially the adverse ones—those decisions you may have been forced to make, knowing that you should have said *No*.

A few years back I met a fellow—we called him Jappa, a Puerto Rican fellow, nice man in his late 40s; he had served 17 years in a federal jail for selling drugs. His story is quite revealing in that he did not do it for greed or personal gain. His wife of many years had been sick on and off for years with breast cancer. The doctors had done chemo, radiation, even performed a partial

CHAPTER 6: BUDGET

Once you estimate your materials and add in your labor you will get a closer idea of the cost of your project. Realize that these are estimates only. And that you may want to figure a contingency figure for over-runs or extra work you decide to do. The budget or pro-forma for the project is an important outline of what you need to follow in order to be successful.

The budget will develop into actual costs which you will track, and at some point, when the project is complete, you will have an exact cost of the project. Right now, this number is an estimate; an actual number will be plugged into your income and expense sheet later. You must know ahead of time that the price of the property, the renovation, as well as all the other related costs will not exceed your income, whether it is a flip home or a rental house for investment.

---

mastectomy to save her life. The couple were hard working people and lived in the Chicago area. Both from nice families.

Then one day she was told that her company was moving out of the Chicago area and that she would be losing her job as well as her health benefits; this was devastating. The bills started to mount up with no apparent end in sight. Jappa was nervous and scared that he would lose his wife and not be able to pay for her medical care. He turned to an easy but illegal source to make money to pay his medical debts: he sold drugs, and for awhile he was able to meet his debts. Then one day he got caught, and it was all over. They took his home, his money, his car, and sent him off to jail to start this 17-year sentence. His wife had to learn how to survive on her own and has remained by his side. Sure it would have been best for him not to break the law to get that job, and rather to work hard to stay afloat.

How easy it can be to go too far when the life of your loved one hangs in the balance. We can easily make the wrong decision when we truly know what the right decision is.

If it is a flip property, you will probably be much more conscious of the costs for rehabbing the house. If you are fortunate and are able to sell the property at the price that you wanted and documented in your pro-forma then you may have hit a home run. But if the property does not sell and you have to hold on to it with all its carrying costs, your profit margin will diminish. If you have only a small margin of profit to begin with, you have to be careful both with the rehab of the property as well as what you end up selling the property for.

If you are flipping properties as a full-time job and taking an income you should be careful when eliminating what you take out for your living expenses. Remember the house of dominoes, whereby you continue to get mortgages for properties over and above value with the idea of taking out parts of that money to live on. All the money you borrow needs to be paid back at some point, so it is important to be prudent. Don't overextend yourself. You are best advised to take out the profit after the property has been sold. That way you will know exactly what you are working with.

Just be careful that your projections are not skewed. Best to figure this out both with wholesale and retail figures since there is a difference between the two. In a volatile market you have to be careful. You should have a good idea about what you think you can sell the property for, either retail or wholesale; you know what you paid for the property; the difference is called your grow profit. From that number you can factor in your rehab costs and possibly project your net profit.

Be careful how much money you plan to put into the property. You do not want to put so much into renovations that you never get it out of the property. You have to see what the market will allow and then price out your rehab accordingly. Knowing that there is a price point that the house will sell at either retail or wholesale, you can also work your numbers backwards and provide yourself with anticipated profit margins and rehab costs.

Along with those costs, there are holding costs: the costs you accumulate after finishing a rehab but before selling or renting—the interest that is accruing, maintenance costs on the property. This is prime money-wasting time; when the project is done you must be ready either to sell or rent. Be sure you know all your holding costs on a property, so you can determine the sale price. You've got to figure everything in by developing your pro-forma. It's important to know this for your taxes as well. Don't forget the interest on your money and labor—specifically *your* labor.

When deciding how much house you can afford, there are certain criteria to keep in mind; here are a few of them: How am I going to finance the purchase: with existing monies or cash that I have on hand, or am I going to go to a bank or personal hard-money lender and borrow the money? Interest rate as well as prepayment penalties play a major role in this decision.

Determine your budget: either how much cash you have now or how much you can borrow to pay for the property. I just don't want to take out a mortgage; now I usually pay cash for my properties, which puts the investment in the lower spectrum of investment opportunities.

Regarding cash: don't spend it all at one time. If you want to buy multiple houses in a period of time, then budget your money properly. This you will see when you do a pro-forma and apply it to your blueprint.

Put a value on your time.

Bad Credit

If you have bad credit, it is going to be a little harder to reach your goals as quick as you want to. You have got to go into the deal knowing how your credit is. You will need to explore your options:

- You may need to work with a partner who has good credit in order to obtain financing. He may obtain the money through a financial institution, and you are able to bring the deal to the table and do the work.
- You may have to evaluate alternative avenues for cash and do smaller deals that you can wrap your arms around.
- You can be creative and find deals where the owner does the financing. I always like this as a viable option: you can hold on to your cash and instead use someone else's money. In this option, you don't need a partner whom you have to pay back or split the profit with.
- Hard money lenders will lend money to a person with less-than-desirable credit. You will pay a higher interest rate, so beware. This is a good option for short-term deals.

Just keep in mind throughout your growth how important credit is; if you have bad credit, work towards improving it all the time.

CHAPTER 7

Funding

HOW DO YOU GET FROM RAGS TO RICHES WITH NO MONEY? How do you plan to fulfill your goals at whatever level they be? What are your goals? Great questions. You have set your plan. You have written a blueprint or business plan, and you therefore have some direction. The ultimate goal for most investors is to increase their financial security. They want more money. It may not be a million dollars, but it may be an amount that will make them comfortable. The best advice I can give is to start today. Stop talking about it; stop dreaming about it. It will not happen unless you take a step forward. You must have a blueprint that you want to follow, one that meets your personal and financial needs and goals.

You want to get started at any amount, but you barely can rub two nickels together to make a dime. There are many ways to get started, but you must understand that the only way is the legal way. To start with, you must be honest and trustworthy. If you don't have those characteristics, walk away; there are plenty of people in jail over real estate, because they just did not do it right. One of the key elements is not to be greedy. Take a step at a time. When you get up to bat, you may hit lots of singles, and that is great. Homeruns are good as well of course, but you're not going to get them every time. Be prepared for the ups and downs, the successes and failures, your roller-coaster ride.

How do I get the money that I may need to get started, and how much will I need to start? Just remember it does not take much to get started. There are ways and means to obtain some cash to get started. Don't wait until you get the money; start prospecting now—find the deal as you plan your money situation.

The amount of money you start with will determine your entry point. If for instance you have little money, $1000 or so, your entry level will probably be in distressed properties in low-end neighborhoods. I can make you successful at the low end and successful at the high end of your investment. It truly does not matter; the formulas, the play, the rules of engagement are the same. Only the type of investment and where you invest will change. You may be looking for some owner financing as well. There are a lot of sellers who want to get rid of their properties and for sure the number of investors that get into the low-end properties is small.

Not everyone is cut out for low-end property sales and rental. Don't count on a line of people wanting to buy your low-end flips; that market does not have a lot of money. You may have to work with a buyer as you did when you

A thought for consideration and evaluation: Don't sell your soul. My brother Richard, the one and only one I ever had, never looked for a job out of college. I hired him, taught him the restaurant business, and gave him a share of it, which is still successful today. I have lived to regret that decision many times.

As a side opportunity we bought a great deal of real estate, mostly commercial property. I had a lot of residential and multi-family houses on the side too. I was doing great. I did 90% of the work on them, the acquisition, the remodel, the rental, everything. He wanted them for himself, and foreclosed on me for all the properties on an $80,000 note that was held by one of our restaurants. I was backed into the corner. He later sold most of these for double the money and made a ton. I have not spoken to

were the buyer. Land contracts and lease purchase options are vehicles to sell properties. You can make money this way, even though you are not going to make that quick buck that you may be dreaming about. Build the portfolio one buck at a time.

If you have no money, and you have great credit and can borrow money, it is true that you don't need cash. For example, if the property is worth $100,000 retail, and your due diligence has estimated that it will take $20,000 to renovate it, you make a play to buy the property at $40,000. So, as an investor you need $60,000 to buy and renovate this property. You can borrow the $60,000 to buy and renovate your house; then you sell the house for $100,000 and have a $40,000 profit for your next project. Some investors may borrow $80,000 and use the extra $20K for extra expenses. The renovation money is considered construction funds and may be available only on a draw. However if your money is private money or hard money you may be able to borrow the extra $20K and buy your next house. Some investors choose to use the extra loan money for their living expenses; be careful with that if you do: don't live off borrowed money.

---

him in 20 years—not that I'm proud of it, but I don't think you should sell out your family for the almighty buck. Some people do. When our mother died a few years ago, he was cordial, but the once great family we had is no longer, and that is not worth it. If you get a piggyback ride to success, don't sell the pig when you cross the finish line. Embrace, be thankful, and remain humble. Do the right things in life that don't weigh on your conscience forever.

You are not evaluated on how much money you have but on how you got to that success, how you spent it, and whom you have become.

This was a difficult time in my life and something that I relive from time to time. But I have also moved on and made millions again.

If you are forced to rent the property, you need to make sure your rental income covers your monthly payment. As I have mentioned some investors will initially get hard money to make the purchase and do the rehab then convert the loan to a regular mortgage. You have got to be able to convert the loan over to a mortgage and feel confident that you have a relationship with a lender to do that. The downside is that if you do too many hard-money loans and are living off your borrowed money, then there is a day that you will have to pay the piper.

The rags to riches story is for everyone. I want to make your road to riches successful.

Whether you have a lot of cash seems incidental at this point. Take a look at what you have and what you can get your hands on. There are avenues of cash that I will talk about. Also there is liquid cash—what you have in the bank. But what is your ability to borrow? Many people may not be able to borrow anything and others much more. What matters is understanding where you stand today so you can build a business model; that's what you need to identify so you don't over-commit to anything you can't live up to. No sense borrowing a million dollars if you can't pay it back. I will provide direction on how to obtain cash so that you can make the right moves when it is necessary to make those moves. The end result is that I would like to put a little extra cash in your pocket so that your personal financial goals will be met. For all of us they are different. Identifying them will measure your success. Don't go into this thinking you will be an automatic millionaire in three weeks.

Initially, you can follow my suggested outline to get you to the point of hitting that homerun. I also recommend joining a real-estate group or getting a mentor who can show you the ropes, someone willing to take you under his wing to work with you. My friend has a website to buy houses, like CASH FOR HOMES or STOP FORECLOSURES; you've probably seen them. There are enough leads that he doesn't want for someone to make a living off his discarded deals. You should network and get close to people who do this type of work.

Avoiding Loans

Here are some ways to avoid taking out a loan to make your first purchase.

Savings

If you have some savings this may be the time to consider using it. You can keep your money for a rainy day and go the conventional borrowing route. This does require good credit; you just need a better credit score today than you needed 15 years ago. Today is especially tough since banks have fallen under heavy scrutiny and are apt not to lend money to anyone. Later we'll discuss stair-step mortgages. But "stair-stepping" is a good way to build your portfolio too: Take baby steps. If you are able to do several zero-dollar-down projects initially, then at some point you may want a multiple deal or a commercial deal. The bigger the project, the more money you will need; the lender will require collateral. If you have been doing your homework and building your portfolio, you will put yourself in a position to borrow money for a bigger project.

Cash

You just need a little to get started, but don't let a lack of cash be your Achilles heel. Have a vision, think about what your goals are, how you want to reach those goals; you can and you will. You need patience, fortitude, and determination to do this. Don't expect to be successful overnight. Don't expect to hit those homeruns right away. Cash is the best way to go if you can. Not everyone will have lots of available cash to pay for a house. There is a school of thought among financial planners to hold on to your cash and use other people's cash. To a degree I agree: you don't want to be cash poor and house rich.

However if you are buying a house for three to five thousand dollars and have the cash available then I say go ahead and pay cash. Why pay interest when you can avoid it? If you are talking a great deal more than that, you may have to research alternative means, and that's fine as well. Don't be afraid not to have a lot of cash to make your investment; there are a lot of ways to finance and rehab your deal.

It is important to develop relationships with your lenders. Always make your payments on time. Keep your contact person informed with up-to-date financials including tax returns. Keep him in the loop, so he feels comfortable about the relationship. Always keep your word.

Personal Assets

You may have assets that you never thought could allow you to buy a property for investment. It could be equity in other real estate, value in a home or other personal property. You will be amazed what you can do.

Liquidation. You can sell things that you may not need anymore to raise cash for your new career. Get lean and mean.

You may have a 401K another type of pension or retirement fund. These are vehicles as well to obtain some funds if you find it necessary.

Income

If you have a job and have an income then you have cash flow. This is valuable for obtaining credit as well as trying to do a rehab while you are working. Any type of job is great. The better the job, the more flexibility you will have.

CHAPTER 8

Assembling Your Team

EVERYONE HAS HIS OWN MANAGEMENT STYLE that he will use to run his business; everyone will do it a different way. Some will do the work themselves, working lean and mean, doing all they can to maximize profits; some will assemble a team of contractors, associates, and employees. So much depends, of course, on how big you want to be now and later. It all takes time. Sure if you are rehabbing and flipping only a few properties a year you may be able to do most of the work yourself. However if you are flipping a few properties per week—that's per *week*—you must develop a team of not only experts that can help you succeed but also people that you can work with and trust. It's vital to your success.

Real-estate investment is not passive like mutual-fund investment. You will need to take an active role in managing your portfolio, making many day-to-day decisions. From the beginning, it is wise to gather around you a team of friends and associates, professionals, and business people who can provide guidance, advice, resources, and services to help you in your new venture. These people will have your best interests at heart; they will work for you, will not cheat you; they will be people that you can trust. It may take awhile to build that team, and it is not necessary to complete it before you buy your first property. You may go through a lot of employees, professionals, and subcontractors in order to get the right group together to form your team; this is normal and ok, because your success will hinge on putting the right people together.

The Members of Your Team

Investment groups and networking. From these types of groups, you will receive endless contacts, containing information that can be helpful to your success. When you are just getting started, being active in a local church is great.

Choosing a Realtor

When trying to determine a good realtor, you may consider a few of the following traits:
- Is this person going to work for you and have your best interests in mind?
- Does he do his homework on a timely basis? You will find that when you see a deal you want it now; you will not want to wait. They can be a day late, and you may lose the deal. It is great if they are a member of MLS, and you have profiled what you are looking for and you are sent listings daily as to what comes up on a day-to-day basis. That's a realtor on the ball.
- Realtors should have integrity; they must be honest, proficient, and diligent. You don't want someone who lies. Be up front; disclose all aspects of the deal. If there is a conflict of interest, disclose it. You don't have time to negotiate a renegade.
- A realtor must be someone who is connected in the community, who knows the people that are making things happen. Someone

CHAPTER 8: ASSEMBLING YOUR TEAM

Get involved, and you will be surprised how many contacts you will make. Investment groups are a way to prospect for properties, sell or obtain materials, and learn about market trends so you can stay competitive. They are a wealth of information. Investment groups are indispensable for building relationships and working deals among members: general networking for the benefit of all. They are not to extort business from new members; exploitation will harm the success of the group.

Realtors. It is a good idea to network with different realtors but you don't have to. They will work hard for you, but remember no one will work as hard as you do.

who can and will bring you the deal first. With his contacts in the community, this realtor should understand market trends, so he can work his magic for you. Also if you need certain things done, he will be able to get them done.
▶ You want someone who will work for you, not someone who blows smoke. He needs to have your best interests in mind when finding and negotiating deals. In return you will be loyal to him as well. Working with a couple of realtors is ok in that you can keep them competitive and honest to the job. If your best friend is a realtor, he is not necessarily going to be the best one for you. It may take you a few realtors before you find the perfect match, but you will find that person. I make the realtors work hard for me. I prefer not to use someone too close. We have seen some dirty dogs out there in the real-estate world. There are some ruthless people that will do about anything to get the deal. They don't care. And you being new to the business should be careful of these types of people.

continued on page 90

You ultimately are responsible; you must do the due diligence and guide the deal with the realtor. I have done as many deals without a realtor as I have with one. It's your call.

All realtors are different with their own work ethics and personalities. There are good ones and bad ones. It's best to do some homework and find the ones that have time for you, who are willing to work the deals for you. They may always talk a good game, but when it comes down to it they may not have your best interest at heart. I have worked with some realtors that are embarrassed to submit the low ball offers that I like to put in. Well, find the one that does not mind, and you will be fine.

Your realtor should be very much aware of your style of business. You have a certain way you want things done; find the agent that fits your mission

If you know the enemy and how he will move, then you put yourself in a good position to slay him.

- A realtor that can navigate the internet can send you information in a convenient format. If you are like me and get too many phone calls, it's great to receive information through e-mail. You can do you research on your own time which is great.
- Get someone who knows how to sell flip properties to the wholesale and rental as well as one that knows how to find the deals for you. This agent will have had to work hard to learn how to do this type of work. It may take time to find that agent.
- Find the agent who specializes in the market that you are buying and selling in. A high-end snooty real-estate agent may not want to go to a depressed area in your market to show properties. It may be beneath him to do it.
- You want an agent who is hungry—one who is eager to make money. Don't get one that does

CHAPTER 8: ASSEMBLING YOUR TEAM

statement and your goals to success. Remember the realtor works for the seller first off, whose property he is listing, but he may act as a dual agent. If that is not the case then the agent works for you. The realtor must understand your mode of operation—what you are looking for and how you want to do the deal. If you are the buyer and are a bottom feeder, then he should know that. There is a great business model in being a bottom feeder, however; investors—stay away from those kinds of deals. Remember that a realtor who sells $50 million worth of property a year may not by your realtor.

I've had some good luck finding realtors that will work hard to make a sale. Recently I found Don, a corrections officer who does real estate part time. I made a few offers on properties, my low-ball, and he did not care about the price. I did explain to him my philosophy in buying properties; he bought in the talk-talk and perform. That's not who you want.

▶ I want you now, not later. If you come later, you may have lost the deal. I want you available when I want you. I may have a question for you and with the right answer your instructions would be to write the contract.

▶ Heart-felt. Get your agent to work for you, believing in what you are doing to achieve your goals. You need an expert—one that will work hard for you.

on it, submitted those offers, and we made a deal. He got his commission. I try to write in an extra commission when the offer is low: $500 is great; $1000 is a little better. About the same time in a different market I found Ed, another hardworking, aggressive realtor. He puts in every offer that I want. He is technologically savvy, which allows us to make even more offers.

I have had some trouble with agents mainly because I am demanding, but more importantly because I like low-ball offers, and more often than not they don't like putting in low-ball offer. Lazy, lazy realtors—stay away from them if you are wise. If you want it done today, then you should demand that it be done today.

Find a realtor that is creative, because there are many ways to structure a deal. Whether it be financing, a short sale, repossession: just about any issue may come up. Think outside the box for superior ways to structure your deal.

Use your agent for information that you need to do your due diligence on the property. This may be especially important if you are working multiple deals. Also, you may end up having more work than one agent can do; that's why you may use multiple agents; however if you specialize in an area or locale, you may have a great deal of the information already. There is so much to do and not a lot of time to do it in. Another flipper is behind you thinking about making an offer on the property you want, so you have to move fast.

A few key tasks to assign to your real-estate agents:

- ▶ Forward any and all hot listings to you when they first come out. You want them first definitely before an e-mail blast, so they need MLS access.
- ▶ Have your agent do prospecting for you. They can do a lot of legwork for you and may have some inside contacts as to what properties are coming come up for sale: you want to be contacted first.
- ▶ Help you with the closing, prequalifications, comps, home inspections.
- ▶ Act as your third-party negotiator to convince the seller to sell to you.
- ▶ Bring you only the deals that fit your buying criteria; let him help you save time.
- ▶ Foster loyalty. You want your agent to be loyal to you first.

- ▸ Be upfront and forthright. Just tell him how it is and how you expect him to work for you.
- ▸ Listen to his advice; you won't have all the answers. Let your agent add a different perspective on your market and your business practices.

There are plenty of bad realtors out there, those who thought getting a real-estate license was their ticket to fame and fortune without having to do any work. Finding a good real-estate agent that will work hard for you is hard. When you find one that will put the extra effort into making you successful, you want to keep that person. Don't be played by aggressive or naive agents.

I like one that will put multiple offers in for you and not argue about your game plans— one that you have had the opportunity to work with.

Accountant—bookkeeper. This team member will give you an accurate statement of where you stand with your business. An accurate perspective of your money situation is essential. They can and should be able to forecast your finances. What is your budget? What will you need in a month or a year? Can and will you have the money that is required? This can be analyzed by a budget.

If you have taxes—federal, state, and local—a bookkeeper can help you determine

SUCCESS

Truman

Harry Truman became president of the United States by accident. Had FDR lived Truman may not ever have been president. How is it possible for a regular guy to become president of the United States?

Truman had a history of failing. He and his friend Jacobson had opened up a clothing store in 1919, only to fail a few years later. He had served in the military and was a successful captain taking a hard stand on what was right and what was wrong, having compassion for the soldiers under him. After his business failed he went into politics and built a reputation for being an honest politician. He never lined his pockets with dirty money. He molded his life around the principles, of hard work, determination, courage, and honesty.

the amount: payroll tax, income tax, 1099 forms for employees. If you have any type of licenses they can also keep you up-to-date and legal, while also ensuring that your insurances are paid in full and have the proper endorsements.

You want to have someone on your team that can keep your accounting organized, so that you keep accurate records: purchases, sales, repairs, and maintenance. You can use a number of programs that will guide you to proper accounting. Do it correctly. If you can't do this yourself, then it would be wise to have someone who can help you. This person could be a part-time bookkeeper, a moonlighter. Or if you cannot find someone, then consider an outside tax payroll or bookkeeping service. You must have accountability. This person is an important part of your team.

Appraiser. You may need an appraiser who will give you a fair and accurate appraisal. You don't want a low ball. Neither do you want someone who may inflate the value. You could get jammed up with this as well. Shop price, dependability, efficiency, and timeliness.

Don't have a closing hold-up because you could not get your appraiser on site.

Contractors, subcontractors. Plumbers, electricians, carpet installers, etc: they work on a specific trade and can do work for a contractor or a homeowner. A contractor is someone who runs the job; he coordinates all the work with the subcontractors, does the coordinating with the local building inspectors and works with the buyer. You are always the main one in charge, and you need to be sure all your ducks are in a row to get the job done on a timely basis. Things need to be done in order and both within a designated time frame and within budget.

Some areas of control and responsibility:

Hiring and firing of employees as well as the subcontractors for the job.

Being sure you collect monies, usually in draw, in a timely manner, so you can pay all your bills including your employees and subcontractors.

Managing Personnel

Don't be afraid to hire or fire someone. It is up to you to hire the right people for the job that you want done. The interview becomes the most important part of the job. When you hire someone for a job it is up to you to explain to the employee what you want done. Then follow up that you are happy with the job that they have done or, if you are not, then have them do it again until it is right.

As the man in charge you have to work your budget so you meet your expectations. Your report card is your budget; you can evaluate your success through your profit and loss as it compares to the budget you forecasted.

You also need to be sure the jobs are being completed. Oversight is important. You cannot just let your people go without supervision. They need to see you there, even better if you can work with them. If you can, the work will be done better and quicker guaranteed. People tend to work harder when the boss is around. Put the right person in the right job, and watch him succeed.

Remember to take care of your people. Pay them appropriately. If you get a big score, go ahead and reward them as you see fit. That will always go a long way. You will learn how to compensate your advisors as well as yourself. The best for a starter in this business is to try to re-invest all the money that you can into your portfolio so when you need to be compensated you will have the cash flow to do so.

It is unlikely that a property management company will be able to keep your interests vested, since they will have many properties and investors. Whose property will they rent or sell? The ones that are the nicest and yield the greatest returns for them. Yours may be on top or it may be on the bottom. Either way, you are best being involved, steering your own vehicle of success.

Having property out of town will open up yet another set of problems, which you may not be ready to address. I have talked about this; you must be aware of the positives and negatives of investing out of town. As stated you will want to use a property management company when you are farther than an arm's length from your property. Get some experience before expanding out of state.

There are certain people you should leave off your team at any cost. We have all met these kinds of people. They want to do business with you while they have their hand in your pocket. They are smart, conniving, ruthless, cunning, and untrustworthy. I don't think you want to start building your investments with them unless you are one of them. These folks should be easy for an investor to spot, but they are hard to get rid of. Do business with the devil, and you will get burned.

Just because you keep these unscrupulous people off your team, doesn't mean you can't learn something from them:

- ▶ They tend to have a lot of ideas and deals in the works; they tend to know some of the trends, what's coming and going.
- ▶ Their approach to building a portfolio may be and probably is different than yours. Good. Pick their brains. See what you can pull together to help you on your road to success.
- ▶ Don't share your ideas with them. You will get stung.
- ▶ Plan your time with them. I like entertaining them, getting them to think you are a friend. But don't let your guard down.
- ▶ You know what you are doing and you don't want to let on to anything in your blueprint.

How can everyone be a chief? It is easy to be an Indian and even easier for an Indian to think that he can be the chief. Sure does look easy to be the boss, especially when the Indian leaves at 5pm to go home and the chief is there to stay until the job is done.

I remember my Uncle Harry telling me the biggest problem in my entrepreneurial career will be employees. I told him, "How could that be? People like me. I'm going to be a good leader." I am indeed a good leader—although at times I only survived. What I do know is that he was right; managing employees was indeed one of the most difficult tasks that I had.

Not everyone can embody the values of a company and transmit them to all the employees. Leadership is a specific function or activity and requires providing direction or training, even at the lowest supervisory levels.

Companies would like to see long-term development of their employees through leadership training. What used to be called *career development* experts now call *leadership development*.

Over the years I developed good leaders at every level—many who just passed through my life to go on to bigger and better things. They took with them a brand, a style of knowledge that was etched on their minds for life.

Workers sometimes act in a leadership role and don't realize that they are doing it. They naturally want to be (and should be) praised and rewarded for a job well done. It is important to recognize excellence. A pat on the back serves well for developing a positive and inspiring workplace. We thrive on it.

Employees want to be involved; they want to be engaged in something that provides a positive feeling of accomplishment, not just stand on the sidelines and watch. I think of all those parents at their children's soccer games who from the sidelines and the stands are yelling directions to the coach. They are certainly not the coach but are doing a good job acting as one. The coach has to take the time to assimilate all that direction and make up his own mind up. Some of those parents want to be leaders, but right now they are not.

You have to have followers. Thank goodness for the soccer players; they are following the direction of the coach. We cannot have all chiefs and no Indians. Everyone at some point will get his opportunity. To be a good follower you will have qualities similar to a good leader.

Not everyone aspires to be a leader as such. It does take someone who wants to do it. Many people are as happy just to follow. If someone wants to be a good leader he will emerge from the pack; he will take all the good qualities of the leaders before him and develop his own style. A good leader is a teacher, a mentor, a role model. His whole philosophy is to lead. He gets people to follow him not because they must but because they want to—no yelling or taunting, no insulting or intimidating, no fear-mongering. These are not productive tactics.

Leaders are developed and nurtured. Some of us have a natural ability to grow to be good leaders. However it is so vital as a young Jedi to learn the techniques of others while formulating your own style.

PART II

Market

THE BEST RULE OF THUMB IS TO BUY LOW AND SELL HIGH. That's what you want to do at all times and under all circumstances whether it is a bull or bear market. The goal is make some money by buying and selling properties for a profit. You don't make any profit when you don't sell. You have exposure when you buy and your money is tied up in the property. The more you sell the more money you will make. If profits are not great for a lower priced house, then you may have to sell more properties to get the numbers that you need to reach your financial goals.

Succeeding in these goals takes intuition and adjustment on your part. You need to be able to adjust to an ever-changing market, making the right decisions at the right time to be profitable. It becomes part of your strategy. Remember that there are costs to holding properties. There are all kinds of maintenance, basic upkeep, and interest on the borrowed money. So think hard about any offer on a property before you turn it away.

Remember that speculation can be your best friend or the devil. It seems great, and we all want to take a bite; what we don't want is to get bitten—and you can get bitten very easily, when you jump into a deal without due diligence. It is important to do your homework and make sure that you have covered all

I have been eying this property for some time in my neighborhood; finally I saw the owner and asked him about selling the home. He was interested. He wanted more than I was willing to pay. However, he had two other properties, three in total, that he wanted to sell. This was a great opportunity for me to increase my portfolio. He was willing to sell all three properties for a price, again higher than I wanted to pay. He offered some financing on the properties, which also caught my attention. This is a great way to buy. I decided to wait awhile to let him ponder a little more, so when I went back to him maybe the price would be a little better.

your bases, so that the odds are in your favor for a deal. Always have a plan, and always have an out clause.

You just never know how the market will turn. You think it should go up, and history tells us this. Just don't put yourself in a compromising situation that could hurt you in the long run. Not good. Be careful. Use good common sense. Don't believe all that you hear; do your due diligence on any deal that comes your way. But when you are convinced on a great deal, then don't be afraid to take a chance and make it happen.

Evaluate the big picture, the entire area, the region, in order to get an understanding of the market. You want to know where property values are going. The more you know, the better your decision. Be overly prepared so you can minimize and downsize in the decision that you are about to make. You can track information easier today due to the vast resources of technology. You want to watch trends. Steve Jobs with Apple took the chance, jumped in, and made a huge amount of money. Take that same thought with real estate and evaluate the trends and get in on it early. Make an intelligent decision based on valid information and data.

As I have shared, the money that you have access to will direct you to the area that you will be investing in: whether it is low-end depressed property or whether it is high-end properties. It's logical for you not to be thinking of a high-end deal if you have no access to money to pay for it. So if you are going to start your portfolio with little to no money, your search is narrowed automatically to a specific area or region. It gives you a starting point.

Also you may know by your gut reaction to a deal. Many people have a good instinct and know how to make a good call—or better, a good buy. The longer you are in the game and the greater amount of knowledge that you obtain, the better you will be at your gut reaction.

Just remember that no one can predict the future. You can certainly forecast what you think may happen, but it all can change very quickly. There are no guarantees at all. As I have shared with you before, go into all deals with your eyes wide open.

CHAPTER 9

Prospecting

PROSPECTING IS A TERM THAT I USE TO SEE WHAT IS OUT THERE, like the gold rushers of the old west, who took a stake in a piece of land, or a portion of a creek and panned for gold. If you want to invest and you have decided your strategy, then it's time to look, to *prospect*.

You have put together a plan, and it is important to stick to that blueprint. Be sure to weed out the properties that you have no interest in, the ones that don't fit into your blueprint. It could be a property that is priced too high, it may need too many repairs, it may be in the wrong neighborhood. Set down a criterion that works for you—remember that there are plenty of deals out there that can work for you and fit into your portfolio. Sift through all the deals and find the ones that work for you.

If you go out every day and make a few pennies, in time those pennies will add up to dollars. Don't go out there and think you are going to make millions right away. I like the shotgun approach to prospecting versus the single shot: you make multiple offers on property. I may have a realtor helping me or may be doing the prospecting myself. I will usually make 3-10 different offers at my standard $5,000 apiece. I see which ones work and which ones won't. I have gotten acceptance on contracts that low. Just do it—that is my mission as outlined in my blueprint. I do not deviate from that plan. I may in time expand it, but today I am ok.

So you decide where in the matrix you will put in. Oh yes, there are opportunities for you to invest with no money, which I will talk about. But at least when you are prospecting, know that you have no money. You don't want to waste your time or the time of your real-estate agent; that's why it is important to stay focused on your mission.

Even today, as the economy works its way out of the financial crisis, you can find many properties to buy. The opportunities are endless. I like approaching property owners who don't realize they should sell their property until you give them the idea to do so. Maybe not on the first go-around, but you should be able to get everyone to sell. That's the game.

Motivated sellers with little equity in their property may be willing to make a deal just to get out from under their present situation. I have seen a lot of these situations where the head of a household lost his job and could lose his

Let the Buyer Beware

Be wise to areas that have the potential to be disasters.

Weather. Some areas are prone to hurricanes, tornadoes, and other natural disasters; these events are excluded from some insurance today.

HOA. Fees have destroyed a lot of cash flow statements. Your mortgage payment and HOA can sometimes be the same amount. You can buy a lot of property only to be saddled with two payments instead of one. These fees can be very high and have put families out of their homes.

Zoning. Business property in a growth area can be a good investment. Especially if you purchased it at a residential or lower price and you happen to be in the path of a zoning redistricting plan. These can be tricky so be careful. It is a home. If a seller has no equity in a property that you are interested in, your thoughts of flipping may be impossible. However, if you can negotiate a great deal then you should consider holding on to the property for a few years, collect the rent on the property and allow the market to change. It may take five years to get your return, but that is ok. You are building a nice diversified portfolio.

If a seller is being transferred and has to sell his house today, he will be a perfect candidate for an assignment of his property including any outstanding mortgage. Put that property under contract with a closing date very soon, give the seller some kind of deposit on earnest money and send him on his way. This gives you a property to flip. Ideally this property is a higher-priced property in a desirable area. One that with a little time you should be able to sell. Many times you won't even have to do a lot to give the property curb appeal. These types of sellers many times are desperate to sell because they have to be somewhere else. They may want to buy in their new area and may not be able to due to the mortgage on the property that you just put under contract.

---

speculative venture. You can make some money on a deal like this. Knowing how the business will grow is the trick.

Public transportation. May not be very important in an upper-class neighborhood; however if you are in a lower class, public transportation will be more important. Especially the bus line. A lot of folks need access to the bus system. You will see this more in the city than in rural areas.

Crime. Low-income areas may have more crime to deal with than nicer areas. With more crime comes a greater concern for safety and security of your property; the rent will be lower, the houses not quite as nice, but it may be all that you can afford. You can obtain information from the police station about where the crime spots are.

City Government. Check to see what services the local government

continued on page 108

There are some real advantages to buying low-cost properties: the main one being that they are the ideal places to start for those who don't have much money, maybe none, but still want to embark on this real-estate adventure.

Initially you will get more income for your investment in a low-priced home, versus paying triple or more for a piece of property and still being able to get only the same rent. You may find that you will get $800 for the home in a poorer neighborhood and get $800 for a similar house in an upscale neighborhood. So really you could buy 3 or 4 more cheap houses; multiply that by the equivalent rent and bank it. This will drive your cash and equity position nicely and put you in the arena to start some serious banking relationships. It's a great way to drive and build your portfolio.

The lower-end properties that you may go after initially will be a plenty. Not many investors will want to do the work that is necessary to make them profitable. So if you deal with the extra work you will find as many properties provides. For instance, in the city trash pickup is provided, whereas in the county there may be other arrangements like taking your trash to the dumpster or dump. It is a great service.

Schools. Generally speaking, the school near a city property will not be as good as the schools in the county. You have a different type of school, with different problems. Families will decide where they want to live based on schools many times.

Utilities. The basic services of gas, power, and water are usually available in cities and counties for a fee. The fees are generally very competitive; however they charge deposits that are often unaffordable for lower-income families.

Organizations. Many areas have neighborhood groups that will have

as you feel you can handle. The average person just does not want to do that kind of work. You will be able to take over the properties faster as well. The homeowner will be anxious to make a deal. In these areas you will find lots of deals. Throw a little cash at them, honestly, and they may think they are rich. This is where you will also find the no-cash-down deals.

Supply and demand will play a huge role in your real-estate portfolio. Both will have an impact on the development of an area targeted for development, purchase, or re-sale. If there is no demand, the price will generally decrease. This may be an advantage for you if you have little to no money and are trying to build a portfolio.

If there is an abundance of properties for sale in an area, the price will go down. There is usually a reason the supply is high. It could become a situation similar to the late 2000s, with the bursting of the real-estate bubble, or a major company closing up, a natural disaster, high interest rates, difficulty obtaining mortgages, people not moving.

plans to improve the neighborhood. They know what is going on in the areas of traffic development, streets, cleanup, crime—all kinds of information can be obtained by being a member of a neighborhood organization. Additionally these groups can be a source for what properties may be coming up for sale. They are a great resource.

Las Vegas is an example of the economic downturn where there is a lot of inventory of medium-priced property that is at 80% of value. With unemployment as high as it is there, people just cannot qualify to buy a home—they have to rent. Vegas is now coming back. Detroit is another devastated area, due not only to the banking disaster but also to manufacturers downsizing or closing, and high unemployment; the worst hit was the low-income area, which even a bottom feeder would not want to buy. Many of those properties have been boarded up and they are talking about tearing them down.

In order to turn around a neighborhood, you need a level of demand that will speed the purchase of homes and drive the demand upward. Someone has to have a vision. The demand may be caused by ease in obtaining mortgages, low interest rates, growth in businesses in the area. The direct correlation between supply and demand will either promote growth or put you in decline.

Prices will rise when there is not enough supply to meet the demand. When that occurs the economy will be stimulated, and you usually can predict growth. As an investor you must see where the growth is occurring and either join in or jump ahead; either way you need to have done your due diligence in order to be successful.

A positive absorption occurs when there is a high demand for rental property, when more needs to be built to accommodate the growth. Shifts in housing needs will play a huge role in how the pendulum swings for the absorption, either positive or negative.

Negative absorption on the other hand occurs when there is more supply than demand; the area is over-built, and there are not enough business or residential users. Again Vegas and Florida are good examples. This is not the ideal situation for a flipper; however a long-term investor can flourish as the prices of property drop. Don't buy until the real-estate market has hit rock bottom. You've got to know when.

There are indications in your marketplace that you can track, observe, and review that may help you in your due diligence of putting in offers to build your portfolio. Watch the retailers as they build shopping centers and develop new areas; you can see the development of roads as new residential areas become a reality, one usually follows the other.

CHAPTER 9: PROSPECTING

New projects require permits and plans that have to be reviewed by your city's engineers and building departments, so you can check there to see if new projects are in the works. Also check recent sales and listings that have been posted on your local MLS. This will give you an indicator of supply and demand in specific geographic areas that will be helpful. If you see too many "For Rent" signs or listings on craigslist as well as the local paper, then maybe you should stay clear of that area.

In areas where there are environmental issues, there are usually great prices. You can buy $500,000 buildings for $25,000 all over the U.S. But take notice: they may have environmental issues, and you will be dealing with all kinds of governmental agencies to clean the mess up. You will become best friends with the EPA. There are state and federal grant monies available for you to start your projects, and enterprise development as well provide additional incentives, which can include money. Easy loans are also available to rehab the property and clean up the mess.

Buying Your First Flip

- Be sure you are sold on the neighborhood. With no money or very little cash your options may be limited, but understand that two blocks in either direction can make a huge difference in not only the quality of the house but also the resale price as well as the possible rental of the house. Especially if you want to maximize your return, be sure you are comfortable in the neighborhood.
- A distressed property, a property under a tax obligation, code violations, or physical and deterioration issues will usually have a distressed owner, one that is anxious to make a deal. You are now an anxious buyer with no cash—also ready to make a deal.
- As always you should inspect the property, and do all the due diligence to be sure you are making a wise decision. Curb appeal is great, but it may take a little more work by inspecting the inside. Be prudent in your decisions. The house next door may be for sale at a cheaper price and may be a better piece of property.

Remember, once you clean up the mess, what will you do with the property? You will want to find tenants that will fill the space. If you can put all the pieces together on a building like this you can make a lot of money. It is a headache that will require you to follow the rules and guidelines.

Timing could be everything: being at the right place at the right time with the right deal, getting there when the buyer wants to make a move. You just don't know what you may get. If you have several deals in the works your chances improve, and that's what you want.

Timing can be important when there are shifts in a neighborhood; these could be related to a number of issues, economy, property or tax incentives, rental versus homeowners in properties, crime, retail and business development, shifts in social factors. So what may be good today may be bad tomorrow and great in a few years.

For sure don't jump at the first property you see for 100% financing. Make sure you are not overpaying for a fully financed deal. There may be a better deal tomorrow. You may want to sleep on the first deal for a day or two in order to feel totally comfortable about it and be sure you did not miss any glaring opportunities.

Stay away from buying a hotel or motel just out of the gate with 100% financing. Maybe down the road, if indeed your portfolio can support the purchase. And don't think of any speculative land deals now. Wait again until you have a strong portfolio. Land speculation is very difficult.

The amount of money you have to invest will determine where you end up investing.

As a bottom feeder your choices are slimmer and you will let a lot of deals go through the cracks. You want them to. Like today a couple of deals come through our investment group e-mail, and we let them go. I want the deals before they hit the front door. By the time they are mass marketed the price is too high; they won't fit into my blueprint.

If you have lived in an area for a long time, you may be able to track sales and values in your head. However if you can't or the area is new, start a file to track the activity. This way you will have some tangible information to make your decisions. Be smart. Work the neighborhood that you can afford, the one that fits your business plan. You should be able to determine that pretty easily. Although if you don't have a lot of money, you will be in the lower-end neighborhoods, where homes will be not only for sale but also for rent.

Once you determine a price range, check the surrounding neighborhoods as well. You may find some good deals on the perimeter; you may be surprised. You can be the investor that changes a neighborhood; that's what I have done many times. A bad element may come into an area: a terrible landlord who does not care or a neighborhood association trying to make a difference in a neighborhood. Whatever the situation, you will see these kinds of swings. It then becomes important for you to identify the swings and know when to buy in and to sell out.

You may want to stay away from a street that has more than three boarded up homes—or instead you can just buy them and make a difference in the neighborhood. I would buy all three. You are not going to sell these properties as quick as you may want to—poorer areas just do not attract the bigger dollars for resale.

The Perfect Flip

Hidden treasures are out there for you and your budget; it may take a little time to find those gems. Don't be in a rush. Remember to do your homework, check all your sources to be sure that you find the perfect fit. You will find the best way to find your deals.

Take the time you need to do the due diligence if you are the buyer. Avoid distressed properties if you can. However in my case I was able to build a nice portfolio with little to no cash on these distressed properties. Most people were afraid of those types of properties due to condition of property, area, value—there are many reasons not to buy and only a few reasons to buy. That's your opportunity to grow. Rags to riches, there are steps and opportunities to get there; don't be afraid to take the steps to success. Remember nothing is easy, just do it today. Make that deal.

Starting Over Again

Sometimes starting over is the best thing to do; walk away and start all over. It's easy to do nothing with a problem; it's important to do something. At what point do you start to do something again? Being obsolete is a state of mind. Can you reinvent yourself to do it better the next time?

Think about a product life cycle and when sales start to decline. Know when it's time to start over with a fresh new concept, taking something that is stale and reinventing it. This does not mean that you are changing your customer base, just providing more options.

How many times do you have to start over? As many times as it takes to get it right. It really does not matter. Find success in the hunt and release the fox when you catch him. Don't so lose yourself in work that you forget what life has to offer. It happens quickly and quietly.

CHAPTER 10

Finding the Deals

Foreclosed properties

FORECLOSURE IS AN ACTION TAKEN by the mortgage company to reclaim a property after the borrower has defaulted on a loan, usually because of non-payment. The lender can repossess the house, like a car loan company can repossess a car. The bank will send out all types of notices in an effort to get the borrower back on track, but when it has exhausted all means, the bank forecloses. The bank, however, does not want the property back; it prefers to have the money.

Foreclosed properties are sold on the courthouse steps. Your real-estate agent is not involved in this transaction, and there are no fees to pay. Any fees will be charged by the trustee who will send out the notices for the mortgage lender.

Foreclosures hurt the credit rating of the person who owns the home, who may also lose the equity he has built up. It provides a lender with the ability to collect on the unpaid debt.

Many investors can make a lot of money buying foreclosures, either from homeowners or from other investors. They want to find properties that have equity in them: the more equity, the more potential for profit. Fluctuating retail prices due to the housing bust have wreaked havoc on the resale value of property. Many foreclosed houses sell at a wholesale price for a quick turnaround.

You can use your real-estate agent after the property has been sold on the courthouse steps. Many times the mortgage company will bid at least up to what is owed on the property. The mortgage company may be willing to do a deal to move the property out of inventory; however more than likely they will list the property with a real-estate agent who works with foreclosures.

The process of buying foreclosures takes a little time to learn, but learn it anyway. You need to track them as they appear in the legal section of the paper. Find out what balance is owed to the bank; evaluate the equity in a property, and what price you are willing to pay for the property—the purchase price is important.

There are two types of foreclosures: judicial and non-judicial. In a judicial foreclosure, the lender goes through the court system and files a claim to recover any unpaid balance. Taxes will fall in this area as well. The court must then decide how to proceed. This process is to-the-point but will take a long time. Non-judicial foreclosures involve a deed of trust that states that a third party or trustee holds the first lien on the property and initiates the sale when the borrower defaults on his loan. When this happens this third party can proceed to foreclose on the property. This process tends to move quicker and is somewhat easier to do.

Result: When the sale takes place, all taxes (city and property) are paid in full; then the mortgage is paid and any and all liens. You get a house free and clear of all encumbrances.

When you buy foreclosures, you need money or at least access to it, so foreclosures are not a good place to start for those who need zero-money-down deals. The trustee is required to take a cash deposit from the bidders. If you win the bid you will have usually 30 days to close on the property. Having the cash to pay for the property is the best. If you don't have the cash before you go to the sale, be sure that you have a line of credit so you can close quickly.

CHAPTER 10: FINDING THE DEALS

In foreclosure properties you may not have the opportunity to go inside the property. You may have to evaluate the property from the curb; this can be a little tricky. Someone with experience may be able to do this pretty well, but someone with little experience may have a tougher time to make a good evaluation. Be careful. If you are a serious buyer, you can knock on the door of the house and talk to the homeowner; maybe you can look around.

Usually, you can get a good idea of the condition of the inside of a house by evaluating the outside. Take a look at the lawn, the bushes, the paint, the soffits. If these areas are in good shape it will give you an indication of how the inside may look. If the outside is trashed, then you should figure the inside is trashed as well. Over the years I have seen that people who buy foreclosures on a regular basis are like gangs of bandits: they work together. Yes, it's illegal, but a little like inside trading, in that one will back out and let their friend have it. The investors may partner with each other. So if you come to a foreclosure sale, be wary of the ladies and gentlemen who attend. I would recommend that you go to a few of these sales. Get a feel for the land and look at the players; see how they play; try to figure out their game before you go with cash in hand ready to buy.

I always travel with either a digital or throwaway camera so I can take a few pictures; when I see something I want to remember, I can just snap a picture.

There are ways to find foreclosing properties:

> ▶ Form a relationship with a bank that does mortgages. You can sometimes get the inside scoop as to what may be coming up for sale—even a list of people who are behind, so that you can contact them for a possible purchase. It would be better for the homeowner

> **When you buy foreclosures, you need money or at least access to it, so foreclosures are not a good place to start for those who need zero-money-down deals.**

- in trouble to make a deal with an investor now than to let it go to foreclosure.
- ▶ Follow the legal ads in the paper, although there are times when these properties go into bankruptcy or are reinstated.
- ▶ Contact the major legal firms that do foreclosures; they usually all have a website, and you can track the status daily. Establish a rapport with several attorneys or administrative people in the firm.
- ▶ Post ads in your local paper, trade publications, online, and put signs in yards—anything that will help you find leads. Desperate people will call you, wanting to save themselves from foreclosure. You may be able to strike a deal with these people.
- ▶ In a gated community, call the homeowners' association and get leads from them.
- ▶ Network with friends who do the same type of work. There is enough to go around—way too much for one person. Form alliances so you can get the best deals.
- ▶ Canvas your target area. Send out a mailing, knock on doors, or put up fliers. Word will get out and people will call.

Be honest; don't take advantage of a distressed property owner. People will do that, and it is not right. Someone losing their home may have $100,000 worth of equity in it. They owe $19,000, and you offer them $25,000 pre-foreclosure. You have basically hoodwinked them out of all their equity.

What you don't want is to be dishonest or too aggressive when approaching people who may be about to lose their homes. They are in a tough spot with lots of bills; you should be warm, sincere, honest, professional at all times. Sure you are buying their home for the money, but maybe you can help them get out of a tough spot and still be in a position to make some money. Just don't be a conman. No one wins when you try to cheat people; that is not the way to go. Once people catch on, you will develop a bad reputation and may end up losing a lot of deals. Put yourself in a win-win situation. Sometimes these people will buy the property back with different terms. And if not, they may be able to rent the property from you.

Strategies at Foreclosures

- Stay behind the scenes; there is always a guy there, maybe in a suit, who is the big shot. He's part of the foreclosure clan: don't become one of them.
- When you go to the sale, mingle; get a feel for who plans to do what at what price. Keep your cards close your chest, like poker. Devise a plan and then execute it. Do it from the background, hitting hard and hitting low—you deal the last blow.
- Pretend you are just there to look, to gather information. Like being a wallflower. Won't they be surprised!
- Be sure to have your money in place. If you intend to bid and buy, you will need cash or a certified check as a deposit to even bid on the property.
- There is a time to be serious and a time to break it up. You will know and learn how to read the crowd.

Foreclosures are a way that you can build a portfolio—just one of the many ways. I suggest you become versed in the many tactics so if one does not work you will have another to fall back on. You will be busy and you will get deals that will come your way.

Be sure you are bidding on the senior lien, the first deed of trust. You don't want to be bidding on a second or third deed of trust, which will do you no good. Be diligent in your research to be sure you are going after the first.

Also, go to a few auctions so you can get a feel as to how it works. You don't want to be a first timer and stumble too bad. Don't assume you are getting a good deal just because you won the bid. You will know this by doing your homework and being diligent in your research. If you set your price prior to the auction then you have set the benchmark for your bid. Adhere to it.

If you missed the foreclosure or did not have the winning bid, you still have options. Unless you really want the property, the logical option is to walk away and go to the next deal. There are so many opportunities out there right now for everyone, and it does not appear to be slowing down anytime soon.

You can try to purchase the property from the person who had the highest bid at the auction. He is going to charge you a premium for buying it from him.

If the bank has bought it back which happens a great deal, then you may have to go through the process, which will take a few weeks. From the trustee the paperwork has to get back to the bank, which will put the deal in their REO department, who will then handle everything. From the REO department, it goes right to the offers, the negotiations, and the sale.

Post-foreclosure

You can buy a piece of property at about any stage of the process. If it is after the sale and say the bank has purchased the property, you can usually buy it at some price, although you may not get the price that you wanted. If a bank has bought it back, I would wait until they have tried to market it for sale. They tend to use a real-estate firm in town with an agent that they have a relationship with, and the bank will want to get a fair price for the property—at least what they paid for it. It may go quick, or as you know, it may take some time

Rejection

If at first you don't succeed, try, try again. Many of the major companies in the world today have failed at one time or another and at least have experienced some form of rejection. How many times did Hershey fail before he hit it right with his wonderful chocolate? Or Pepsi? How about what Lee Iacocca did for Chrysler?

You can figure you will get rejected many times. Sometimes you may fail. You may feel helpless to the point of giving up. You may be hurt. You may get depressed because of your own self-pity. Remember if success were that easy, then everyone

to sell. The longer the property stays on the market the better the chances for a reduction of price. I watch those deals. Be patient, give it time. Sometimes it may take six months or more, but that price will come down. This is when I shine and put that $5,000 bid in on a piece of property. Nothing like getting their blood to boil, especially when they stand to lose a lot of money on the deal. No one wants to take the loss, but at some point in time they may be ready, and your offer may be just right.

Redemption Period

The redemption period is the period of time after the sale during which the seller may take the property back or stay in the property. If you are the successful bidder, you do not want to do any work on the property prior to closing. If you do you are leaving yourself open to the possibility that the owner may redeem his interest in the property. If you plan to do some pre-closing work, be sure that you have something in writing that allows you to do the work and be paid for that work if the seller redeems the property. Just be patient and wait.

---

could do it and there would be no challenge, nothing to work for. When you get to the top, when you are successful, you have climbed the mountain; it is wonderful thing.

If you have failed acknowledge those failures, learn from your errors, and move on to bigger and better things, you will get stuck in a cycle of failure, making the same mistakes. Rejection and failure are not easy for anyone to take. They may bring on depression. Try to remain strong. You are not the only one.

Don't get defensive; don't have a chip on your shoulder; remain positive in all that you do. Try not to second guess situations. If you have done your due diligence, evaluated both the positives and negatives, then you will succeed, because of the knowledge that you have gained.

When a lender takes the property back they are required to maintain that property. The lender may not want the property on the market for a long time as it will cost him money. It also has a negative effect on his credit ratings. That's why you may see lenders willing to make deals at the end of a quarter but for sure at the end of the year.

Lenders will try to spruce up some of these foreclosed properties to get a higher value in an effort to recoup some of their loan monies. If you can make a serious offer to the bank prior to any work, you may be able to get a better price. Of course your ability to negotiate is vital at this point. If you can close quick and take the property as is, your chances will be greater.

Be sure to do your research before you buy a house at foreclosure.

- What is the present tax value of the property today?
- Are there any building code violations on the property? This will make a difference in your rehab costs for resale. This will also help you negotiate with the lender on a better price. If the property has been condemned, the value just went down. You should now be able to estimate the value of the rehab and be able to work that into your negotiated offer to purchase.
- You will also be able to find any environmental issues that arise prior to sale, which will also affect the price. Do your due diligence on this as well.
- Go to the court house and do a title search to see what you are up against. Not everyone knows how to do a title search accurately. It does take a little time, patience, and training. This is a great tool to have in your portfolio of expertise.
- See if the property has been appraised. Sometimes the lender will have this information and will give it to you in their effort to get a higher price. Your goal is to obtain any and all information that may help you buy the property at the lowest price.
- You will also have competition; yes, there will be very qualified people doing all that they can to beat you to the punch.

Have in mind what you are willing to pay for a piece of property prior to going to the courthouse steps. Be smart and put all your information together to make your offer.

REO ("Real-Estate Owned")

This is the department in the bank that prepares the property for resale. If you can get hold of the property before it goes to the REO department, do it. The less money the lender has in the property, the better your chances of making a deal. Remember to put your offer in writing, have an earnest deposit, and be ready to close quick. I try not to have any contingencies.

> Be sure to do your research before you buy a house at foreclosure.

Foreclosures provide another opportunity to grow your portfolio. If you don't like the process or are too unfamiliar with it, just start learning about it. It's fun to be knowledgeable about all aspects of the real-estate business. When you network and are climbing the ladder, this is a subject you will be versed on.

Short Sales

A short sale is the sale of a house at a discount so that it sells fast. For example, if a lender is holding a $100,000 mortgage on the property, a buyer in a short-sale purchase may be able to obtain this property for $80,000, and the lender takes a 20% hit. This requires some time and effort and a good real-estate agent with experience with this procedure. Sure you can do this; it will take some time and you will make some great connections that you can use over and over again. If you have a buyer for that property at $120,000 or more and $100,000 is owed and you can buy it through a short sale for $80,000, you just made an additional $20,000. Not bad for some time and effort.

A homeowner in straits with his mortgage may turn to a short sale as a last resort. Even though he will not come away from a short sale with any equity, he will be released from the responsibility of the mortgage, which may be his goal. It will also save his credit score. In a short sale, the savvy investor can get both increased equity and decreased mortgage principal.

Pursue a short sale only on a property that you think will flip easily. This is a situation in which it will be helpful to pull out your list of potential buyers or investors to whom you can flip the property.

Short sales are a lot harder to identify than your regular foreclosures, but you can find a short list of homes available from the lending institution. These are usually houses where the lender has made an attempt to work with the homeowner, but he is still in default. A good lender will do that. After several attempts to work with the homeowner the bank may decide a short sale is in order and put it out there for a realtor to market. They offer great discounts for potential investors and homebuyers. The lender tends to modify rates, term, anything to keep the house from being foreclosed on, and in this way the bank avoids legal costs, internal administrative costs, and advertising. It is a win-win situation for them.

It might be difficult to convince a lender that it is time for a short sale on a particular property, because the lender will be taking a loss. An experienced realtor with good negotiating skills (or you if you've got them), however, can negotiate a price with a lender for a short sale. The seller does need to give his consent, but sometimes the lender will forgive the difference between what is owed and what the house is sold for. It is worth it if you can be convincing.

Even though the government wants lenders to work with borrowers, which costs time and money, at some point the lender may just give up trying. This is prompted by an investor making contact with the lender on a short sale, which is a viable option for the lender to consider. Lenders want to minimize their losses. A short sale does this and also moves dead inventory, which is especially attractive to lenders at quarter- or year-end. They are under pressure to make their balance sheets look good.

Many banks will bundle deals. If they have a lot of inventory, they may put ten homes in a package and sell them all at one time to a sub-wholesaler at a great price. They get rid of some good properties, as well as some terrible ones. But the buyer has to take them all; that's the deal. They may not all be in the same town either. So these sub-wholesalers will work with local realtors who know the market. They may first try to sell them at market price. The final price will usually be determined by the market and the success of the realtor, but the price may eventually come down, and you may get a deal.

For a short sale, you will need to submit the following:

- ▶ A hardship letter from the borrower saying why he has to do the short sale, i.e., why he cannot make the payments. This is an important element.
- ▶ Copies of the borrower's tax returns and present income statement. Is he working or not; can he pay the mortgage?
- ▶ Any and all information about the condition of the property. A home inspection is good. Details of any citations from the local building department, or something from a contractor will be valuable.
- ▶ Value of the property today as is. A copy of the local tax assessment will be helpful as well.
- ▶ The lender has a great deal of work to do in order to make the short sale happen. There are a lot of calls to make to verify the documents they have received. They have to decide if the price offered is a good deal for them and that they can substantiate the loss.

Each lender is set up differently, as a broker or as an investor; you can deal with all the different lenders and learn what they require for a short sale. It is helpful to work with one lender at first and learn his system.

Bankruptcy Opportunities

If you want to follow the bankruptcy trail you can check public records for pending bankruptcies, talk to bankruptcy lawyers, as well as having a working relationship with trustees, who are empowered by the court to manage the case. Sometimes the family or mortgage can homestead his property and stay in the home or they can force a liquidation of assets including the selling of the property. If you are in a position to buy the property at a fair price, you may be good. You probably will not get the best deal in town as the trustee will get some comps, maybe an appraisal; notwithstanding, the trustee will do some homework before you get a price to purchase the property.

For Sale By Owner

For sale by owner is usually a valuable tool, driven by aggressive owners who feel that they can sell the property themselves. In cases they have been successful. This takes some time but truly, and the price listed may be a retail price. Remember your benchmark offer; unless you can purchase the property at wholesale or lower, it may not be the deal you are looking for. Also, you will not have the marketing tools or expertise that an experienced realtor will have.

Absentee Owners

As the baby boomers start to inherit properties from their parents, they really may not want to fool around with them. That business is not for everyone. Someone inherits a property, and they decide to ignore it. It won't take long for the property to go downhill in value by lack of care and maintenance: grass growing, mail in the mailbox, peeling paint, maybe a lockbox from a realtor on the door, newspapers on the porch; there are plenty of them in all cities. You can find these homes everywhere: the children live out of town; they have lives, and either don't know what they have or don't want to fool with it. The properties tend to go into disrepair. The cities usually try to enforce some codes and regulations on them but have a difficult time: the code department's long arm does not usually reach beyond the city and nearly never crosses state lines. I have tried to negotiate with these absentee owners and have had a very difficult time. Many of them do not understand the market conditions in an area that they are not familiar with. Like anyone else they tend to think that their house has a greater value than it does. It is a tougher client to steal something from. You have to work especially hard to get them to the table to negotiate a price.

Auctions

I have bought a lot of properties at auctions. It's great to do a pre-auction. A real-estate auction company from out of town was selling several properties in the area once, and I was able to bundle three of them into one package. They were not good deals individually, but I convinced the auction company that they were better off bundling them and selling them to me for one price. Basically I got three properties for the price of two of them. I rehabbed one of them and am presently collecting $700 per month on a $60,000 completed rehabbed property. The other property, which I paid $5,000 for, I 80% completed and sold for $30,000. The property that was two hours away that I paid $12,000 for I sold for $35,000. One-hundred percent financing for 30 years, no call on the note. That's a nice check to get every month. Overall it was a good deal for everyone. If you can get one or two of those a year, it's a lot of fun.

Tenants

Depending on where your property is located and its condition, you may find landlords ready to sell their property because of their tenants: they are giving up on the idea of getting rich quick. I have been approached over the years time and again to buy someone's property due to the tenants. When they get frustrated, you can move in. You will see these frustrated people at the supply house, court, or investment groups meetings and such.

You Cannot Always Eat Caviar

How about a couple of saltine crackers and some Cheez Whiz? It's ok—you don't have to eat caviar every night. Well shoot—I don't even like caviar, but some people do. At the end of the day you want to have a few nickels to rub together. Taking those nickels and spending them on caviar may be a foolish choice, although tempting to some. It's best to walk away and savor the nickels.

Have you eaten any crow? Sounds bad, smells bad, and *is* bad. Real bad. No one wants to eat crow. We may have made a mistake, not done what we were supposed to do, said *No* instead of *Yes*. We put ourselves into positions in which someone is making us feel bad. It could even be a simple mistake. No thanks.

Jay Leno was asked one time about going out on dates with his wife of 31 years and what they do. He answered that they go to a fancy new restaurant, but sometimes prior to going out for that expensive and rich meal, he will go to a drive-thru burger joint for a bite to eat. Nothing like an unpretentious person who has humble roots and sticks to them.

Do what you like and what feels good to you. You can't go wrong with doing what has brought you success.

CHAPTER 11

Valuation

How to Choose a Property

The basic premise and principles of evaluating a property will be about the same in any location, whether you buy property in Roanoke, Virginia, or Detroit. My formula for success will work anywhere that you want to develop your portfolio. Remember there will be times that you may want to go to the opportunities. Don't spread yourself all over, causing havoc in your life.

- Amenities to property (bus stops and schools for the lower end; waterfront and view for the higher end)
- The numbers don't lie. Work the cost of the rehab against potential rental income and resale. If the numbers don't work, move on.
- Estimate your cost for rehabbing that new location. Different areas will have different requirement restrictions and codes. Cost of labor and materials will vary as well, maybe double, depending on your location. If you are working in your geographical area, you will have greater management control over your costs. If you are doing projects out of town in different locations, you may not have the control you would like to have.

- How much can I make? Put a value on your time. What are you worth? What am I looking to make on this deal? Personally if the location was good, but I could get in and out and make something large or small, I would consider it—even if it did not fit my blueprint.
- Know when to get in with developing locations; there is a time. If you are doing a deal for a long-term investment that generates a nice income, shelve it; enjoy it. However if you have a location that you want to flip for some income, timing is critical; you must know when to sell.
- Evaluate each property on its own merits. They are all different and all the buy-ins and resales will be different.
- Don't be anxious, control your emotions; pretend you don't care.
- Sometimes land deals are great, but they are not for the novice. Location is vital, knowing which way the area's moving. If you know which way the development is moving, you may be able to catch a location. It is speculative and risky but could be financially rewarding.

Home Inspections and Appraisals

Just remember home inspectors can be a double-edged sword. They will work well for you if you are buying but may not do well in terms of selling. They tend to be detail-oriented and will find things that maybe you missed. You care when you are the buyer and are trying to negotiate the purchase. All the negative items on a home inspection can be used to reduce the price of a property. They may not be a big deal but I will make them a big deal when I am negotiating a price.

If you have done business with the same home inspector, you may be able to add a little influence on his report. However full disclosure is necessary.

Appraisal or Not. If you are targeting a specific area for flipping and rehab you will eventually know the estimated value of a piece of property. You should be able to do your own comparison ("comps") pretty easily. Properties selling in the area, MLS listing, FSBOs, paper listings, as well as craigslist will become great tools to evaluate properties. You have to look at the values of other properties in neighborhood. Using the city's tax information will also help you determine value.

Condition is your bargaining chip for negotiation as well. If you do decide to use an appraisal firm to get an appraisal, you will have to pay for it. Be sure you have an idea of how they may value the property: low, medium, or high. They all have reputations; find out the reputation of the one you're thinking of using.

When going for a bank loan it's important to understand the appraisal process. You need to know the value prior to asking for your money. This will tell you how much you need to borrow. Either with the rehab money included or not. Usually a bank will want before and after build-out appraisals.

In today's market, it is much harder to get loans due to the increased demand for better credit scores as well as the tightening of the reins by the banks. If you have a good credit score and equity position, you can get money.

Developing relationships with appraisers is important. You will not get the runaway appraisals that were done 10 years ago, but you can get fair and equitable ones, done to your liking. Like in banking, develop a relationship the best way you can.

Many times an appraiser will do a before and after value for you, usually for the purpose of obtaining a loan. Also an appraiser will give you an idea of what a property is worth so you can do a cross comparison in your property taxes.

Your real-estate agent can also be a valuable tool to use in helping come up with your independent value.

Condition and Attributes of the Property

Renters always ask about attics and basements. In tough economic times, families will double up in a home to save money. They may sublet a room. They turn a spare room into a bedroom to overload the property. This in most cases is illegal and will cause some problems for you. If you flip the house, basements and attics can be a selling tool.

You will develop a keen eye over time for the potential in prospective properties. Don't play your hand; there are great possibilities in all kinds of run-down homes that people do not want; it's your responsibility to see the pot of gold and make some money. Making money with no money. Your information, your knowledge is valuable.

When you are prospecting you will find properties at all different levels of repair. Ugly is cheaper than good looking. If all you have to do is curb appeal, then you may be in pretty good shape as far as a quick flip property. It's more like do-it-yourself type projects versus a complete renovation.

Challenges are always fun to do, especially when you can be part of the transformation of the property, see it move from disrepair to a showplace. It becomes especially nice when you can add some creativity to the project at whatever level; that will also help you get that extra dollar when you sell the property.

It's funny to see cosmetically challenged properties: metal cabinets, a weird paint color inside and out, a beat-up driveway or sidewalk, dog markings throughout, outdated carpet, a shed that is ready to fall down. These types of repairs are generally easy to make and will change the look of the property completely, so go ahead and move forward. Just doing a few of these things, painting the outside, cleaning up the yard, and putting in a new door will give the property greater visibility. This could mean thousands of dollars more in your pocket.

The longer you are in the real-estate business the better you will become—practice does make perfect. Everyone has a different level of inspection. Some investors can just do a drive-by and tell the condition of the house. Some people may get out of the car and look at a few things:

Quick Inspect Checklist
▷ Roof
▷ Heating and air
▷ Mold
▷ Plumbing
▷ Insulation
▷ Siding
▷ Asbestos
▷ Sniff

- **Roof**. Roofs are tough so be thorough and careful when prospecting: they are expensive to replace, and doing so won't increase the value of the property. If you truly have a bad roof the value may diminish because the new owner will have to replace it. You cannot sell a house at a premium dollar without a good roof. I have purchased flip and rental houses before that only had a good roof; I just did not want to mess with replacing a roof. You can spend seven to ten thousand dollars easy on a roof; in some flips that may be the entire renovations cost allotment. So be careful; it's not hard to buy some shingles, flashing, and some tar and go at it. That won't cost much and it may do the job. Roofs are difficult to repair by all stretches. Flat roofs are trouble; stay away from them if possible. When you inspect a property, look for obvious patch jobs and trouble areas, then go inside and look for stains on the ceilings and walls; that will give you an idea of what may lay ahead. Sometimes roofs have two layers of shingles and you should be able to detect that. If you do, be prepared to replace that roof soon. Lifetime is not a lifetime anymore—20 years is about it. Certainly it is ammunition for negotiation; no one wants to pay a premium for a property with a bad roof. If you find a bad roof play it up big in your negotiation; if it is good don't mention it or play it up as bad and needs to be replaced.
- **Heating and air**. They are always a big ticket item. Take a moment and take a look at the system. Evaluate your options on the cost of conversion of heat if you plan to put in a new system.
- **Mold**. Any kind of mold in a property must be dealt with. Sometimes paint will hide a millions wounds. Be sure to have your tenant or buyer sign a mold release.
- **Plumbing**. Plumbing has become a no brainer. It is getting easier and easier to run. Especially with pex pipe. Almost anyone can do it. Look at the pipes inside. Old lead or galvanized pipe may be a problem. However it is cheap and easy to correct.
- **Insulation**. Sometimes you can add some insulation to a property but truly this can be an unnecessary expense. You be the judge. They

do have inexpensive do-it-yourself procedures that can save you a lot of money. It really won't add a lot of value to a property in terms of resale and it won't get you more rent.

- ▶ **Siding**. I am not a big siding person but there are flippers and investors that love siding. They buy a house and immediately replace the windows throughout and put siding on the house. No doubt this will give you a fresh new look. For curb side appeal and resale this is attractive. It is sometimes better to shop this out for a price to a subcontractor. Lots of people can do this work on the side. It generally is easy to do but for the specialty cuts and bends you need specialized equipment.
- ▶ **Asbestos**. Do not disturb. You may see some around borders and pipes in older homes. I have been told to leave it. If you have some, you can get advice from the DEQ, and he may recommend that you encapsulate it so it does not get disturbed by accident.
- ▶ **Sniff**. Use your nose. If you by further inspection have a chance to get inside the house, your nose may tell a lot of untold truths. Some odors you want to smell for:
  - ▷ mold or mildew
  - ▷ fire damage
  - ▷ gas or sewer smell
  - ▷ water soaked or pet smells in the carpet
  - ▷ odors from the kitchen area.
  - ▷ pet smells of all kinds
  - ▷ age smell, usually musty and not pleasing

There are indications that you have to look at to see if there is any truth behind the smell. If there is, dig deeper; you may find the real answer. The seller will have to pay dearly for these problems in negotiating the price.

Cool stuff. You may get lucky when you go inside a house and see some cool stuff that will enhance your resale value:

- ▶ Nice hardwood floors under carpet—that's a good one
- ▶ Vaulted ceilings that may be hidden with a drop ceiling. Or could be accented with a skylight or some nice track lighting

- Drop ceiling in general, hiding a nice ceiling
- Kitchen cabinets that have been painted and could be refinished
- Landscaping that is overrun and can be cleaned up
- A good looking almost new furnace that no one has touched in years, Just a service call and you are in great shape.
- Beautiful wood siding that has been covered by vinyl.
- A fireplace that has been covered up and all you may need is a mantle.
- A claw tub that with refinishing and new fixtures could be worth a million dollars.
- A cupboard in the kitchen that either was covered up or destroyed in some fashion.

Remember, a negative that you find in this property is projected as a negative to the seller and once fixed, painted, or repaired it is now a positive to your buyer.

Ugly is what ugly does. A plain ole ugly house that no one wants: yes, you can get it cheap. But take a good hard look to be sure that you can make some improvements to the outside to give it that curb appeal. You should be able to do it. In Part III, I will talk about porches, doors, painting, and landscaping, as ways to show off a property.

How to Choose a Price

Most values are not scientific as hard as you try to make them. There is no magic formula or standard that you can use, no rule to get an exact value. You can come close to a ballpark number. In most cases it's what the buyer is willing to pay and what the seller is willing to sell it for. If you have a meeting of the minds with a written contract and consideration, you have a deal.

So does it matter as to value of a property? You have to start somewhere so take an educated or uneducated guess and see if you can make a deal.

Buy a piece of property right by maximizing your equity: below wholesale, way below. Fix the property up right. At that point you will have value or equity in the property. Often you can refinance the property to allow you to

The Journey

Is it the hunt or bagging the fox? Many of us live for the hunt, not the trophy. It's the journey that keeps us moving towards success. Sure along the way there are trials and tribulations. Many things may get in the way that may slow you down, events that may act as speed bumps, obstacles that will dishearten you or diminish your enthusiasm during that journey.

That's the motivation to keep you focused on your goal: bagging the fox. The fox ultimately is no big deal. Seen one, seen them all. We cherish and live for that journey—that's the adrenaline rush. I love the journey.

take some money out of the property, enough to let you buy another piece of property.

I call this stair-stepping, using one house to buy another. By repeating this process several times you can and will be able to build a real-estate portfolio by using other people's money. If you own your own home you can take out a second mortgage and accomplish the same thing. You need cash in order to grow and/or the ability to borrow cash to buy properties.

If you are in the low-end market—say, the beaters that sell for around $10,000—then it's not a bad idea to have $10,000 handy to buy that deal.

You should always be prospecting, always looking for a deal. That's why when someone comes to you with a deal you want to be able to jump on it. Quick. It's like the early bird gets the worm idea: you don't want to miss a deal.

In your blueprint of success you have predetermined the price range of the properties that you will be looking at. So when deciding how much of a house you can afford, the house comes to you. A $50,000 house may wholesale for $40,000. However if your price range is $10,000, then $10,000 is your offer. Don't compromise your offer due to the value of a piece of property. Especially in bad economic times when people want to get out from under their mortgages, the baby boomers are looking for other options; older retired folk may not have options to work with. There are many reasons why someone will sell their property today. You just have to decide if it fits your profile.

So how much of a house can you afford? How much do you want to put into the purchase price and the renovations? Decide if you are going to flip the house or hold on to it for a long-term rental, knowing that the sale of a property may take a little time. Your available cash will play a huge role in making your offer. Just starting out I suggest that you stay somewhat conservative in making your offer. You will prepare a pro-forma so that you can evaluate your upcoming offer and potential purchase. Ask yourself:

- How much available cash do you have?
- Are you going to borrow money? From whom and at what rate?
- What is the cost of renovation?
- What are the extra costs of purchasing and selling the property?
- What is your current income? This will depend on whether you are doing this part time and have other income or whether you are taking living expenses out of your properties. This second option could be a tragic flaw.

In poor economic times you have got to consider the carrying costs of flipping property. Your carrying costs may be lower if you are using cash; however hard money is going to cost you dearly. A lot of new builders got caught in the housing bubble when their properties did not sell, and they were paying large amounts of money on interest.

When deciding on a house that you are ready to purchase, you may want to take it to the next level of evaluation. Certain flip properties will sell better than others. What does the market demand? What is selling today? Where is it located to make it attractive for a re-sale?

There are many methods of determining value of a property. Investors who are landlords use some, flippers use others, and wholesalers use all depending on what kind of a deal they are working with and the buying criteria of the investor they are purchasing for.

Amateur wholesalers find a property and then find buyers for it. Those who know what they are doing build a buyers list of active investors and look for the types of properties that they want. That way the day you get the contract is the same day you sell the property and you are now on to your next.

Value of Property

Brick and mortar. This is the actual cost of a property. How much per square foot it cost you either to stick build the property or rehab the property. This is actual cost.

Income approach. This is based on the income potential of a piece of property. Whether it is a commercial or residential property, lenders want to see what the income will be or is and what the expenses will be. There is a certain amount of subjectivity to the process, so be prepared to back up your income and expense report with actual leases or bills that you have paid.

You will get a greater value for your property using the income approach. With income and over time as your mortgage payment stays the same your rental income should increase nicely. I have many properties where the property has been paid off for years and the income on the property doubled.

Methods used by Landlords

There are various methods of valuation due to the fact that there are various types of property in different locations. A property in a low-income area that typically does not appreciate much, if at all, cannot be judged with the same formula as one in a high-end area that grows in value. The reasons for this include not only appreciation but the speed that it will sell, as well as low-income tenant drama versus upper-end tenants that pay their rent, etc.

The Hooch Method of Valuation (contributed by Dallas Powell). This method is to be used for low-income property in both white and minority areas. This is basically a junker formula. The Hooch Method is great to quickly determine a property's value. It is a formula used by landlords, because the determining factor for a landlord has to be rent, not the After Repair Value (ARV) as a flipper would use. A landlord couldn't care less what the ARV is unless he is intending to sell the property within a short timeframe.

The Hooch Method of Valuation is:

> (monthly rent x 30 – repairs [including splitting up the utilities on a multifamily if needed]).

The maximum offer would be:

> (monthly rent x 35 – repairs).

Never go over 35 on junker properties when buying wholesale. Remember, I am talking about wholesale, not retail. The Hooch Method is specifically designed for low-income areas. There is room in this method for your profit. So let's say you think there is $5,000 of repairs on a house you found, and the place will rent for $900:

> $900 x 30 = $27,000 - $5,000 = $22,000. This is your offer.

Triplex example: 1 bedroom $425; one bedroom $425; 3 bedroom $595.

> Total rent = $1445 x 30 = $43,350
> total value of the house with no repairs needed.

Now let's say that you have about $5,000 in repairs.

HERE IS A TIP

When you decide on the price that you want to pay, reduce that price in half. So if your offer is $10,000 make it $5,000. You want to establish a starting point for your negotiations, letting the seller know you are serious and you are not offering much for the property.

$43,350 - $5,000 = $38,350.

This is the total that you will offer in the rent x 30 scenario.

There is room with the Hooch Method to make double payments and end up with very little cash flow per month. Double payments on your fifteen-year note will pay the house off completely in five years considering all expenses.

2% Rule. The two-percent rule is useful for nicer areas. In this scenario you are talking about property that appreciates some, lawns that are taken care of, a high-end blue-collar or low-end white-collar area. You shouldn't see many houses that are in need of repairs. People in this area are NOT living paycheck to paycheck. They have a little bit of expendable income. Most houses are also not rental property like you would see in the low-income areas. There will be many owner occupiers with a few rental units here and there.

Using this rule you determine the value by the rent equaling two percent of the total purchase price. So if the rent was $900, then multiply it by 50 and you have $45,000 for your offer. You also must subtract repairs in this method. There is less cash flow on these types of houses for a landlord but less drama to deal with as well. They also have more appreciation than the low-income housing.

My general rule of thumb is to never get more than a 15-year note. And with that in mind, never pay more than (rent x 50) on ANY house purchase, or it will not generate cash flow. Bounce some scenarios against the Cash Flow Analysis explained below and you will see for yourself. If you extended the note beyond 15 years and paid a little more than the 2% rule, then you can make the property profitable, but I, like most wise investors, am in the business of making money for myself, not for the banks.

1% Rule. Do a search on the internet and you will see more people talking about this 1% Rule. In this scenario the rent should equal one percent of the purchase price. So $900 rent should mean that you pay $90,000 ($900 x 100) minus repairs for the house. This is the rule that the novice investors use and get burned on. I have run across many landlords that have gone under because of this. I then try to buy their property and they are so far upside down that I cannot even make a sensible offer. You would have to put a significant amount of money down to have a positive cash flow with this formula. This formula is only used by idiots in my opinion. But if I were selling a house I would be using this formula as if it were tried and true.

Cash Flow analysis. Here is an example of a quick determination of value based on profit per door on a triplex. I use this formula on every house I buy along with the other listed formulas, as I want to make sure that the house will bring the minimum cash flow I require. And the big question is will the property turn a profit or not. Many investors want a minimum of $100 cash flow per door per month. This formula is based on a 100% loan, as if you were going to pay yourself back for what you put down on it too, which is what a wise investor does.

> Gross income: $1,445 per month; $17,340 per year
> Less expenses (50% rule of thumb): $8,670
> NOI: $8,670
> $43,350 @ 7% / 20 years: ($1,865)
> Yearly Cash Flow: $6,805
> Or $567 per month or $189 per door @ 3 units

Other methods of valuation include the Gross Rent Multiplier and Capitalization Rate, but these methods are not needed for a wholesaler. You are trying to determine a ballpark value. The investor will do that as well as along with the GRM, and the smart investor will be figuring it by the CAP rate.

Flippers: Maximum Allowable offer (MAO). Flippers use a different formula based on the property's Maximum Allowable Offer (MAO). Flippers are determining the After Repair Value (ARV) of the property, subtracting repairs and holding costs, and deciding if there is enough profit in between.

Most flippers I know won't touch a property unless there is a $20,000 or more spread between the ARV and their costs to purchase, repair, and hold the property. So when figuring this stuff out, you run the same numbers and subtract your fees and you then know what to offer.

Many wholesalers like to be between 65 and 70 percent of the ARV. In my opinion that is high and if a wholesaler came to me with a property in that range I would tell him to come back when he had some real deals. But I buy cheap and am not the typical investor since I typically do my own wholesale deals. I like to work the seller down much lower than that, and I suggest that on your initial offer you lowball it and then let the seller work you up.

Let's look at this formula based on a high 65% of the ARV. Let's say that you have found (without a doubt) that the after repair value is $100,000 and it needs $15,000 of repairs to make it worth $100,000.

> 65% of the ARV minus cost of repairs equals MAO (maximum allowable offer. Notice the maximum! Don't go over or you won't be selling the property.)
>
> Or
>
> 65% of $100,000 - $15,000 = MAO
> $65,000 - $15,000 = MAO
> $50,000 Your Maximum Allowable Offer

So you take this $50,000 and reduce it by the profit that you want and you have your actual offer. Let's say you want to make $10,000.

> $50,000 - $10,000 = $40,000.

So you offer the seller $40,000 for the house.

CHAPTER 12

Negotiating

YOU NEED TO BE ABLE TO SELL YOUR OFFER. Why is the property you are buying not worth as much as the seller wants, and how can you justify the ridiculous price you are offering? That's the technique you need to learn and develop. As time goes on and you become familiar with the process you will use techniques that will help you. When you do your due diligence on the property you should have an outline of the improvements you want to make and what they will cost. You will have a contractor's price for the work, and your own price for the work. You will negotiate your deal with the contractor's price to substantiate your argument.

You will get better and better at this with experience. It will take some practice before you become the pro from Dover. Also remember without a signed contract there is nothing lost. You can always walk away from a deal. Talk is cheap, and it is not legally binding. Talk all you want. When working with a prospective seller, there are many questions you should ask:

- ▶ Who owns the property?
- ▶ Why do you want to sell the property?
- ▶ How much time do you need to move?

- Do you have the authority to sell the property? If you have partners, who has the authority to negotiate and ink the deal?
- What did you pay for the property and when?
- What did you do in your rehab work and how much did you spend?
- Do you have any pictures?
- Is the property involved in any legal suits right now?
- Are there any judgments or liens on the property?
- Do you have a tenant, what kind of lease and how long is it for?
- Do you owe any taxes on the property?
- What is your mortgage? Whom is it with and are you behind on your payments?
- How is the property heated, and how old is the unit?
- What do you think the property is worth?

Special Situations

Death do us part. If the owner of the property has passed and the property is with an estate that will greatly influence the price. A lot of executors want to clean up the estate, so the price may be negotiable. If the executor is from out of town they may not know the market conditions in your area and you will be at a great advantage.

Equity. If the property is paid for and there is not a blaring mortgage on it, the seller will have more latitude to make a deal at any price. The higher the mortgage, the harder it will be for the seller to make that deal. If a bank owns the property, they will at first try to get out of it what they have in the property. The longer they have it in their inventory the lower the price will be. I have seen some crazy offers on properties. There are times when at the end of the year they want to clean up their dead inventory for the regulators and may

CHAPTER 12: NEGOTIATING

By getting some of this information you will get a good feel for the status of the property and be able to put together an offer, if you decide to. After awhile when you see a property from the curb and with this information, you will be able to put together a reasonable offer. It's not that hard, especially when there are similarities with other properties, especially if they are in the same area as ones you have researched before or already own. That's the beauty of targeting an area and specializing in that area. You become an expert and can save a great deal of time, effort, and money. You will be able to get the best of the best deals.

No matter what you pay for the property, even if you are able to steal it, make the seller feel as though he got a great deal and that you are the one who made it happen. Even if you stole it so to speak, you may have just saved the seller's personal financial life. You were able to fill that need. Again, it's a win-win; make the seller feel good about the deal.

---

just about take any price. So don't be bashful in your offer.

Bottom-feeder earnest money. Like I have outlined before, as the seller you want to request the largest amount possible as a deposit. However, as the buyer, and especially as a bottom feeder (which, by the way, is not an epithet to be snuffed at or ridiculed as unprofessional or unethical; we are buyers, buyers with a purpose to succeed), offer as little as possible. Even if you have a great deal of money, do you want to hand it over to the seller? Personally, I like going to the seller with a promissory note to denote my seriousness as a buyer. Why not? If the seller is willing to sign a contract with little to no money down and a promissory note for either the deposit or for the purchase of the property, then I say, Why not? Go for it. When you have no money and you want to get into the game, then you must be creative; this is a way to be creative.

So when you have no money, use the promissory note as a way of negotiating your deal. Remember

continued on page 146

As the buyer, don't offer a lot of information if you can help it. It is not necessary; the seller is now only interested in his situation, which is to sell his property. Learn to listen, be silent, and let the seller lead the conversation. Don't be afraid to ask questions, though. This is the information that you will use to negotiate your offer. You are building ammunition to use against the seller for your offer; you will have an edge if you know as much, or more, about the property than he knows. Don't show your hand; keep your thoughts to yourself. You don't want to appear too anxious. If you need to, act distracted or disinterested; walk out if it gets stale.

Let the seller know you are working on lots of other deals and that you don't need this one. You can take it or leave it; it makes no difference. You are doing the seller a favor by buying his house. You don't have to; you can walk away any time.

Most people think that they can negotiate a deal—that it's a piece of cake. I have not seen many great negotiators who were not also veteran negotiators;

that in this situation you may be dealing with a desperate seller. If that is the case it is ok. Don't take advantage of them but do get the best deal you possibly can by low-balling the offer, promissory note in hand. You may be thinking it is a bad deal for them and you are taking advantage of them. But in reality you may be saving their life. They can always say *No*! You are not forcing them to do the deal. They have decided to do it. It is not your fault if the seller is uneducated. How many cars did you buy from a used car salesman and felt like it was not a good deal afterward? Caveat emptor. But let the seller beware too; it goes both ways. In this case the buyers are the sharks in a pool full of guppies.

Contracts. Have there been any other offers on the property and what were those offers? You can get a good idea what the seller is thinking by evaluating what the seller has turned down. You may be able to get that information or maybe not.

CHAPTER 12: NEGOTIATING

you have to learn the art. Dallas Powell and I are two of the best at negotiating and getting a great deal, but so many people think that they can do better.

Have a plan prior to negotiating your deal. You have selected the property you want to buy. You have done your due diligence on the property, and you want it. You may even have a price you want to pay for it. Now make the plan for how you are going to negotiate with the seller to get to that price. There are many different ways to skin the cat, to get to that acceptable magic number, which you must be able to stand behind: if you are talking a cash deal be sure that you have the cash ready to buy the property. The worst thing is to negotiate the deal and then not be able to stand behind it.

I have a friend named Frank who buys a lot of foreclosures at the courthouse even though he really does not know how to buy property. The trustees love him because he overpays for all of his properties; one of his problems is that he gets wrapped up in the heat of the sale and before he knows it he has paid too much for the property; he wants to win at any price, but really he

This information may be difficult to obtain from a real-estate agent due to disclosure laws; however, the seller may give it to you. Either way if you can see this information it will be helpful to you.

has lost. To an extent he is negotiating with the trustee who is acting as an auctioneer for himself. He never has a maximum price in mind before negotiating because he has too much money. He loses a lot of his margin of profit by paying too much. Later on the resale will hurt him. Negotiating well becomes part of how and who you are in the act of a deal; you personally will play an important part in how you negotiate a deal. We all do it differently.

You need to lead the negotiating. You need to be the alpha dog, the perpetrator, make them come to you. Come from a position of strength, not one of weakness; that's what will make your deal come to fruition and make you successful. It's how you make it happen. It's all up to you; don't let the opponent get the upper hand in negotiating your deal. And don't be afraid to walk away; there is another deal just around the corner.

Since you are going to build a large portfolio your first deal is not going to be your last deal. You may have several negotiations going on at the same time. Multi-tasking on different deals is fun. Just be careful if a couple of them come through at the same time. I stagger the closings so I don't get caught in a tough spot.

> You must have a vision; be persistent, have a lot of patience, but most of all be determined—tough not transparent.

You must have a vision; be persistent, have a lot of patience, but most of all be determined—tough not transparent. Stand your ground and don't give up. I like gaming people: if the seller decides to walk away from a deal but then sometime later comes back to me, the price of the property just got reduced. I don't want to revisit the old price. There is a price to pay for not doing the deal the first time; let the seller know this upfront.

Real-estate agents, buyers, and sellers work in tight circles. It is relatively a small community. They consider themselves professionals. They tend to network well; they attend meetings, seminars, continuing education, as well as share stories by word of mouth. You must develop a reputation of honesty and integrity—that you do what you say you are going to do. Otherwise sellers will steer clear. Do the right thing and it will come back to you in spades. If you are inefficient, lazy, and dishonest, word will also travel fast and your business will suffer. You want repeat customers, especially the investors who buy and sell a lot of property.

Our approach to negotiating properties sometimes comes across as "take it or leave it." It is easier to use that approach through a real-estate agent than with the homeowner himself. When dealing with the homeowner, use a higher level of diplomacy. You can be tougher with an agent who can sell your offer with a little more finesse. That is a good tactic: when I put in my low-ball, take-it-or-leave-it offers, which are many, I leave it up to the agent (when I use one) to make the deal. That's what they are paid to do.

You will have greater success in a down market like now because the market is so soft. People are not buying properties like they were ten years ago, especially the lower-end properties in depressed neighborhoods where folks may not have all the credentials to buy. In these areas you will see far more rental properties than in higher-end neighborhoods. This creates a great opportunity for the person getting ready to build an investment portfolio. You may develop a reputation as a low-baller or a take-it-or-leave-it negotiator. It may work against you sometimes, but in many cases when properties come up for sale, agents and homeowners will start coming to you. You will develop a reputation quickly based on your performance.

There are different approaches to building your investment portfolio when it comes to negotiating and buying property. You can take the high road and do little negotiating, paying almost market value, or the low road and be the low-ball king. Some real-estate experts will not promote the low-ball technique. I prefer the low ball. How many low-ball offers do you have to make to get one of them accepted? You will know that answer in a short time and, true to fact, may establish a reputation as a low-ball king. But, you are not running for elected office: why should you care if you hurt someone's feelings by putting in a low offer. You are not in a popularity contest. You are in business to build an investment portfolio. Many real-estate agents may put you on the bottom of the pile; homeowners may just throw your offer away. Real-estate agents are bound to present to the homeowner every offer on a property.

Your agent will be able to feed you information that will help you decide how to move forward on your deal. Having a good understanding and knowledge of the area and what may or may not work, your agent will be sure that you are not exposed to any mistakes. He will also negotiate any and all counteroffers and can act as the devil's advocate during negotiations. You as the buyer do what you can by holding the trump card. Your agent will be dealing usually with another agent or the property owner himself.

The real-estate agent commission is built into the advertised price of the property, so why should you care? You make your offer; the seller upon acceptance pays agent's commission. This applies unless you are doing a FSBO, in which case negotiations will be up to you. There are all kinds of options on which way you want to proceed. You can cover a lot more territory by using an agent.

Don't Chase the Rabbit

There are deals, more deals, and tomorrow there will be even more deals. I have jumped in too quick too many times. When you are following your blueprint and remaining focused, it's all-important to have deals in the pipeline. If for instance you are prospecting, and you see a great property worth $60,000, your opening bid is $5,000. If I am doing two properties per year, it's early spring, and I am on either the first or second property; I may put in ten bids. This way I see what's happening, like fishing downstream; you never know when you catch one. If any of the deals come through, great. I usually try to delay the closing by including an inspection clause—a feasibility study. Heck, for $5,000 I made a score—and $3,000 a grand slam, so I have time to find the money if I need to.

It is easy to get wrapped up into a deal, sort of like getting sucked into buying a piece that you can do without at an auction. That's why you should work a couple of deals and make sure that you have your Maximum Allowable Offer in place. It makes no sense to chase the property and pay too much for it. You don't need anything that bad and you don't want to pay more for the property than you intend to pay. It's hard to walk away; learn how. You will be surprised that later the deal may come right back to you. Maybe not today, but later.

If by chance you buy something that you shouldn't have, for any reason, do a few improvements to the property and move it; flip it. Curb appeal can make a difference. Don't try to put the square peg in the round hole. It either fits or it does not fit. You will know. Be objective in your thinking and make the right choice.

It's All in Your Head

Knowledge is the key to being able to do your due diligence on a property, so you can intelligently make an offer and negotiate a deal. This will not happen overnight. It will take time. Take the time to learn all you can. The bottom line is that you want to be more knowledgeable of the market, the property, the HOA, basically all aspects of the deal, than the seller and the agent. That way you come across as the expert and what you are saying about your offer and the reasoning behind it may in fact be the truth. And if you convince the seller, he may meet your low-ball offer. This is what you want. It is not easy; you've got to do your homework and be prepared. That's why I like specializing in an area: I know it better than anyone.

It also pays to be knowledgeable about each particular sale; a little research or exploration into these areas might help you negotiate the price you are willing to pay:

- ▶ How quick does the seller want to make a move?
- ▶ How desperate is the seller to sell the property? Is he facing foreclosure? Is he behind in his payments? Does he have other financial constraints that have forced him to sell his property? There could be marital or health issues that are forcing him to sell. A lot of homeowners got upside down on their homes, taking out second mortgages to do other things with. This caused a lot of financial stress to homeowners. A house worth $1 million in 2006 may be

worth only $200,000 in 2013. The payments would have stayed the same. Many families want to get out from under the large payment and get to something they can afford.
- ▶ Has the property been up for sale for awhile? Whether it was an REO, an FSBO, or an MLS, see how long the property has been offered. If the property has had no offers in 30 days the chances are better that the seller will look at your offer. The longer the property is on the market the lower the price you want to offer. Also it will indicate to the seller that maybe there is something wrong with the property or that the price is too high. Either way the seller will be thinking.

Get into the head of the seller if you can. Know your enemy before you fight him. He may have the same attitude toward you, so in the act of negotiation show no sympathy and go for all that you possibly can.

You won't know until you try; that's a key element in making a deal. How will you know the answer until you ask the question? How will you know about your offer until you make an offer? You have got to start somewhere; how about at the bottom with a low-ball offer? You may get lucky, and the offer will be accepted. When you do low ball an offer be sure that you have a good reason why you are low balling and then put the offer on the seller's plate, telling him what a great deal it is. You have got to get them to a point where they feel like even your low ball is a high offer. You know it is a low ball; they do not.

If it makes it past the trash can, then your door will be open for negotiation, which puts you a step closer to making a deal. Even if you committed and something comes up—just cold feet or some vital information about the property—until you sign the contract and provide legal consideration, you can walk away; that's the beauty of a deal and negotiation: when you are in charge and control the deal, you can walk away.

Points for Review

- ▶ Don't chase the deal. Let the deal come to you. There are way too many great deals out there to chase it. If you chase the deal you may overbid on the price, and you don't want to do that.

- Stay firm. Know in your mind what you will pay and that's it. This is consistent with your blueprint and will indeed give you the results you are looking for. That's why you want the seller to come to you.
- Tit for tat: You may put out a straw bidder, one to establish the bottom price in an effort to get the property at a price that you are willing to pay. You want this $80,000 property for $10,000, so you have a straw bidder or friend put in a contract for $7,000; you have set the bar for the seller.
- Don't communicate too much. Keep your comments direct and to the point. Be direct. No nonsense. Get the job done.
- Be professional to any and all counteroffers or conversation relating to the property.
- Pitching an offer is important. You will never buy the first property if you don't try. Trying is making the offer—any offer.
- Your real-estate agent can be your eyes and ears when making that offer. You are in the background and the seller may never know who you are. He doesn't have to know.
- You can read a person through his body language. By the way he talks you can get a good or bad feeling on whether the deal is going to happen.
- Always be professional in your negotiations with the seller. If you make an offer and it does not work, try, try again.

GOOD TO KNOW:

Everyone wants to win; everyone would like to think that he got the best deal. Not always the case; sometimes you win, sometimes you lose. Just remember the bird in the hand philosophy.

- ▶ Find those deals that are too good to be true. Once you taste blood, meaning finding one of those deals, you will want more. So keep on looking; they are out there.
- ▶ Check out the house. The condition of the property will give you a good idea of what the property may sell for; remember they are all different. When you go inside, do a mental audit of the furniture, appliances, wallpaper, paint, toys, and TV.
- ▶ Cash talks. It seems that it may always come down to cash. If you have a nice deposit, can verify funds in the bank and close quick, you will get the attention of the seller and/or his agent. People talk a lot of smack. Don't be that person—if you are serious and have the cash, then make the deal.

They say take-it-or-leave-it has no place in negotiations. I guess it depends. Offers and counteroffers are like a cat and mouse game. You decide where you start and where you plan to end. You know in your mind where you want to end. High-end properties are going to be a little more difficult to low ball. They are especially harder with individual homeowners who are in the retail market. Dealing with retail is much more different than dealing in the wholesale market. Obviously the retail market is going to have higher-valued properties; these may have mortgages of up to 80% of the home's value. This is a tougher piece of property to sell again, as opposed to wholesale. Once you are in the business for awhile, you will gravitate to the wholesale market.

It's an Art

The ability to negotiate a deal is an art. I have the **$5,000 Rule**, which has been successful many times. It is a tool that you can use to establish a price and hopefully pick up properties cheap. If you put in multiple contracts on properties, sooner or later you will get one, so I recommend having deals in the pipeline. Offer prices that are ridiculously low: the **$5,000 Rule**. Let the sellers come to you. Chances are they will. If you are not in a rush you may have your hands full. This will take some practice and maybe some nerve, since the prices you want to offer may be silly. Who cares? Try it; you may like it.

CHAPTER 12: NEGOTIATING

Establish yourself as a no-nonsense negotiator: here is the price, say $5,000, and I am not going up. The buyer may be interested and sell you the property at that price. Know when you plan to close the window. The buyer may counter your offer. Know where your point of acceptance is, for instance $7,000 or $10,000. You should know before you go into the deal. I am working with a realtor in Danville, who will submit any price that I want. I have been submitting $2,000 or $3,000 offers on houses there.

Your success rate on deals that are substantially lower than what the seller wants to sell a property for will depend on your ability to sell the seller on what the property is worth. Obviously, with that in mind I am going to present evidence of how much needs to be done to the property. Although you may end up not renovating these areas, they do allow for great arguments to bring the price down:

- the kitchen has to be completely redone—new cabinets, new floor
- the bathroom needs new fixtures and updating
- the roof leaks and needs to be replaced
- cracks in the foundation with a leaky basement
- electrical needs to be updated
- heating is old needs to be updated be sure to add the cost of air conditioning

Let the seller know how much money it is going to cost you in getting the property up to snuff; this may make him feel bad and consider your price.

Not a bad idea to throw in a few goodies when you are buying a property—things that may not normally go with the property: the appliances, wood stove, washer and dryer. I would consider them enhancements to make your deal just a little sweeter. Remember that it does not hurt to ask, and you may just get them. The seller may not have any interest in these things at all.

You can get the seller to do some additional things like pay for some of the repairs through credit or decrease in the purchase price. This may be included in your negotiations or price, or if you like after you have agreed on a price. You hit him with the repair list and ask for a credit; you may get something, and it is always worth asking because all he can do is say *No*. You can strengthen your case at the last minute in a negotiation. Why not ask the seller to pay for some additional things (for example, closing fees)?

Wheel-and-deal tips of the trade:

- You can be speedy or slow—depends on what side of the deal you are on.
- Be cautious, careful, and watchful; be honest.
- A deal to get is one to secure.
- Know the wheeler's background; check the temperature.
- Have backup cash.
- Watch yourself—project all outcomes; have a Plan B.
- Think about your portfolio and cash flow.
- Plan on the deal's termination and liquidation.
- Keep it simple; no complication.
- Be honest.
- Be thorough—cover all your bases.
- Get another opinion: Two are better than one.

You don't have to be a rocket scientist to make a deal; use your knowledge and intuition—your gut. Run the numbers. Look ahead to what's next; if the deal you made is a bad deal, make a plan. Once you have done real estate for awhile you will develop a better feel for what is good and what you should stay away from. You will know when to walk away and when to stay. Remember there is another deal just around the corner. When one door shuts two may open for you.

No Regrets

You will think sometimes if perhaps you sold your property too quick and could have gotten more for it. Or if you buy a nice property, that you could have bought it for less. Don't worry about what the other person makes. If you sell a property quick, be satisfied. You hit the mark. I have seen price swings of

$3,000 that have either moved a property or did not. Don't be greedy. Selling it quick only means that you can do another deal quicker. Lots of small deals will add up quickly in your bank account. On the low end if you bought that property right and can make money on it then you should be satisfied with that deal and move on to the next one.

You will always feel like you can do better. There is always a story of an investor who got the killer deal. Don't worry about his business. If you like the deal, if the money works and it is something you can win with, then what is stopping you? Do the deal and be happy with it. The guy who has to brag about his deal may not have received such a good deal in the long run.

Many times I personally view it as a game, like chess or monopoly. To the victor go the spoils. That's not a bad attitude, but the attitude and belief of a winner, a champion in the travails of successful investing. The more offers you make, the more houses you look at, the better you will become in making great offers to buy. Don't be afraid; take the approach that every house you look at you make an offer. There could be days that you make 100 offers. Let's worry about the funding later; you never know what the seller is thinking, and one out of a 100 may take your offer.

CHAPTER 13

The Purchase

THE ACTUAL PURCHASE PROCESS CAN BE A CONFUSING MESS OF DETAILS. Unless you have experience purchasing real estate, seriously consider retaining a lawyer and a title company to ensure that all of the details are in place. Without hesitation or reservation I will tell you that you should have an attorney or closing agent at a settlement company prepare your deed. Eliminate the chance of a mistake; shift the liability to a third party. Also, they will have title insurance if there happens to be a mistake.

- Find the property that you want to purchase through the various means, prospecting, etc.
- Decide what price you want to offer, after you do your due diligence on the property.
- Make an offer. This may take a little time, some bargaining, and negotiation. Start somewhere; make an offer. Remember, no offer is foolish. You never know what the person will take or reject.
- Settle on a price and reduce it to a contract with consideration. Be sure to evaluate the terms. Ideal: low cost with zero down payment. The number will depend on your situation. Be keen.

A Purchasing Checklist

▷ Do I have title insurance?
▷ Are there any encumbrances, liens, or judgments on the title? You need fair and equitable title to the property with protection.
▷ Have the terms of the contract been fulfilled and in accordance with the law?
▷ Have I misrepresented any of the facts or information to the lender, the seller, or my attorney?

You as the buyer want to be sure you are getting a clean title. If the title has a defect, the defect will be paid with sale proceeds. If there is not enough money to clear the title, the seller has to come up with the money, or he cannot provide clean title, in which case the buyer will probably not want to buy that property. You can do a quit claim deed or a deed of gift, accepting the encumbrances on the property that you are buying. This approach has its risks. But remember, any and all liens and encumbrances come off ten years from the day of recording, so if you are buying and holding, you may be good.

I have made some great purchases with bad titles. If you buy a piece of property that has a defect in the title when the property passes to you, you can wait 10 years for that defect to come off. I did a deal where two judgments were on the property in the name of one of the owners who had passed away—basically, an uncollectable judgment. I took the chance since I purchased the property at the right price, which was good. Using the property as rental income was my option. Flipping the property was not an option. Good deal for me again as long as I hold on to the property for 10 years.

If you purchase a property at foreclosure then the property will pass to the buyer with good and equitable title. You are ok.

When you get the title:

- ▶ See if there are any liens on the property. You may find there is a second deed of trust or an equity line.
- ▶ Tax liens, either local or federal, or state tax liens may be on the property as well.
- ▶ Follow the chain of ownership to be sure there is no break in ownership, that it has remained consistent over the years.

If you have questions about any of the issues with liens on the title or anything else, the title company will straighten them out. Always have the title company do a title search before closing. As good as your search may be, it is best to double check. The title company may go back a little further than you did or just be a little thorougher than you were to be sure you get clear title. In a situation like this, it's best to be safe.

I just purchased a property where an older, sickly man had lived for 30 years. His grandmother's possessions were still in the house. I ended up making several offers on the property and only to find out that he did not own it. His relatives owned it, but they were all dead. I lowered the price, offered a little cash to take it *as is*, and it worked. The house has some liens on it, but as 10 years pass the liens will as well. This was a risky property; I will not be able to flip the deal right away, but after it is rented for a number of years, I will be able to do so.

Contracts

Always make your offers in contract form. You may initially talk an offer through to a point where you know where both parties stand. Once you feel comfortable as to the terms and conditions then go ahead and make that offer, but be sure it is in the form of a contract. It must be in writing signed by both parties and have some type of consideration to be valid.

This contract, whether initiated by your attorney or not, will make its way to your attorney or closing agent to fulfill the terms of a contract and close the property and record it. Be sure you include all the details within the contract. It has to be written; here are some key points that the contract must stipulate:

- Do the appliances pass with the property?
- If there are tenants, will they put down deposits?
- The amount of the deposit on the contract
- Closing date and location
- Who pays closing costs?
- Financing
- Dual agency requirement (if you are using a real-estate agent)
- Will there be any inspections?
- All disclosures, mold, termite, dual agency
- When to take possession
- Who will pay the property taxes
- How long the offer is valid. Do not keep it open ended, but include a drop-dead date.
- The price you are willing to pay, with the terms and conditions of the financing
- When does your deposit count and when does it not? What is the effective date?

You may have already discussed all the counteroffers on the property; if you have, then take the contract to the seller for signature. If it is a blend contract whereby you have discussed the deal with the seller but really you have not confirmed the price and all the details of the deal, then have the contract ready to go to the seller. Either you bring the contract to the seller, which works great, or have your realtor bring the contract. If the contract is not what the seller is looking for, then be prepared to negotiate the deal further, usually done with a counteroffer. You as the buyer should cross out the changes, write in what you want to change, and initial the changes. Leave a small space for the seller so if he accepts your counter all he has to do is initial the changes and you have a done deal. Again you want to be honest and up front with all the terms and conditions of the deal, so there is little to no room for error. That way no one gets surprised at closing.

Use contingencies in contracts effectively; a seller prefers to have as few as possible, but they can help the buyer. I recommend a small refundable deposit.

This is your exit if you think for a minute you need one. A contingency is a condition in a contract that must be fulfilled for the contract to remain valid. Best to put your intentions in writing to the parties involved.

Common contingencies:

- financing
- home inspection
- a marketable title
- sale of another property
- appraisal

Be careful on any type of performance contracts. Something may look great to you today, but in six months with things a little different you may no longer want to fulfill the performance terms. Many times it will be about money, which is tough unless you sell the property or have a nice cash reserve.

Closing. Be sure to use a reputable title company or lawyer to do this for you. There are many; develop a relationship with one and be loyal. When ready to close, consult your settlement company or your attorney—one or the other needs to be brought into the loop. Then, organize what funds you will need, assuming your offer was based on either cash you have or cash that you have lined up for the closing. All that remains is setting a date.

Transaction costs. It will cost money to close a deal. Many of the expenses are all going to be the same, but many you can shop to get the best price. Don't think you should do this yourself. You could make a mistake that could be costly.

Fees that could be added to your closing costs at closing you should try to negotiate and be aware of:

- **Application fee.** This is a fee that is charged by the lender or mortgage broker to work your loan. They typically want to cover their costs, which could include credit checks. Most banks won't charge you up front but will add it to the costs. A mortgage broker may require this fee up front. Typically they also can be negotiated. Ask first.

- **Credit report charge.** This fee is for pulling each of your credit scores, Equifax as an example may be a separate line item or it may be included in your application fee.
- **Home inspection.** FHA may require one or even you as the buyer may want a home inspection on the property. This price will vary from area to area. You may decide after the inspection not to buy the house. You will still have to pay the home inspector. You may pay him up front upon completion or it could be a line item on your closing statement or HUD. You can save some money if you are able to do this yourself.
- **Appraisal Fee.** This is the fee charged by the insurance company for an inspection of the property to determine its value. This is a specialized field and does require a level of training. You can shop this and find the appraisers are different. They will all charge a different price. Again you can pay direct or add it to your closing statement or HUD. If you obtain a loan, most lenders will require an appraiser to determine the value. Appraisers can do most residential homes, but it does take someone more specialized to do a commercial job. Properties can be appraised by the conventional brick and mortar approach or for a higher value they can be appraised by the income method.

Always be conscious of any and all unexpected costs that can range from back taxes, a roof, a lien by judgment. There are a number of expenses that may catch you by surprise. Just be prepared as best you can.

CHAPTER 14

Financing the Deal

IF YOU DON'T HAVE A BUCKET FULL OF CASH stashed away to finance your new investment business, you will be thinking about your options—and there are plenty.

You want to obtain the best mortgages you can possibly get for your situation; whether it is about amount, terms, or interest, you really want to shop your deal. Your mortgage will be one of your largest expenses. That's why when I can, I pay cash. If I cannot then give me a short-term loan so I can get it done with. That philosophy has worked for me for many years.

It is best to set up a savings or checking account in a bank so that you have a beginning. You are developing a relationship and that in itself is important.

Applying for a mortgage may be a little tricky. The amount of money you put into the property as a down payment, your equity, is important when trying to put together a payment amount for you to budget. If you are financing the property for 30 years you need to know what your monthly payment will be. The financial institution you are borrowing from will analyze your income to see if you can afford to make the payment; they will do a good job with this. They will also give you the payment amount and itemize the interest and principal for each payment.

Loan applications can be complicated and require a great deal of information. One thing is for certain: you must disclose all your information as requested by the lender. I found the best thing is to prepare a checklist of what is required, and then pull those items together into a package for presentation to the lending institutions. With future loans, you will only need to submit your loan application package with up-to-date information.

The key here is to reduce debt, pay on time, keep your debt-to-equity ratio in check at all times, and monitor your credit to be sure you are doing all you can to improve it—a little at a time.

For the longest time I was not worried about the immediate. I always looked for the long term. I therefore never had more than a 10-year mortgage. I structured the mortgages for 5, 7, and 10 years. I called that my stairstep mortgage.

MORTGAGE BROKERS

Mortgage brokers are people who will take your credit information and loan request and shop it at different lending institutions. They will try to get you some competitive deals. The brokers will take a commission for their work, which will vary in quality. The brokers may charge a commission or points that will go to them for their fee. During the go-go 90s, mortgage brokers popped up everywhere, and some people made some serious money. As a borrower you had a lot of options. Mortgage brokers pushed the envelope to a lot of deals then, putting the economy in a tough spot. Some mortgage brokers even misrepresented information from borrowers to get them qualified.

The mortgage broker can do a lot of work for you that you may not want to do or not know how to do. After a while a mortgage broker will have a checklist of what is required and should have a pretty slick system to get done everything that needs to be done. Mortgage brokers generally give advice to their clients. It is important for a mortgage broker to

It hurt my day-to-day cash flow; however, in the long run my properties got paid off quickly—ones that I could use over and over again to build my portfolio. After awhile it seemed like I was having a bottle of champagne each year as I burned another note that I paid off, growing both my portfolio and my equity position.

Most borrowers would prefer not to pay points. A no-point mortgage is great and the best to get. A private lender may charge you points, plus an organization fee, high interest, and other add-ons.

listen to the client and actually see what he needs for his situation. It could be for his personal home or an investment portfolio. For most people a home is the largest investment that they will make in a lifetime. So it is important to be prudent in your decision making. A good broker will take the time to work for your investment portfolio and give it direction.

You want the best deal you can get for your loan; instruct your broker to find it. There are hundreds of lenders; he may work for just a few of them. You want them to get you the best deal out there, to shop the deal, to think outside the box, especially if you have a good deal and good credit.

The broker you hire when applying for your loan can also handle the closing as well. The documents can be tedious and a broker with closing experience can make it work for you. He can close the deal for you with little to no problems.

Prequalification is a competitive advantage when negotiating a contract of purchase. You can save some money and time by pre-qualifying for a loan. Most lending institutions will let you come in to their office and pre-qualify. Based on your income and credit as well as the price of the property, they can tell you how much house you can afford to buy. So if you qualify for only a $100,000 home, there is no sense looking at $200,000 homes. You can and should stay within your price qualification range. Don't waste your time, your bank's time, and your realtor's time.

Beware of prepayment penalties. Look at these closely. As a buyer you want to be sure there are no penalties charged.

The banks like you to pay off a loan from time to time. This further enhances your relationship with a bank. It will give you greater leverage to borrow more money later on. At some point in time the banks will put a cap on what they will lend you and cut you off. That's why you want to use multiple lenders.

At some point you may qualify for a private banker, one who will specialize in your portfolio. They may require you to move all your business to their bank. If and when this happens, be sure to get a substantial line of credit so your future needs will be provided for.

In your own portfolio watch your interest rates. If you have an opportunity to lower your rate, and thus improve your cash flow, you should consider refinancing your loan. If you are taking over a loan, you should evaluate the interest payment and see if you can get a lower rate.

Some elements to watch for when securing or refinancing a mortgage.

1. Avoid loans with any penalties for prepayment. If your existing loan has a prepayment penalty, don't re-finance it.

2. Be careful of the closing costs. Shop around for the best ones

3   Don't refinance at a fixed rate onto an adjustable rate mortgage.

4   Don't finance the property with all the equity out of it. Leave some equity in the property.

5   On an equity line evaluate the interest rate, the increased payment, and the effect it will have on your monthly cash flow. Some finance experts suggest paying off your credit cards, which generally charge much higher interest. Throw them away and use only the equity line.

6   When you take out an equity line and use it for a flip, pay off the equity line when you sell.

7   Make a financial plan when borrowing on your equity line—have a plan you can live with.

Fixed mortgages. This is a loan where the interest rate stays the same during the term of the loan. This is good during a volatile market, when interest rates are more likely to fluctuate. It protects you if the rates increase. Advantages:

- Provides a solid, current pro-forma statement and balance sheet so you can plan cash flow over the life of the loan.
- As rents go up your mortgage will stay the same.
- Lower interest rates

Adjustable-Rate Mortgages. An adjustable-rate mortgage is a mortgage whose interest rate is adjusted by the bank every so many years. Those years are specified in your loan, usually every 3 or 5. You may hedge your bets by doing this if you think you can predict the interest rate 3 to 5 years down the road. However, a fixed-rate mortgage with a low interest rate is better; you know what you are paying today tomorrow and 3 to 5 years down the road.

Assumable Mortgages. I like assumable mortgages. They are mortgages that you can take over from the seller. In today's economy people are overwhelmed, many over-financed, jobless, and need to get out from under their mortgages.

So when you are prospecting, advertise that you want to take over a mortgage. This is possible. The question is price and down payment. Don't chase the price. Come up with a fair price. Certainly since the seller may be more desperate than you, you are in a position to get a favorable price, with a zero down payment.

There are some advantages to assumable mortgages. The obvious one is that you may be able to put zero down and buy a property. Hold on to your cash. There usually is no credit check, but be sure you make the payments on time each month. Don't draw attention to the account of an assumable mortgage.

You can make a deal very quickly between the buyer and the seller. There is less paperwork and red tape in an assumable mortgage than a conventional type of mortgage. However, be careful of a fast talking broker or real-estate agent; always seek legal counsel. Divert the liability to someone else.

You have no exposure to banks with your personal information. Plus, when applying for a new loan you should be able to use the new property as an asset. If you bought the property right and with a proper valuation you will have added to your net worth, enabling you to borrow greater amounts and more often at your financial institution. It's a win for the seller and a double win for the buyer.

If you are assuming a loan of any type, you will be best advised to obtain legal guidance. Never assume you are smarter than a real-estate agent or an attorney. Retain a person who is qualified to handle these types of transactions.

Balloon Loan. A balloon note is a note that can be amortized over a period of time, with a balance due before the end of the amortization period. For example, say you borrow $100,000 at 10% over a 30-year period of time, with a "balloon" or a call in 5 years; that monthly payment should be about $877.75. At the 5-year point, you would owe the entire balance of the loan. This is good for the lender in that he basically collects mostly interest for the first 5 years and will receive most of the principle at the 5-year end. This can be bad for the borrower because he has to come up with a bulk of the money at the 5-year end.

However, note that interest rates could change for better or worse. The borrower could have other available funds coming that can retire the note. There are many financial circumstances that can occur in one's portfolio that would prompt the borrower to have a balloon as it would also for the mortgage holder. This does keep the payment low for the borrower as well. As a result, balloon loans are ideal for flips; just be very sure that your property will sell so you will have the money to pay the balloon.

During the term of a balloon payment loan, it is a good idea to make as many principle payments as you can. This certainly will reduce the amount due at term of loan.

REMEMBER:

All the money you borrow will be at a price that you will have to pay back. Be careful of how much you borrow and how much you leverage.

Construction Loans. These loans are usually for new constructions. The money is withdrawn from the bank in parts (called "draws") as the project gets completed. Upon completion and final draw the borrower usually has to put permanent financing in place.

Land Loans. Loans for undeveloped land only. As a conventional loan you usually extend this type of loan out for a long period of time, since it may be awhile before the land will be developed.

Bridging Loans. Working with two different loans and combining them into one.

Take-Over Loans. These are perfect when you are trying to do zero financing. Look for these. Sometimes they require little money down and enable the buyer to get in with zero cash. A few of these types of loans in your portfolio will help you grow your worth.

Permanent Financing. You can use any alternative means to finance a project. Whether it is a new construction or rehab. When the project is done the lending institution will usually want to put that loan on a permanent basis, which you would negotiate. For example you may want a fixed or variable loan; you can negotiate the term and the interest rate. Since you really may not know how much you will use for the construction or the rehab loan, you only finance the amount of money that you have used.

Line of Credit. Like a credit card, although interest may be lower than a credit card. It is usually based on assets that you have, as well as your ability to pay back the loan. There are a lot of lines given on equity in homes or investment properties. That's why if you can do the first property at a low cost, you should do some non-traditional financing on as much cash as you have. This will give you immediate value or equity in your property, and that's what you want. Soon, you can use that equity to obtain term loans with banks for future growth.

If you are an investor and buy many properties you may have a line of credit that you are working with so you can do deals quicker. These types of credit lines are good to have; they are helpful and almost necessary if you are doing a lot of flip properties.

Equity line. This is a line of credit that uses a house for collateral. Once you have grown enough to purchase your own home and if there is equity in the home, you can take an equity line on your property; this will give you a flexibility to move money and spend money on your investments.

You may be ahead of the game and have a home, one that you can pull some cash out of and use that to start your investment portfolio. You don't have to sell your home; you are just leveraging it, but as with any other investment, you could lose it. If you don't make any payments, you will force it into foreclosure. Don't let that happen. If you take some equity out of your home in any form as discussed, pay it back as soon as you can so that your well is not dry, and you don't overexpose yourself. You don't want to put your family at risk.

CHAPTER 14: FINANCING THE DEAL

It's like that old saying, If you bed with the devil you may be playing with fire. Be aware of the interest rate you are being charged. The interest rates today are the lowest that they have ever been; take advantage of those rates today.

When you refinance your primary residence for either an equity line or cash out, be aware that you will have a higher monthly payment. Will you be able to handle it? Look it over and be sure you can. It's your obligation. You don't want to lose your primary residence. And never borrow more than your home is worth.

Talk to your accountant for any tax ramifications of refinancing.

Home-Equity Loans. A home-equity loan provides a homeowner with cash, loaned against the equity in the home he already owns, rather than the equity in the home he is buying. If for instance your home has a value of $100,000 and you only owe $20,000 on the house, you can take out a home-equity loan on the part you own free and clear. These loans can be approved, with no money actually dispensed, just available to write checks or make withdrawals against as necessary. A sort-of piggy bank. This is called a home-equity line (see above). So when they need money they can go to their home-equity line of credit and draw from it. Once you draw on it, then you are required to make the payments as set up with the lender.

This is a great way to have cash available when you need it. For instance if on a $100,000 house you owe $20,000, you may have a $40,000 home-equity line of credit from which you can draw at will. You could do a small flip or rehab project with this $40,000, and when the house is done, sell it, pay back the $40,000, and start again. Before beginning this arrangement, be sure you can make the monthly payments.

Home-equity loans may charge you the borrower a higher interest rate on the amount borrowed. It is a greater amount of exposure for the lender in that they now have taken a second position to the first deed of trust.

171

SUCCESS
In General

You can count on 10% of the things that happen in life. The real issue is how you handle the remaining 90% that is out of your control. Ninety percent is a large number; how do you react to such a situation? Many people's thresholds are not very high, and they find different—and sometimes destructive—ways to handle situations. Some use alcohol or drugs as a crutch; some become isolationists; we all will act differently.

Always be on your guard; money can be the root of a lot of evil. I saw that with my brother Richard whose wife was a gold digger; the larger the wedge that she put between him and his family, the better. It indeed caused a lot of hard feelings that never were able to be resolved. So you have to ask yourself, Is the money worth it? Truly, could all the money in the world buy you happiness?

As we know, tragedies take no prisoners. Tragedy does not evaluate her targets by their financial statements. Tragedies affect everyone, and they know no bounds. They don't care if you have money or you are poor. I think of John Travolta's son who passed away suddenly. All the fame and fortune that John Travolta has did not help his situation.

So are people with a lot of money really happy? Did they sell their souls to get that money? Can you ever be normal again?

Interest-only loans. These are ok for a short-term deal like a flip. But not the best for a long-term hold deal. You do not pay on the principle; you only pay the interest. If you are doing a flip or a development project you want to be able to keep your payments low, so an interest-only loan should work for you. In the end you will pay the principle off. On a long-term deal I would want to amortize the loan so I am paying down some of the principle of the loan. For me the quicker, the better.

Recourse financing. This offers greater protection to lenders, because it offers additional protection on the loan. If you default, they can get the property back; in addition they can go after you personally, including any additional assets that you have. The borrower is subject to a greater liability. You may also be liable for fees, penalties, and extra interest. Just be sure you make your payments on time. For the seller, non-recourse financing is better, but usually non-recourse financing has more stringent requirements and higher standards for loan applicants, including lower debt-to-asset ratios.

Credit cards. Consult your spouse on what your plan is; get her involved. Discuss the amount to be borrowed and how you plan to pay back. When you have the money to pay back be sure you do. Don't abuse your credit card; with interest rates so high, your monthly payments may be high too. For the short term (e.g., rehab projects) and emergencies, they are perfect.

Credit cards are good way to track your expenses as they will show up on your statement. Don't get carried away. Multiple credit cards can cause some serious credit problems, if you don't plan your cash flow properly. Think it through.

Lease Option. This is an easy way to control a piece of property without a large cash investment or down payment. This type of deal gives the buyer a lease deal with all the conditions of a typical lease, but it also will include an option to purchase the property usually at a specific price. You usually pay a little more each month. The extra goes toward a deposit, and at some point as designated in the contract your deal will be consummated. These types of deals are a little dangerous for the buyer, who must budget for a larger monthly payment. The seller not only has the buyer on the hook for an immediate payment that is larger than usual but also has him committed to a level of ownership, like helping to defray the costs of repairs and maintenance. They take that added responsibility that a tenant may not normally take on.

Owner Financing. Whenever you can, try to get owner financing. You can save some money and minimize your exposure by borrowing directly from the seller. There are advantages to seller financing. Most of the time you can get better terms than at a bank. You are usually in a better position to negotiate the terms of your deal. This may relate to amount borrowed, interest rate, term financed, points, insurance, as well as any other items that are involved in the transaction.

Some people just don't like debt. I did not care when I was younger. When you have debt and are paying interest, it does take away from cash flow. The older I become, the less debt I take on; I would prefer the investments to be in cash—using cash flow to maximize the future investment purchases. Borrowing money is always risky. Whatever you borrow you have to pay back with interest. You have to be disciplined to make those payments each month so you don't lose the loan. There are times you may want to take those risks, and there are times you should not. You should evaluate the terms of the loan before you borrow the money.

Be honest with yourself and honest with your calculations. If it is a chicken, then call it a chicken. There is a difference between a chicken and a donkey. Some people will work numbers so that they can obtain a bank loan—numbers that look good to a creditor. If by chance they are spurious, then have the real numbers handy so you know what you are working with. Not borrowing enough to complete the job is super catastrophic and could cause you to lose the deal. You don't want to go into a deal in heavy debt. All those bills that you have that put you over your budget, without a source to pay those bills—it sure will take some time to dig yourself out of that hole.

CHAPTER 14: FINANCING THE DEAL

It is possible, just hard. You may want to do a project so bad that you are willing to risk the extra debt.

Just be sure you don't jump into another project like the one you just did, without a little cash flow foothold. You want to be secure somewhere, so you have something to fall back on if you need it.

SUCCESS

Be strong in the virtues, the beliefs that you hold dear. You are the hero. This doesn't mean that you are always right, but that choosing the narrow path is always within your power. When you are wrong, you have forgotten that fact, but you can always immediately remember it and start making right the decisions.

If there are people in your life who try to control and coerce and manipulate you, remembering that you are in control of your own life will be all the more difficult; at times it will seem impossible. In my life, even when I was right I was wrong, or so my mother and my wife tried to convince me. Is it even possible to be wrong all the time? I am not sure anyone is wrong all the time, but it is possible to be made to feel that way.

Stay constant, stay focused, be determined; God will reward you when it is your time.

CHAPTER 15

Venues for Financing Your Deal

BANKS, SAVINGS AND LOANS, HARD MONEY LENDERS are about as different as apples and oranges. They are all fruit, yes, but all taste a little different. You need to be aware of that.

Banking relationships are important for long-term growth. This may not happen today, especially if your credit is not outstanding. It may take some time if you have bad credit, so as you are growing your portfolio, continue to improve your credit score. Your first test will be your credit cards, negative reporting from existing creditors, how you paid back a car loan, your student loans—any judgments against you. All these things will develop a credit score. Banks will look up your credit score, and that will be a basis of your loan application. Your reputation will follow you. Good character will be a major factor as well. Used to be you could go into a bank and borrow money on a handshake and your character; not anymore. You need that credit score.

How long have you owned your business? It will be harder to borrow money for start-up companies. You know what they say: You can borrow money when you least need or want it. What you need today may be further than an arm's length away. One avenue to take is to work on your portfolio by using your own assets. Or get it privately financed—you know, beg, borrow, and steal so to speak, to get a few properties under your belt. Polish that balance sheet, develop that track record, get some experience, and bingo: you will now have some history to show your bank.

After awhile by your due diligence you will be able to compare deals with terms. In time you will try to establish relationships and through those relationships you will get good deals.

Playing one place against the other is also good, but you must have a strong deal with great credit. By the same token, if you have a sketchy deal and have mediocre credit you may have to take what you can get, which may not have the most favorable terms. Just be careful you don't put yourself in a tough spot by being overzealous on a deal you shouldn't take.

Not everyone gets the best deal on a new car. But everyone will tell you that they did. Heaven knows you could shop until you drop and may never get what they got. Work hard to network and see what is going on, who is doing what. Make your contacts, and see who has the best fit for you.

Commercial banks. Establish a relationship with several local banks. Have your main account at one bank. Set up other accounts, even savings accounts. You can start with your bank. However there will be a limit on how many properties they will work with you on. Their exposure will be limited. So when you come in with maybe your third or fourth, don't be surprised if they say *No*. That's why you have a relationship with other banks, so that you can stair step your loans. Your portfolio will look a lot better to a bank, if you don't over expose yourself to that one bank. Diversify your money and your holdings.

Used to be you could borrow money over the phone with some basic information. But today loans are much more difficult and go through a rigorous evaluation process; the banks want to see balance sheets, credit reports, as well as your cash flow and the property's cash flow. If you have equity in a property they want to see it. They will want to attach it as well. They want their hands on all they can get.

You know if you go in for a loan and do not have financials and tell your loan officer, "Hey let me get that to you later," it may be a red flag. Versus having a package of all the necessary information ready to go.

Lenders will change their policies. Relationships will change from bank to bank. The loan officers in a bank will also have a different philosophy in lending. You can go to the same bank talk to three different lenders in different branches and get different results. It's good to have a relationship with someone who knows you well. If you don't get the answer that you want, go to someone else and then someone else until you get the answer you are looking for. It may take some time.

This philosophy applies also to different banks. Establish a relationship with different banks, so if one turns you down for a loan you will have options.

Just be sure you do your homework when pitching a loan to a bank. You want to have all your ducks in a row and look professional, like someone who is knowledgeable. Someone who deserves a loan.

> Establish a relationship with different banks, so if one turns you down for a loan you will have options.

There are many different high-tech but user-friendly programs that you can use to formulate cash-flow projections and track your properties, to show your due diligence to the bank. They will want to see what you have done and evaluate that progress to your blueprint to see if you are worthy.

Partners. Talk only to potential investors whom you trust. You have got to have a good feeling about the people you invest with. Likewise you must be honest; portray yourself as a doer. If someone is going to invest his money with you, he has to trust you. You must do what you say. Develop a track record of success.

If you have any type of partner, generate a limited outline as to how much of a capital contribution each will make. Is he a source of capital? Be specific in your agreement; be sure it is fair to you and the other members, and most important sign promissory notes with interest to ensure payback on money borrowed.

If you set up a partnership, general or limited liability, decide how much if anything each partner will put in. It does not have to be equal. Be sure the amounts are documented. Be sure you document in a promissory note the terms of payback.

I once did a deal where a friend of mine purchased two fixer-uppers. I did all the work on both of them and paid for the work; when the two properties were done, it worked out that I got one house, the cheaper one, and he got the other, more expensive one. He was happy. Although he is happier now that for the last few years he goes by and picks up a rent check on a property that was paid for in cash. I suspect that he has recouped all his money by now.

Investors. There are a lot of people who have money but do not have the knowledge to flip or rehab a property. They may not have the time. They could be looking for someone like you with the necessary knowledge. You need to find these people; they are your friends, at real-estate groups, on craigslist, among stockbrokers and financial planners. You just have to look.

Best to start a partnership or a company, and put all your cards on the table before you start. Remain a person of integrity, and you both can make money.

Friends and family. This may be a good source of funds for your project; they may want to be part of a great idea. You always want to be sure you are forthright with family and friends. You can pass the hat, and if you make a good deal and win, they are more likely to do it again. The nice thing is that you may be able to borrow the money at a low- or no-interest loan. Just remember that your responsibility to pay them back is vital due to the personal relationship you have with them.

Document everything. Your family may be the first group of people you talk to about investing in your real-estate portfolio. Even if your relationship is super, write it down anyway; have an agreement so both you and they are comfortable. What happens if it fails? If it is in writing, there are no questions. Don't assume anything, and expect the worst. If it turns out great, then how do you deal with the success, i.e., distribution of profits? If it is in writing, then there should not be any questions as to how to act. Plan for failure and plan for success.

Private investors. You want to pitch the private investor like you would pitch a bank. Do your homework and put together a nice package, one that he can take with him to study. He may be a little easier on reviewing the package than a bank. However he will have questions, so be prepared. A private investor wants to make good loans. He wants to get paid back; it is your responsibility to pay him back. Where should you look? Internet, craigslist, newspaper, networking with friends or social groups, stockbrokers and financial professionals, friends, business associates. If this deal is a flip, there are several things you can do that will help you sell the investor:

1. Show him the property. Take him to the site. Show him what you plan to do. Pictures are also a good way to illustrate that.

2. Put together a pro-forma, a cash-flow statement, so he can see how much the property costs, how much you plan to put in it and how much you will make.

3. Show him how he is going to get paid back.

4. The closing costs may be a lot cheaper borrowing from a private investor. However the interest rates generally will be a little higher than a conventional loan.

5. The time it takes to get the money is generally quicker as well. You can pitch a deal and close a deal with a private lender quicker than with an institution.

6   Once you've been successful with an investor, it will be easier to go back to the well for your next deal.

7   Lots of people have money to invest. Many of those investors want to diversify their portfolio and are looking for ways to invest. They may be unhappy with their 401K as well as the market.

Online lenders. I would be careful with these, especially if you are new to the business. You do not want to go down a stray path. You may have to do some research on the lender. People that you know may know a quality lender; this may be the best way to find a quality lender that meets your needs.

You may want to stay with institutions that you have developed a relationship with; you usually are better able to negotiate a rate with those lenders that you know best. Be careful with banks that sell their loans; you may think that you are working with one bank and then end up dealing with another—a bank where you have no relationship, where you are only a number.

SBA loans. These are a little tougher for residential real estate but a good source for commercial properties. The SBA does not give loans, but it guarantees them with a participating bank and usually at a lower interest rate. It takes a lot of guess work out of the bank's hands.

Venture capitalists. These types of investors usually want a larger return on their investment. They are able to pool different sources of money from all different people. They can raise a lot of money. They want companies that will grow quickly. This large flip may be a large commercial building; you already have a buyer; so you want to broker or flip the deal. These investors are smart and will want to take an active role in the project. Ever watch *Shark Tank* on TV? That's the idea; they want to get in and get out quickly.

LLC/Sub S. If you go the corporation route of setting up your portfolio and desire to go quicker to the mainstream of developing, some people will sell equity or stock in their company. Stockholders will want to see financial statements and will want a return on their investment—a dividend.

Angel investors. These are investors who tend to have disposable money, that don't mind investing in projects or property. They want to be involved in growing companies, ones that offer promise of great returns on their investment. Angels can be individuals or group of investors. As they come, they are golden.

Owner financing. One of the easiest ways is to get seller financing. Many investors don't want the headache anymore and are happy to sell their property with—yes—even 100% financing. You will never know unless you ask.

Best if you don't have to put any money down. Negotiate an interest rate; the seller may want to charge a higher interest rate on the property, but try to keep it low. The seller may also want to balloon the payment in a short period of time, maybe 3 to 5 years. Pick the later and give yourself time to either flip the property, to get enough rent from it, or to refinance.

A lot of people would like to do owner financing in so much as there are serious tax advantages to this for

Take Time for Your Family

It's good to force yourself to take a vacation. Do it today. Entrepreneurs, business leaders, and families tend to put different values on their time and spend it differently.

I can remember working so hard for my family—well at least I thought I was. I would work extra days and weekends, thinking it was ok because I was doing it for them. And truly it was for them. I wanted success to afford the nice things in life. It was for them even more than it was for me. But looking back I don't think it was nearly as important as I thought it was; today I regret that I didn't spend more quality time with my children. Spend time with your family; don't pass up opportunities to be with them.

Today I try to spend a lot of time with them, but now that they are grown, I want more. You may be taking a right turn in life, and they a left: be sure to travel together. You can make money at another time.

them, i.e., capital gains taxes. It provides them with a nice payment for a long period of time. Remember that the buyer will be paying a lot of interest at first on the note, which in the end is a much greater return for the seller.

Owner financing does have its downsides: you will have less room to negotiate; you may not get the area or property you want—owner financing is much more available in low-end neighborhoods and with properties that do not have a mortgage on them.

Federal and state lenders. These are a tad more difficult to obtain. I would start by associating with an investment information group, local economic incentive groups. Check out state and local grants and financing situations.

Insurance policies and companies. You have a couple of options here. You can borrow the equity off any insurance policies that you may have. You may not have a lot of equity in a policy, but it is an option. You can also approach insurance companies for loans as well. These deals tend to be larger loans in nature: commercial loans, office buildings, shopping centers, very solid projects.

Mortgage companies. During the 2000s there were plenty of mortgage companies that thrived. Money was aplenty until many of the mortgage companies went bust due in part to the housing crisis. Now the ones that exist are pretty good. They tend to have access to a lot more money lines than an average single bank. They do charge points, sometimes higher than your standard bank. Watch those hidden costs.

Savings banks and credit unions. They usually operate like commercial banks, so don't count them out for possible money. Credit unions are expanding their customer bases and actually going out of their comfort zone of lending to a specific customer base and attracting new customers. Many times they offer much more attractive packages for borrowers which may work for you. They also may have looser credit and borrowing terms.

Mutual savings banks. Mutual savings banks are something of the past. There are not as many mutual savings banks out there as regular banks but there are some. You may find some long-term investment opportunities here for your money as in certificates of deposits or regular savings, and they may pay more. But for the active investor this type of bank may not be for you. It's all about establishing a relationship with the institution that will fit the needs of your portfolio.

Hard-money lenders. I am not a fan of hard-money lenders; however they do work, and they can help you buy property. They usually collectivize the project more than a bank would. You will find that they will lend money quicker than banks or mortgage companies will. To them, a credit report score may be less important than it is to a bank. On the other hand, the interest rate is going to be excessive: 15-18%, and maybe they will charge you points. There is usually a prepayment penalty on deals, too. Just the same, the money is easier to obtain, although they will do their homework.

Believe me many of them go into a deal wanting it to fail so they can get the property back. Nice to get a rehab back completed for resale. The hard-money lenders that I have met are cold, heartless cutthroats. Not like banks, who have lollipops and free pens to give out. These hard money guys are smaller operators and seem to get as many deals as they can handle. However, there are mortgage companies and banks that you will need for conventional monies. Best to develop a relationship with them as soon as you can. Think about getting a loan at each bank—you may eventually need to. One, two, or three properties per bank. Use normal to high values, creating value in your assets to borrow money from another bank and so forth. Don't let anyone know that you may be over-financed or under-collateralized. Present a successful portfolio. The banks want equity and value to justify their loans. At some point in time you may consider a line of credit with one or two of the banks or mortgage lenders. Or even a line of credit on your equity. This will give you operating leverage to buy more property.

When they find a deal, many investors will use hard-money lenders to rehab the property. They buy a property for $10,000, need $20,000 to rehab the property and another $20,000 to live on, which is not always a good thing for an investor to do. I don't recommend this at all, but it is done. You have to be careful of a domino effect of disaster. Just keep in mind nothing is for free. Whatever you borrow you will have to pay back.

You've got to have avenues to pay back the hard-money lender. You don't want to be in a position where you have to amortize a payback to a hard-money lender at all.

Hard money is going to cost you more money in holding on to the property. When you obtain a hard-money loan, you need to move quickly either in your sale or permanent financing of the property. You don't have idle time: that hard-money loan will cost you a bundle to carry.

In your relationships with all your lenders, don't burn any bridges; rather, develop a style of honesty and integrity. Pay back your loans. Network with people you can help and who can help you. It's only a matter of time and you will be successful. Be patient.

PART III

The Property

DON'T DILLYDALLY AROUND. You must be pro-active in renovating, marketing, and selling your property. You don't want it to do nothing: you won't make any money. There are options, but the goal is always to maximize your income and avoid risks or financial exposure.

The key element to flipping is buying a property as low as you can and then being in a position to sell it. If you cannot sell the property then you are not flipping; you will be holding on to it; this brings up another topic: property management, which I will discuss later. Flipping properties is not as easy as you think. You've got to understand the market; don't get stuck with a property that will not flip. A lot of flippers, as well as speculators in new construction, lost a lot of money during the 2009-2012 housing bust.

If you have some money or don't need cash today, you can offer nice financing packages on properties you have for sale, either with or without down payments. You decide how much of the property you want to finance, but doing so at any level gives you a nice source of long-term cash flow. Check with your accountant for any potential tax consequences. This does require a level of financial planning; you should know what you are doing before you do it. Think ahead and ask around. Someone else may have a better idea.

Maintain good relationships with your subcontractors, your employees, and real-estate agents so you can have consistency in your business plan. You have to be able to ride the ups and downs of the market. It will not always be good. When it is bad you will need to be able to adjust properly and consistently. Bad times will not last forever.

It's better to have the reputation of a flipper who does quality work versus one whose work is shoddy and whose customers are unhappy. Callback complaints are tough to deal with; they are a liability to your patience, time, money, as well as to customer perception. Who needs it? Do it right the first time; take your time and be proud of the work—even if it cost a little more the first time around. If you are renting property you will be able to get more money for the property, which means getting a better tenant, which in turn means higher value of the property: not bad having the nicest place on the street. You can be ok with that.

When your plan to flip doesn't work and you cannot sell the property, you may have to consider renting it. This will buy you some time until the market changes. You may have to give the tenants a short-term lease, so that if you sell the property, you will have some flexibility with your tenants. A lot of flippers want nothing to do with property management, but rather put all their properties up for sale. Property management is not a bad option. You may be surprised at your success.

So the plan is to improve the property, recoup all your money invested, and then sell it for a nice profit. This is a great strategy, especially if you have got a little cash and do not need any cash for awhile. Do a few of these types of deals, and you will see some cash flow. It's always good to have a piggy bank. You may not have one to start, but down the road you may want to have a cash reserve: a person, a retirement fund, a savings account where you can access a little money to make a deal. It's nice to have that comfort level. Call it your rainy day fund. There will be rainy days too.

CHAPTER 16

Renovation to Hold or to Flip

MAKE YOUR PROPERTY JUST A LITTLE SPECIAL. Do something that will attract a person to either rent or buy your property. It's easy to do what everyone else does, so step out of the box and make your property nice. An example of this may be paving a driveway versus leaving it gravel. Adding a deck, a carport, mulching, making a larger living room with no dining room. Or, adding a bedroom of sorts to a large basement so instead of a three-bedroom so you now have a four-bedroom.

What Degree to Fix a Property

When you wrote your mission statement and laid out your blueprint, you decided how you were going to develop your business. It doesn't mean you may not deviate from that model very much, as long as you know what you are doing and why. The rags to riches formula of success starts on many different paths. I specialize in junkers as the best of bottom feeders you can find. If it is a flip property you will have to decide how much renovation you want to put into the property to get your flip. This depends on your purchase price, neighborhood, condition of property and your available cash. Many people overspread on a flip. They will redo the property as if they were going to live there—over-thinking it like they are predicting the buyer. You cannot predict the buyer.

I know some flippers who always replace cabinets in a kitchen. I don't always do that. If you put in an in-ground pool, will you ever get your money out of it? The answer is usually *No*. Don't call that curb appeal; it is not curb appeal at all. If the cabinets are decent you can refinish them, paint them, decoupage them, put new knobs and hinges on them and wow. You may have saved a lot of money here real quick.

A factor in flipping depends on the flipper's plan as to whether he plans to wholesale the property or sell it retail. In today's economy with the housing market in the tanks, you would have a hard time flipping retail unless you get the right house and the right person. This is always a crapshoot. Or you may move it quick at a wholesale price—to either an investor or a retail customer. Either way I would suggest you put some money into curb appeal. If you spend some money on the outside yard and house, maybe a new tree, you will be amazed as to the results you will get. I immediately put a sign out for sale by owner.

Don't wait for the sun to shine, you must make it shine. If you truly are a bottom feeder and thinking about holding onto a property for a long-term investment, then you really must think about how much you will put into the property. Years ago I would put in ceramic tile, trying to make it nice. The tenants would ruin that tile quick. It cost a lot to put this down. It did not take long to decide on 12x12 vinyl squares. I do the floor then do the base cabinet in the kitchen; I always leave a couple of pieces in the base cabinet as well, because the supply house will change patterns every 6 months. It is easier to change one or two tiles than it is a whole vinyl floor or ceramic. They will do damage. Think ahead.

CHAPTER 16: RENOVATION TO HOLD OR TO FLIP

If the plan is to hold on to a bottom property in a modest- to low-end area, here is something to consider. How much will I put into the rehab? Each city has a building department, which has a set of standards. Many states follow the BOCA Code for renovation or new constructions. Many will have a code enforcement group that will want to ensure safety and structural integrity. That the building is not dangerous.

> Don't wait for the sun to shine, you must make it shine.

I think code. First and foremost I look at electricity. Fuse boxes and 100-amp service have proven not to be enough power. Lately I make sure the electric service is up to date: 200 amp service, circuit breakers, grounded outlets, and GFCIs. As a general rule I have been putting ample outside lights and electric baseboard heaters. Even if the house has a gas furnace I have in the past put in electric as a secondary source. A lot of poorer people will not be able to turn the gas on in a property; that's generally one too many deposits people just can't afford. This enables a tenant to choose his means of heat.

I look hard at the kitchens and see what needs to be done. Replace or refurbish the cabinets, upgrade sink, and put a new floor down. Same with the bathroom. If the walls and ceilings can be repaired then that's what I do—plaster, sand, prime, and paint. Even as a beginner rehabber with no money, you should be able to do this. It may not be perfect but you have got to start and you need the practice. This is all part of the stepping stones of success.

The point is if this work is a C+, but all the neighboring houses appear to be D's, you have succeeded and for starters that's fine. As long as you know that in a couple of years as the neighborhood gets better you may want to improve your property to a B and eventually an A. You have time. As the neighborhood improves, the tenant mix will improve and so will the quality of your property. During that process you can increase your rent.

That's when I go fishing. A $600 rental when upgraded can get $700 or $800—you can always discount the rent to a prospective tenant, but it's hard to increase rent.

Sometimes it is very difficult to gauge a rehab with certainty, so I encourage you to prepare a budget and do all you can to stick to it. Things will go wrong, but if you are lucky and prudent, your rehab will come in under or at budget. If by chance you run into an unforeseen problem—termite or fire damage, a bad water line, broken sewer, non-functional or inefficient heating system, a leaky roof—you may end up over budget. Don't think that you are going to spend $7000 on a $25,000 roof replacement. I'm talking about a $2000 repair.

At some point you may just draw the line. I have done it many times where I have said I have spent too much money. Complete what you have done, so you can get your certificates and get a good tenant. I figure at that point you collect rent for a couple of years and when you lose that tenant you can do more work. That's considered a stair-step development to property. I have had properties for twenty years and am still making improvements to them. Everything in due time, I say. Usually the property will appreciate in value, and you will be able to increase the rents as well as being able to reduce or retire the mortgage. Even if you are planning to sell the property in the future, sometimes it's best to accept a respectful offer in the moment, even if it is for less than you had hoped, so the buyer can finish the project. Decide when a project has become a money pit.

When you are doing a property and trying to figure out how much to spend it may take a few tries before you get a feel for budgeting. At first get a price from a couple of contractors, maybe from a medium- and low-end company. Also, put together your own estimate; then do a line-by-line item comparison of the estimates. It's really helpful to put it on a spreadsheet; there you will see and compare the differences in the line items. My friend gets a price from a low-end rehabber, and he gets a turn-key package on his rehab. He barely has to go to the property, only to check progress and make changes, which sometimes he is charged for and sometimes not. It's really a crapshoot as to whether you are going to get a better job or a worse job until you develop a working relationship with your contractor. Sometimes when you can do the work yourself, you can add more to the job than when you contract the job out. You are afforded that versatility which you sometimes cannot do with a contractor without a substantial additional price.

CHAPTER 16: RENOVATION TO HOLD OR TO FLIP

Remember you can also do half yourself and half with a contractor. This may balance your budget as well. Watch your pennies all the time.

Sometimes you can act as the general contractor, sub out work you cannot do, and do what you want to do. This gives you some ownership in the job. If you are not working full time this may be the route to go. If you are working, your time may be limited.

At some point the job will be complete, and you will want to see what the job actually cost you. You may be surprised or sad. I have done some jobs and have been amazed how much I overspent. I was much too high and was happy when the job was over and there was income. Heck this house was huge though, over 4,000 square foot duplex, three bedrooms, in each duplex. I did a small two bedroom ranch during the time that I was working on the duplex. I had that property complete for less than $10,000. It was easy.

Just remember although the work is the same all these rehabs are different. Always evaluate the work that you have done; keep good records of your investment.

Motoring Up

You get started in the morning, and you cannot stop. You are in perpetual motion, like a well-oiled machine, pumping and pumping, making it all happen. You feel the adrenaline; you are making all the right moves, the right calls; everything is working for you. You feel your heart beat by each decision that you have made. It is great to feel in control of your destiny.

The only issue is being able to keep yourself sane! You must keep yourself in a self-check mode. Why make yourself vulnerable to anyone or anything? Just don't do it. It is not what you accomplish, remember, but rather how you do it. You don't want to put yourself in the corner with no way to escape. Determine your exit plan before you engage. This requires a level of planning and organization which you want to do before any project. It is important to expect a positive outcome; you don't go into a project thinking that you will lose.

CHAPTER 17

The Renovation

WHEN YOU BUY A PROPERTY TO FLIP and want to do a major renovation, you must be very careful of the expense for such a project. It's one thing to do small projects—painting, floor, countertops, outside work; however, when you consider a major renovation, you can add some cost to your project. If the renovation requires a building permit, a zoning variance, or even a set of plans, you indeed will be adding some additional costs to your project. There are usually hidden variables in those types of projects as well, which can affect your end result.

Carefully and properly price out the renovation. If you plan to use a subcontractor, get at least two quotes for the work. If you plan to do it yourself properly, plan out the materials and the labor and leave a little wiggle room in there as well for the unexpected. Before you get started on your renovation you need to decide if the renovation makes any sense. Evaluate the cost and how much more you will be able to get for the property. It's all about the profit. When the renovation is complete, will you be able to get that much more out of the property at your retail or wholesale price? Will it increase your profit? Also, will it increase the marketability of the property? Will you be able to sell the property quicker? You really need to have a finger on the pulse of consumer market trends, as well as the needs of the buyer. Doing a major renovation just for the heck of it can be costly and decrease potential profitability.

By now you may have a good feel as to what is selling in your neighborhood, and what characteristics people are looking for—for example, nice decks, added living space, open kitchens, furnished basements with a possible bedroom or family room, or even an enclosed sunroom off the back. These are major projects and must be budgeted and planned.

For years I have had a unique ability to see the potential in any property. If it is a no-go, I know right away; I can usually come close to the renovation cost off the top of my head. This is a great asset. Review the cost estimate sheet in the Appendix. On the other hand, for years I have tried to pick unique and fabulous colors for the exterior of a house, to brighten up the neighborhood. To my dismay even when they look good on a paint chip or sample section of the home, they have been disasters. So that being a weakness I decided to get a little guidance on picking colors for the outsides of houses. Colors do make a huge difference. Potential buyers can be drawn to a property by a unique color scheme.

Do something clever with your property. See if the house has anything to make it really special when it is done. There are trends in our society that trickle down to neighborhoods, that will attract people when they are looking for a property. Try to be ahead of the curve on those items, but first you must be able to identify some of the things people want.

Make your property just a little nicer than the one next door. You can:

- add a fence
- add a washer/dryer
- use stained glass
- add a deck
- create garden areas
- make it pet friendly
- install thermo-double pane windows and screen doors
- upgrade to a larger hot-water heater
- update all electric and HVAC
- finish front porches
- improve the yard

These will help you in your overall plan whatever direction you may take—rental or flip.

Comparisons

When doing your flip renovations or your rental, take a moment and see what the area houses look like. Be competitive with them. A front-porch rejuvenation or a deck will stand out in a neighborhood and set your property apart from the others. If the neighborhood is run down, yours with a little money and curb appeal could be the best house on the block. If you are buying all over town, this task is a lot harder than if you are buying in a neighborhood and trying to dominate a market.

I mentioned stairstepping your renovations. You don't have to do all your renovations right now and today. For the long term, you can plan projects that will enhance the value of your properties.

Just recently I added some fencing to a back yard on the street side. I was able to get some free mulch from the city for a berm, did a little planting, and bingo changed the look of the house in a minute. I have owned the property for five years, so doing something extra was just fine.

It is important to keep your rehab in line with the housing profiles that are in the neighborhood; in an historic area you need to maintain consistency of style and grace. Most of the time in an historic area you will be required to maintain this consistency through the ARB or building department or zoning. The restrictions will be less stringent in lower or modest neighborhoods. If your rehab stays one step ahead of the neighborhood, you will get a better tenant to rent it and a higher price on a resale or flip. If you turn a basement into a family room you will be able to sell it for more money or rent it for a higher price. Think about that extra bathroom in the basement as well.

Keep it simple, stupid—a cliché, but it has some merit. Do a lot for a little. Focus on the important areas that will yield you the greatest return. That will save you a lot of money and headache. For instance you may consider redoing the kitchen. Ok, but instead of making it large and dreaming of the expanding family, maybe the thought should be making it smaller, more efficient and user-friendly, and thus providing more space for living, which can be accented with more light and open space. That will work. Think outside the box. The days of families resting around the dining room table are gone. People are on the go; they are busy. It's just time now to make some changes to our living space, which have been long overdue.

Do what you can when you have the money to do it right. Keep your project simple and within a budget, think through the use of materials so you can save some money. Kitchens can be expensive. Be careful. Clean up your space.

Arrangement of Living Spaces

Personally, I like the open kitchens and large outside decks. In the past I have added decks to homes. It does give a family more space, and they seem to like it.

Outdoor living. The hottest new thing today is extending your living space to the outside—a kitchen, living area, or even a bedroom. People are feeling the connection to nature. You will not see a lot of this in the lower-end homes in the poorer sections of your town, but you will in the upscale neighborhoods. Try to incorporate some of the outdoors to your innovation in an effort to get top dollar for your property, either for sale or for rental.

You can accomplish some of this with large windows, sliding glass doors, large decks done in any type of platforms, trellises, spas, and the like. Don't make the homeowners feel entrapped in their own home; open it up create lots of space.

Put in livable kitchen space. You may not want a so-called dining room as it was in the past versus a kitchen that spills over into the dining room as one and the same. So the preparation of the meal is within the conversation of the family and guests. You can take a wall halfway down, put in a countertop, and change an entire look of a home. Add a large window or deck to this type of area, and you'll be in heaven. The kitchen has now become the new living room. Let the space flow easily. Try not to tuck the kitchen in a back, dark corner.

This type of thinking achieves open living space. I just completed a property where the kitchen, eating area or dining room, living room, and front porch were all one and the same; they were one. It was actually pretty cool. I am not sure that the tenants got it, until they moved in and enjoyed the space. This type of living does bring families and friends together. There is no escaping from the family in this type of house.

Mudrooms have grown in popularity. More space for more stuff: closets, laundry rooms, outbuildings. And here recently there has been growth in the need for basements and attics. Not sure why everyone wants them, but it's a question I get asked a lot. With the economy so bad, some families want to turn them into extra bedrooms. That's usually against code; I recommend against doing that. Then there are those families that have a lot of stuff. Lots of stuff. Stuff all over the place and nowhere to put it. It's best for a home that is strategically laid out in the living areas to have a basement and attic. Where is the family going to put the Christmas tree?

Major Renovations

You need to be aware of the structure of the house: what walls are load-bearing walls, what you can easily take out, and what you have to be careful with. You can take out a load-bearing wall, but it does take some expertise. You need to secure the wall and put in a header that can carry the load of the house, and you must support the header properly. When you decide to take out a wall there are many things to consider: duct work, wiring, flooring. So look into these areas as well as the factors of time and money.

Load-bearing walls are all the outside walls of the house. The interior load bearing walls are the ones that run perpendicular to the floor joists. Think hard about what you want to do to make the best use of the space at the most economical price. When you are renovating a flip property, you want the most bang for your buck.

People want space; they have families that don't want to be on top of each other. So if you want salability then try to get as much space as you can that is airy open and comfortable.

Don't spend your money just to spend it. Why design a whole new kitchen if you don't need to? Can you get by with what you have? If you move it or reconfigure the sink and cabinets you are looking at a big job, with rerunning electric and plumbing. If you need new cabinets or are a flipper who does new cabinets all the time, maybe you can get a special price from your lumber yard who sells them. Buy box cabinets from a local cabinet shop; overall they can be reasonable, if you don't go too crazy. Do make sure your property has plenty of cabinets; potential buyers will be impressed. So evaluate the amount of money you may have to spend versus the gross possible gain you may get out of it.

SUCCESS

Dare to try something new, to take a chance in life. Nothing ventured, nothing gained. Taking chances is not for everyone. If you decide to take a chance, be sure it is everything that you are looking for. Don't do something just for the heck of it. Have a goal in mind. Know what you will have to put into it and how much your returns will be. Evaluate all your options, your strengths and weaknesses, so you minimize the effect of any potential loss.

Trust your instincts. Whose expectations are you evaluating yourself against when it appears that you are happy and life is going well? What do you think is best for you? You may know what is best for you, but not be able to move forward on it. It sure is a terrible place to be.

You want perfection but really perfection is impossible, and you may find yourself just pushing the bar higher and higher almost to a point where it is out of reach. Don't push that bar so high—just do your best in all that you do. Those who seek perfection usually pay a high price. An Olympic athlete may train his entire life to win gold, but he may come up short on the Olympic trials

CHAPTER 17: THE RENOVATION

Remember a new countertop and fixtures and faucets may just do the job as you want it. The same holds true for an extra bathroom. You may be able to add a half bath pretty easily. However, the real question is do you have the space in the house for either an enlarged kitchen or extra bathroom. On a rare occasion you may have the space. I had an older property with an upstairs porch that the previous owner had enclosed to be a sunroom, creating a weird overhang on the ground floor. It was easy to enclose, added a master bath off the master bedroom and a half bath for guests. So the entire house had four bedrooms and now two and a half baths. It was nice. It made the house much more rentable. So in this case it worked out great.

---

and never stand on the podium. He could have spent his entire life in pursuit of that medal only to now be broke and not able to ride a bicycle. The mother of Gabby Douglas, the 2012 Olympic gold medalist for gymnastics, went bankrupt right before Gabby won the gold. Some of these people double down; it's all in for the gold. Many people pressed me when I was struggling with the restaurants not to think of the repercussions of failure. And there is a fair share of failure in the world.

The pursuit of perfection keeps your world small; it does not allow you to grow personally and professionally in other areas. You limit your options. When you as a perfectionist trust yourself, you know your strengths and weaknesses. You learn what you can and cannot do. If you make a mistake you will know how to rebound from it and move forward.

For most of us finding a happy medium is just fine. You can find peace and long-term happiness by being good; you don't have to be a perfectionist all the time.

Always be sure that any of your flips have a laundry area. Some of the older houses did not have them. When you can add them, be sure to do so. In a back porch area, the basement, anywhere. It is important.

Enclosing a porch could be dangerous; you really must evaluate a porch before modifying it. I just did a rehab and did not enclose the porch, but I really fixed it up to make it a special sitting area. This porch was off the kitchen, and it made it a nice space. If you need the space for larger closets or an expanded room, then the porch may be an option. Because porches are on the outside of the house, you must consider whether you will have to add a header when you penetrate an exterior, structural wall.

Don't be afraid to do this type of work if you think it needs to be done. It's usually not that difficult to do and will give you added value for your property. But it does require planning and perhaps an engineer's evaluation.

Always assess the roof. Sometimes you can tell how many layers are on a roof: you are allowed only two; after that you have to strip the old roof down to the plywood. If the roof has been leaking and there is interior damage, always fix the roof first, then repair the interior damage. Replace the sheetrock and any rotting studs, to be sure there is nowhere for mold to grow. Then monitor closely for continued leakage and mold growth.

Plan Your Project

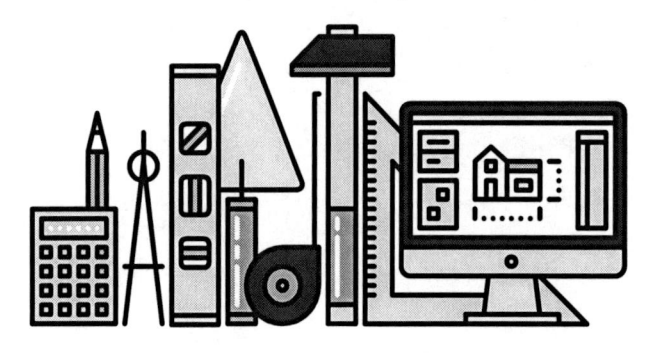

Know what you want to do. Have a plan. You can write or draw it out if you like. You can make an outline or you can be on the job and provide direction as to what you want done first, second, and third. The worst thing is to have to do something over after you have just done it. Always have your materials lined up to do the work; in addition, have your labor and subcontractors ready to go as well. It's just good business to have a plan. Then with the plan in place you will execute that plan and then evaluate it. How well did I do? Did you hit your projects and come in on budget? This is good management and enables you to review your performance. It's a learning experience for your next project.

Used to be people wanted large master baths with a spa and separate showers. This is just not working today, there is a trend toward smaller, more efficient master baths that work.

Let your space work for you and the tenants; do something special to your house. The areas in which you spend most of your time should be largest. The places where you don't spend much time should be smaller. Be practical and smart when re-modeling your property. Think about how you can maximize your space for the optimal usage at the most reasonable price.

Take your time, make a plan that will maximize your investment in your project. You will have only so much money to spend with the initial cost of the property you will have a certain dollar in the project. Try to stay on point and ignore the line of reasoning that says "If I do this and I do that, I will get a higher price." It's not always the case. Be smart about your money and you will make money.

Take your time, make a plan, a blueprint. Use the existing footprint of the house to your advantage to transform it into something just a little bit better, so your property stands out in the neighborhood as unique—one that you can either sell or rent at a price comparable to other houses in the neighborhood. By doing those special things to the property you will be able to exert some control over the values on the street.

Even though you may want the best-looking property in the area, you must stay within the market for the area. If the property is worth $50,000, don't put $100,000 into the property. You want to use good sense in how you spend your money. Likewise, you don't want to do $25,000 worth of work and do shoddy work. Being able to pull a project together and to have the plan is an asset for you. This unique ability will help you obtain a financial partner at a time when you may want or need one.

Your Workforce

It is important to use good people, but your budget will determine this. When you are getting started, you may have to do the work yourself, with help from friends. Spare your cash; don't go crazy. How you structure your deal will determine how you will finance the rehab. As an example, zero cash and no rehab loan dollars mean you will be doing work yourself. If you borrow some money for rehab, you can afford to hire some people. If you have totally funded the purchase of the property and the rehab, it will allow you to hire better tradesmen.

I discourage the use of a general contractor. But you can solicit bids from people who renovate property. I have a formula as to how much the rehab will cost you. When shopping a contract price, get the contractor to meet you there. Even with a low budget try to find the best, most skilled workers for the price.

Buying Materials

All prices are not the same. Once you decide what you need for materials it's time to make that purchase. I prefer to build a relationship with a wholesaler. You want to become the wholesalers' go-to guy. I have been able to obtain volume and contractors' discounts. No sales tax for resale and sometimes I am able to get seconds or discontinued product cheap, real cheap. Having a warehouse, a base of operation is great to have if you can: a garage on a property that you can lock works great for storage of surplus materials, leftovers, good buys, just about anything.

When you buy overstocked materials at a wholesaler or even at an auction you have to pay for it now, and you will have some holding costs so make sure you get a great deal to make it worth your while.

When someone is demolishing an old house, I may go get some scrap off the house—which is free. I love the historic windows and the old German lapboard siding. New lap board is over $3 per foot.

You will also learn what type of materials to buy. There are some jobs where you can get away with builder quality materials. You don't always want to go cheap; however, decide where you want to spend your money. Usually in the show-and-tell stuff. I also try to eliminate lots of colors when

I paint, so that I don't have half cans lying all over the place. Try to keep it all one or two colors, so it is consistent. Good for touch-ups as well if you already know what color it is. With prices rising, you must think of any and all cost-saving ideas to save a buck. I paint my porches brick red; now my porch color is "Spanky Red."

If you need items like carpet, tile, or linoleum, you can sometimes buy that as an overstock or close-out item. Ask the wholesalers you know to call you when they've got overstock, so you can be one step ahead. I don't think I would store these items, but if you are in a project and working your plan they may just fit in perfectly and save you some money.

I have been amazed at what I have been able to buy at auctions—from products to entire houses—saving me a great amount of money. Wholesalers who have closed up or plants that have a surplus of materials and tools will sell off at auction. I remember buying a pallet of double-hung windows, assorted sizes all for $200. Had to have been 15-18 windows. That's the type of buys that you want to get. It may take you awhile to use up the different sizes but remember the price was just right.

Decks and Porches

Decks. I love to do a deck. Anywhere and anytime. If there is an opportunity to build a deck off a kitchen or a rec room I want to do it. Today people like to grill and hang out on a deck. Make it a nice size so it can accommodate the people in the house. If you have a back entrance off to the side that just does not look great you can change the look by adding a deck, say 10x12 feet, perfect with steps. The size is appropriate for the materials that can be purchased with minimal waste. Decks don't take long to build and are not too awfully expensive.

Porches. Nothing like a nice front porch, wraparound porch. Whatever you have to work with, dress it up. So that your potential customers will be attracted to your house. There are a number of things you can do to jazz it up: new pickets, bead-board, or tongue-and-groove ceiling and decking, nice steps, creative paint job, shutters on the windows, nice front door. Even the neighbors will like what you have done when you improve the front of your property.

Kitchens and Baths

Most buyers will not have the vision you will have to remodel both the bathroom and kitchen. It is a nice add-on for you and you can get that extra dollar, for a nice up-to-date kitchen, especially in a higher-end property that can command the higher retail price. In a lower neighborhood where you cannot get the price, you should consider your options and decide to what extent you feel as though you need to remodel both your kitchen and bath. Maybe you can do one and not the other. Or possibly just do a refurbish: countertops, paint, faucets, and floors.

You can dazzle a buyer by upgrading a kitchen and bath. Make them open, airy, fresh, up-to-date, new. That will attract a buyer quicker. Evaluate your price point and your cost of the rehab in those two vital areas.

If they are bad, change them up. If you are at the higher end of a flip, make them great. Recognize when a fixer-upper kitchen and bath just won't do the job, when a little extra is needed; you have to make the judgment call. Modernizing your kitchen and bath can sell a house. It will be one of the most expensive areas to remodel, so be sure you estimate the cost properly.

Kitchen cabinets. Women like nice kitchens, lots of space, nice cabinets, dining area, nice floor. Depending on how much you are putting into the property, the kitchens are an area you may want to pay some attention to. You must evaluate the expense of refurbishing or replacing your key items in the kitchen.

Buyers will look closely at kitchens and baths. Sometimes paint and a new floor will work—then again, sometimes not. Most families spend a lot of time in these areas, so you may want to do an extra good job in there. Here are some suggestions for the kitchens:

- ample light
- nice working cabinets with unique knobs
- new contemporary countertops
- windows
- new floor
- open areas to other parts of the house—dining room or living room
- pass-through counter
- ventilation
- new sink with sprayer
- exhaust for oven

...and for the bathrooms:

- new fixtures
- nice size vanity
- new toilet (or maybe only a new toilet seat)
- extra shower head
- new floor
- tiled walls
- great lighting

If you are flipping the property you may want to consider up-to-date new appliances. They complete a kitchen for sure. Include if you can, install a dishwasher and garbage disposal. New buyers will like the add-ons. If it is a rental property, don't add appliances; they are just additional items you have to maintain. You don't need to put a washer and dryer in the home. Let the buyer bring his own.

Know in advance what your allowance will be for the stove and refrigerator. Maybe the buyer may have his own and will not need yours.

Decide where you will put a microwave—you don't want it just on the counter. Plan for it, with the appropriate outlet.

Energy and Environmental Upgrades

Energy-efficient houses are now coming to the forefront, especially extra insulation and double-hung replacement windows. There are many federal, state, and local programs that will pay for upgrades to properties in different areas, and all you have to do is apply.

Lead paint is another area in which governments are getting involved. It's great for the property owner. Yes, you do have to do some work, but in the end it is worth it.

Many cities now have programs for energy-efficient renovations to your property. Many cities will do this for you for free. All you have to do is ask and apply; it may take time. Most people are not aware of such programs and with no applicants there may be lots of funding just for your project.

Regardless of whether you upgrade a heating or air-conditioning system or add some insulation, it is important to look at a house's energy efficiency. With higher energy costs, homeowners want not only something nice but also something environmentally sound. This is an added plus, but you will have to evaluate by project.

Odds and Ends

- Ceiling fans. The price of ceiling fans has come down a great deal over the years, and I have usually recommended putting in ceiling fans maybe the kitchen, living room, and also master bedroom. With a light kit they provide great light, movement of air, and a look. People tend to like the ambiance that it creates.
- Don't forget to put ground-fault receptacles in the bathrooms and the kitchen areas.
- Good lighting with nice fixtures around the outside of the house is a great idea.
- Carpet. In a re-sale, carpet is nice and will help sell a property. In a rental situation, I recommend tile or an alternative. No carpet.
- Paint. A fresh coat of paint will do wonders both inside and outside. For a rental I have used the same color so I don't get confused on a re-paint job; it's always easier just to do white. For a flip, it can be best to allow the home buyer to pick colors.
- Windows and doors. It's always a good idea to put up a real nice front door. Add the mailbox and house number. This will give the house curb appeal. Depending on the intended use of the house—sale or rental—and the condition of the windows, I will assess what I have and make a determination of what I need to do. If the windows are old and single pane, it's not a bad idea to upgrade to thermo pane, double-hung windows. They are really cost efficient. They are not too difficult to install and people really like to have them, especially if they are buying the property.

Parking and Landscaping

When I can I like to improve the parking situation. Many of the older homes in the inner city have just street parking. How special can it be if you cut in a driveway, either pave it or just put down some crush and run. You can do some basic landscaping and a walkway to the front door.

If you have an existing driveway you should be able to assess what you need to do to get it right. Sometimes a new blacktop or sealer. Make it stand out and be attractive. Don't forget the landscaping here as well.

For next to nothing you can make the yard look great. A few plants and I can make backyard borders on properties where it is appropriate. For privacy I also use trees as borders and shade—something that does not require a lot of maintenance. Many cities will give you free mulch. All you have to do is pick it up. This type of mulch usually acts as a good base. This will help with curb appeal either for flipping or if you have to rent the property. It is important to maintain it.

You want to keep your properties always looking good. That's why in your repairs and maintenance you should follow your stair-step approach to your short- and long-term plan for the property. Be sure your properties are the nicest on the block. Make them stand out. That will also give you a big up in renting those properties as well.

Just remember when you renovate your property to have a plan in place, whether you are going to keep the property for the long term and collect rent off it or whether you plan to flip the house. Do good work, use good materials, and do your best in making sure you maintain a reputation of quality.

Playing Your Hand

Whatever game you decide to play either at home or in business, you must keep your hand close to your chest.

Be careful; know when to hold them and when to fold them. Know when to go all in and when just to let it alone. Look at the situation carefully. I am not one to overanalyze a situation; maybe I should after all these years, but I prefer to think on my feet.

So we learn over time with experience how to read the players, what they are thinking, how they play—which is what we do in life when doing business or dealing with family matters. You really want to know what you are in store for before you go knocking.

You may not want to go all in on a poker game unless you have a good feeling of what it is you are about to do. Expect the unexpected. You never know when you will be trumped.

Make good sound decisions that will advance you up the ladder of success. You cannot start at the top—although some can. You know whom I'm talking about: those of privilege who started on top without the background and knowledge and took a tough fall into the hole—oops. Those people who started at the top really should have been smart enough to prepare for the unexpected. Because it will take you more effort and time to climb the ladder, don't fall into the same trap. Know your competition and anticipate the unexpected.

CHAPTER 18

Managing Projects

IF YOU HAVE THE CONTACTS THAT I TALKED ABOUT EARLIER and if you are a wheeler and dealer, you may be able to pull together a huge deal with zero dollars, using the leverage of your expertise. You can make a lot of money. Investors want doers; they want someone on their team that will work. How many of us know those people? How many of us know of those opportunities for a big deal? A development, a land deal, or even a shopping center. You probably should think smaller, manageable projects—ones that you can grow into and that are available for zero down, ones that develop both your handy-man skills and your project management style. You have got to learn what comes first.

Let me provide some insight as where to begin:

1. Curb appeal. I like doing a complete clean-out of the property. Maybe some basic demolition. I want to see what I am doing. During this process I am formulating my blueprint and planning my costs. You are learning your trade. Cleaning out a property—and some are really bad—does not require a lot of cash. You got dump fees, time, cleaning products.

2   If the weather is on your side, it's a good time to work on the outside. Paint if necessary and get the yard looking good. At any point you can put a "For Rent" sign or a "For Sale" sign for the purpose of premarketing your property; you may hit a home run and someone may purchase it right then and there.

3   Formulate your blueprint, your plan for the renovation, with associated costs. Think about the amenities that you want to put into the property that will help you either sell it or rent it. Costs are a big factor. An example:

   a   New cabinets, used cabinets, or fix the old
   b   Upgrade heating system or put in new
   c   Electrical upgrade. If there is a 100-amp panel, I go to 200. Am I adding baseboard heat? How many outlets and lights am I adding? Can I use what I have?
   d   Water. How's the water pressure? Most of the time sewage is ok. Plumbing work is usually pretty easy, as compared to electrical. With the introduction of Pex and Shark fittings, it has become a real do-it-yourself and learn-as-you-go project.
   e   Build out. How bad are the walls and floors? Sometimes covering a bad ceiling with new ¼-inch sheetrock is the way to go and easier. As you determine your plan for renovation, you are estimating the costs as well putting together an affordable budget. If your dollars allow you to go to the studs for new electric, heating, plumbing, and walls, make that decision. If you're on a tighter budget, then you cannot afford to strip the walls to the studs; you will have to make do. You can put quarry tile on the floor at a high cost, or you can buy a $24 can of oil-based floor paint. In the low-end rehabs and in places where pets will be allowed, I recommend painting the floor.

CHAPTER 18: MANAGING PROJECTS

4   Once your blueprint is complete it's time to put your plan into action. You may or may not need a building permit. Most local ordinances will require you to get one. Not a bad idea to obtain one, although maybe not for a specific aspect of the work. I usually get a general permit that covers everything. Don't think you can sneak a major job through without a permit. Most of the construction materials today are coded with dates. Pex for plumbing is new; they will see it and gig you. You are allowed to replace like kind as in repairs and maintenance. Lots of activity to a property will attract the attention of city officials and renters and investors.

5   Ready set go! You are on your way. Take your time; be thorough; do a good job. Basically the rule of thumb here is to do all the hard things first; that's what I like to do because when you are winding down the project and tired of it you don't want a hard list. Do all the items that require rough-in inspections and things that will be hidden in the wall or underground. Either way you know when that is complete all you will have do is cover up. Sheetrock repair or replacement, paneling or the like. Spackle, trim out, and paint.

Remember with zero dollars there will be times that the cash flow is not good and you will be forced to do a non-cost item on your property. It could be demolition, spackling, yard work. You want to go in order, in sequence, but there is no real rule.

Personally, I love to see progress, so there are times I will finish out a room, prime, and paint it, so I can get a feel of how the property will turn out. It also allows me some great satisfaction on how well I am doing—motivation to move on. It's nice to stand back and praise yourself on your job.

6   Almost done. The project is winding down, and you're tallying final coats of paint, inspectors, bushes, and grass seed. You're cleaning the house and getting it ready to market.

All along, while doing this great project you are prospecting for your third and fourth projects. As I have discussed prospecting takes time, but by now you should have started your next project; aim to have them overlap. I call that having one in the pipeline. This way you can move your materials to the next project without scrambling to find a new one.

Along with the budget that has now been done, you will want to get started. As discussed you may start the items that need to be done first and that require a building permit, as well as demolition if any. The items to do with a building permit will probably take a little longer to complete, but along side of those

It's Our Time

It's our time; our time is now. You have made the right choices and you have trained and trained. You have prepared yourself to take the prize—the prize of success that you have been waiting and praying for. It happens to all of us at different times of our lives. In 2012, just by chance an 81-year-old retired Vietnam vet who came from a small town with a simple life won the super lotto, $300 plus million. Tell me that was not incredible. Sure would like to win $300 plus million at twenty-five.

Sure enough, it's your time. You go to work every day and do the best you can, working to the best of your ability, thinking it may be possible.

Be smart; be energetic; be constant, well-disciplined, and passionate about your mission.

Don't give up hope; there will be a lifetime of distractions and temptations that can lead you astray; instead, work hard to stay focused on your plan. Don't forget your family. They will be there for you as you have been for them.

Continue to put the effort in; get up and go; do the best you can in your work, your faith, your family, thinking that your time is now. Even

projects you will want to do some of the smaller projects that will give some show and tell. Consider completing the outside first so you have a nice curb appeal; build interest in your project.

So in essence you will formulate a plan of both short-term and long-term projects. Some of them essential and some not at the moment, but important.

I like being able to see completed projects at week's end so I usually try to plan a project or two that I can look back on and say ok then that looks great. This makes me feel good about the project and myself.

---

if your time isn't *right* now, when it comes you will be ready to accept God's plan. You are in the plan.

Don't try to figure it out. It may drive you crazy. You just stick to the plan that you have outlined. Always maintain the high moral ground, being as prepared as you can be. Constantly learning and training to be better than you were yesterday. Your day will come very soon. Be patient: if it is not today, it may be tomorrow.

Remember Jeremiah 29:11: "'For I know the plans I have for you,' says the Lord, 'They are plans for good and not for disaster, plans to give you hope and a future.'"

I am ready for this to happen. What about you? I have been ready for awhile. Why do we think that our lives at times are disasters when in actuality we should be counting all our blessings? We have forgotten to take time to be grateful for all those wonderful things the Lord has provided us.

When we realize all the good we have received, we can embrace any disaster as a blessing of good fortune, which requires only time and faith to bear fruit. We must grow beyond our own shortcomings and fears to be stronger disciples of the Lord.

Utilities are something you are going to want to think about. You may need power at the property for being able to work. There are choices: if the electrical looks good in the property you can have the power turned on. This is the best option. If not, then there are alternatives. If you are increasing the panel to 200 amps and running new circuits, you can either put in a temporary panel which is great or use a generator for power. It's just nice to have power at the property. Running extension cords form the neighbor's house is not safe at all.

You may also need water, so not a bad idea to have the water turned on. Not knowing how much plumbing you plan to do, it's good to be able to have water. If nothing else, to clean paint supplies, concrete, pressure washing, to find leaks to name a few. Other utilities including gas may not be important right now to do.

You may never have enough time to get a project completed. Your time estimates for each task will really vary. And the accuracy of your estimates will improve over time. Whether you're held back by the attitudes and skills of your workers or by unforeseen repairs, rest assured something will come up to prolong the project. My personal make-up is that I like to work a little extra each day, maybe even have a weekend crew, three guys who have regular jobs and want to pick up some weekend work. By doing this you can usually get more done, and the project will move a little quicker. Some projects, however, will just take time no matter what you do. I prefer to get in and get out of a project, so I can move on to something else.

Hiring weekenders, friends, and students

There are a lot of people that you can hire on the weekend who do moonlight work from their regular jobs. Many are talented and want to make a little extra money. Often you can get them at a good price. During the summer, on weekends, or after school, students can be a good source of labor.

If you are working with part-time people, you want to be sure you are there and are working with them, giving them all the direction that they will need. You will need to buy materials for them, answer their questions, inspect their work, and pay them of course. At the end of the year, you will need to send a 1099 form to those who earned $600 or more.

Time Management

Use your time wisely, don't waste it. Plan the week ahead of time so you know what you are doing and what is expected of you. Use a daytimer so you don't miss opportunities or meetings that you have committed to. Plan big projects around long weekends and vacation time as well, especially if you have a full-time job. With some good weather and a few bodies you can get a lot done.

Buying materials always seems like a waste of time. I laugh at myself when I charge $50 for every visit to the supply store. As a habit I try to buy the materials either at night after work or first thing in the morning. And I try to be one step ahead of the people working for me. If you are going to start work at 8am, that's 8am and not 10 because you did not have paint or gas for the lawnmowers. Be prepared. Also, I like to have a few jobs going at a time, so if it rains or you run out of materials for one job, there is somewhere else your people can go to finish out the day. It's a good way to avoid the workers just standing around; if you are like me, that will drive you nuts.

Send only one worker to the store, never two. The second worker always wants to go to get out of working. It's never been a two-man job. The second worker should be given some tasks to do while the lead goes to the store. Time is money; I measure my success by how much I can accomplish. There is always something to do.

I always try to leave a clean and organized workplace when I go home in the afternoon. I like the job to be clean and fresh in the morning when I get there—puts you in a great mood.

Many wholesalers and credit-card companies have rewards or discount programs. Do what you can to qualify, so you can save some money. Every little bit helps and over a period of time you will save a considerable amount of money.

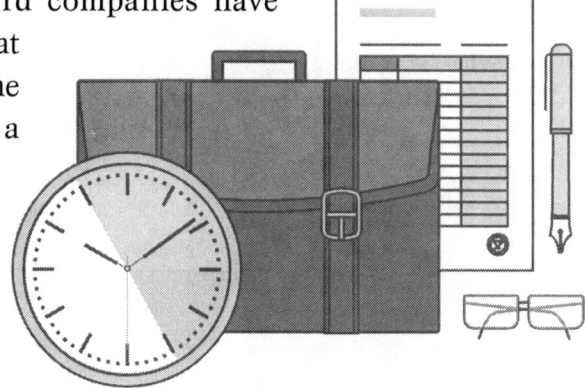

If you are doing a rehab and don't get the full list of supplies, you could end up running around all day like a fool picking up odds and ends. What I like to do is plan ahead of time. If I know on Monday what my repairs are all week, I will try to make one trip to the supply store. I try never to go during the day but rather in the evening or early morning. Nights are great since the supply stores are a little slower. I get as much as I can for all the jobs and set them up. By bringing all the supplies to the different jobs, when my help shows up, I am set to go. If I am by myself, that's ok too. I still buy the supplies the night before or in the a.m., so I can get started.

Having a truck or van with items on the truck also saves some time.

If you know your project will be short term, a flip or a mortgage in a period of time, you can set up lines of credit at supply houses with minimum payments due and full payment when the property is sold or mortgaged. Start with what credit line you can get and allow it to grow.

Plan your work properly. I like cutting perennials, weeds, and brush in the fall or winter to avoid unwanted growth, so when spring hits your weeds are gone, and you are looking good. Also do your heating and air conditioning work on your off season; trying to get air conditioning fixed in the summer time is tough to do.

Note that if you plan your work properly you can save some money. Also, if you are able to do several jobs at one time that will also save some money. If you have some HVAC work to be done, have your contractor do all the units and not just the one unit. Coordinate your jobs and save considerable money by avoiding charges for multiple service calls.

> If you plan your work properly you can save some money.

At all times, try to maintain a positive cash flow. This is hard, since it is natural to spend money. I am guilty of this for sure; there is always a project and someone to pay. But there will be an emergency or a great deal that you may need some cash for, so be as liquid as you can.

Be safe and cautious. Try not to extend yourself. Don't take crazy risks. Be prudent in your decision making. It's the best thing that you can do. You want to avoid the silly mistakes.

When you complete a job, reward yourself. Take some time off and pat yourself on the back. You did a good job. Take a long weekend or vacation.

Some things you want to keep in mind before you start: Think the project through and be sure you will get a return for your investment. Is it worth your while to do that project or is it a waste of money? Does it really need to be done? This is your due diligence on the project: looking before you leap. Sleep on it a night and see if you feel the same way in the morning. Some people will put pools in their homes and will never be able to get their money back. So whatever you do, be sure you will be able to realize a return on your investment.

Planning and development

You will have to be sure you plan the project properly. Scheduling is very important, making sure your people show up on time and do the work that they are supposed to do. The work usually has to be inspected before the next phase of work can be done.

Make a plan. Think about what you will do to the property. Prior to buying it you should have taken the time to make your blueprint. It may be a short-term plan, including some cosmetic curb-appeal work, and ultimately a wholesale flip. Or it may be an extended renovation and keeper for your portfolio. Either way, you will have some insight as to what your plan is and how to execute it. The cost factor will also determine what you can do. You have a plan for your entire portfolio in your blueprint; you just have to follow your plan, staying focused and on budget for success.

This process may become complicated if you are doing multiple projects—you end up doing a lot of juggling, but proper management is crucial to the success of a project. Not many people can envision what a project will look like upon completion. You've got to have an eye, like a coach seeing raw talent and being able to develop that talent over a period of years.

Stay Strong

You may not want to be an eternal optimist, but I want you to be: to take any situation and make it a positive, remembering that you can work it out and be successful. Through your life you will face setbacks, speed bumps, tragedies, and maybe a brick wall or two. These things will only make you stronger. Remember you are blessed by these things because they are God's will, and you will survive and be a better person.

Life has its way of dealing some serious blows. Death is one that is the ultimate and cannot be escaped. There is nothing after that in your life except for praise and peace for the person who has died. This may not help you right now in coping with the broken heart of losing a loved one. It never is easy; don't pretend it is. Learn to cope with death in your own way, hoping that it will make you closer to God. There is peace knowing your loved one has finally gone home. You will develop resilience in the face of tragedy.

We all at some time or another will face our eternal destiny. So we must now do all that we can to embrace life and all the pleasures that we are afforded. It's a beautiful thing to experience, and truly we are lucky to have been so blessed. Remember we all will not be rich rock stars, but we can have peace in our lives without being rock stars.

Remember that what you have learned yesterday and what you learn today will be the tools to succeed tomorrow. Get all the information you can get, so that you too can be enriched with success.

Some Ideas on Prioritizing your Projects.
What do I do first, second, and then after that? Here are a few ideas:

1. Building permit items. For example electrical, plumbing, mechanical, or structural. All these items are critical. Some may even require a drawing in order to obtain a building permit. If that is the case, I hope that you recognized this in your pre-purchase due diligence. You may be required to retain someone who is licensed. That will probably cost you a little more money. Budget those expenses properly.

2. Some essential repairs will include broken windows, paint, a new front door, gutters, plaster on the inside or a leaky roof to name a few. Don't create more work for yourself than what needs to be done. There is a limit. Draw that line.

3. Think about those items that will bring you the added returns on your investment or more rent. The deck, new flooring, washer and dryer hook ups. Stay away from dishwashers. A new counter in the kitchen, a vanity in the bathroom (but not a new tub; it gets complicated quickly). These are the items that you want to do because it makes sense.

Money-pit projects.
Rehabs and renovations can become money pits. You can sometimes spend more money during the last 10% of a project than in the beginning 50%; it is crazy. If a rehab project has a reasonable cost associated with it, I don't think anyone is going to blame you for that. But as the house nears completion you may get the urge to do things to the house that you personally like; this will quickly put you over budget. Don't spend money that you don't have to spend or that you simply don't have. Doing the job right is so important; you must stay on course. Don't make the mistake that I made. Take a moment; hire the

professional, if necessary. You don't want to have to come back and fix something that you did not do right the first time.

You will have to watch every detail of the project as it moves along. During each phase you can either make money or lose it by not being able to control and manage your expenses. It is critical during all stages of the project. There will always be something that you did not expect that potentially could eat into your profit.

CHAPTER 19

Landlording

The Decision to Rent and Not to Flip

When you have zero cash and you want to get big in real estate in order to make a lot of money, low-income maybe depressed property in undesirable neighborhoods may be your only option. Don't worry; it's a super niche to be in.

The properties you buy will be harder and usually slower to sell. You can make some good money by renting instead or in the mean time. There are some nice advantages with renting your property:

- ▶ You can get your renovation money back through collected rent.
- ▶ You can hold out or wait for the right buyer to pay you the price that you want.
- ▶ If you wait long enough your property will increase in value. I bought a quadplex at 502 Day Ave in the mid-eighties, paid off the note in a few years, and enjoyed the income. With the four units I was able to get $1500 to $2000 per month for many years. The $25,000 I paid for the property in the 80s is now worth over $200,000. It just so happens to be in the right spot for growth.

- ▶ There are some serious tax advantages you can enjoy throughout the term of the mortgage and while you have repairs and maintenance.
- ▶ It will help your credit across the board.
- ▶ It will give you personal income and wealth. It will also allow you to buy more properties.
- ▶ You will now be in the property management business which is a new set of rules. It's not as easy as you may think. If you have a mentor, learn quick, be a good student.

The rental business does provide a steady cash source—I don't say *income* as I don't want to confuse you. There is gross income and net income. Net income will be yours. One of the pitfalls of property ownership in the rental business is that an owner thinks that the gross income is his and spends it on everything except expenses—taxes, mortgage, maintenance.

However if they're done right, rental properties are relatively safe: most rents enable long-term, steady growth. They may or may not provide a positive income based on your ability to manage the property; this will depend on your ability to control its expenses. They are relatively easy to manage for most people; however, as we've discussed, there is a world of difference between a good property manager and a poor one.

A cardinal rule is that your tenants are customers and if you treat the customers right—knowing that they have become your income source, then you will be ok. When you mistreat them, it's only trouble for everyone. I believe the old adage that the customer is always right, and I draw the line in the sand with a good solid lease.

Negatives of rental property:

- ▶ If you don't keep responsible tenants (i.e., the kind who pay), you will have a negative cash flow. Don't rob Peter to pay Paul. You've got to pay your mortgage; they've got to pay their rent.
- ▶ There is much more maintenance for landlords than for pure flippers. Maintain your property so that you don't fall victim of code officials.

Property Management

It is not as easy to manage property as one might think. I put someone in charge of a couple dozen properties for a year to help me, a nice, middle-aged friend of mine. She had done some property management before, and I thought that it would be a great short-term fit to manage these properties. From the first day it was a disaster. She could talk to people, and find a tenant, but was not capable of collecting rent, except from little old ladies. Nothing was ever open to rent because she hated to go to court. The files were never complete, which was evident in the judge's rulings. She did not kick anyone out, and she did not provide reports of rental income, or expenses, or anything. I loved the fact that she worked thirty hours a week and accomplished little to nothing. How was that anyone else's fault but hers? Within four months the uncollected rent was about $54,000 or seventy percent of potential rental income. She had me on my last nerve.

Something had to give. It was difficult, since I had a personal relationship with her. Over a period of three weeks, I hired three very experienced people. These candidates were very capable of doing the job well. Each one trained for a few hours with my first employee, and each one quit within a day. Not that they could not do the job, but she filled the introduction to the job with gloom and doom, and they all got scared and quit, citing silly excuses for leaving. In desperation, my friend Ed stepped up. He was a middle-aged man with a military background and great common sense. No experience whatsoever in real estate or property management. Within thirty days, he had been able to assess situations, obtain eviction notices, collect more rent, pay bills, deal with proper accounting situations, and establish a system of checks and balances. Clearly, a novice can do a great job managing, buying, and overlooking properties. It is about commitment and some understanding. You need a commitment on your part and you need to know if you can do it and make it work. All the experience in the world does not give you a pass to success.

Unfortunately Ed was not able to maintain the success of his first days on the job. Within three months 80% of the homes were vacant. The others were boarded up by the city, no bills paid. Ed just about ruined a great portfolio. It took me nine months to turn twenty-five properties around to make a cash cow again. You have to know what you are doing.

At some point you will decide whether to hire someone or do the work yourself. Like any other business that is just starting out, you will be the cook, waiter, and bottle washer. You may have to do it all; be prepared to make that commitment. From repairs all the way to accounting, there is more to it than meets the eye. Yes there will be a lot to keep up with but really not much more than if you were running another business, although it is different and that is why it is appealing to people. One thing is for sure: you don't need a lot of people to help you in the beginning; doing the work yourself can be gratifying, and you have total control. Better to manage your time thus enabling you to manage your business, hands on. You can't blame anyone else but yourself

Trust

Are you a trustworthy person? Or do you lie and cheat to get ahead? Do you break the law to succeed? These are all the wrong reasons and ways to get ahead in life. Best to always play by the rules and be a leader of men. One lie always leads to another, and before you know it, you will be in a hole that you can't get out of.

It takes a person with strong convictions to do the right things in life and not cross the line. Not everyone has the strength to live by the Golden Rule. It takes strength to forgive someone for what he has done and then move on.

I have always trusted people to do what they say they are going to do. So many times they did not make good on the word. How disappointing it has become over the years. I just seem to attract people who are deceptive and untrustworthy; maybe that is part of God's plan for me: to help all those that I can. I don't have any regrets in helping people. Even though, as some say, it may be abuse for failure, but you can also congratulate yourself for its success. Best to start yourself in as many roles as you can, so you to learn all aspects of the business.

If you need help, decide what areas you don't like or where you feel you are the weakest and get a little help. There are all types of property management. The basics are the same in principle; the difference is in the type of property that you are renting and the type of tenant you are working with. No sense doing a criminal background check if you are in a tough area where criminals live; this is your decision. Maybe this is an area you are trying to change. Initially you may not get the quality of tenant that you like. Background checks may be a waste of time. Bad credit, almost a given. It's tough to get an up-front

to me, I keep going into that lions' den over and over again. You have to trust yourself first before you can trust someone else. Protect yourself when you extend yourself to someone whom you want to trust. Be cautious.

Trust takes time. It's not an all or nothing situation. You don't have to be all in, like when you have a royal straight flush in a poker hand. Trust will take time and energy to develop; both parties have to test the waters and see if they can trust each other. Take baby steps if you have to. Don't be afraid: always do your part. If that bond of trust is to fail, let it be on the other person and not you. In time, and without betrayals, your bond will grow strong, and you will be able to trust the other person implicitly.

You cannot control another person's actions; you cannot redirect his intentions good or bad; you cannot control his thoughts, how he acts, or what he does. You may be able to have an influence on someone in order to point him in the right direction; then just hope for the best.

Keep in mind that we are all individuals all working hard to achieve happiness means to us. Anything that you can do to help the people God brings into your life is great.

cash deposit when they first move in unless it's tax refund time. So you may want to increase the rent. If a place rents for $600 you can charge $650 just to offset upcoming expected losses, damage, nonpayment of rent, or anything else that may occur.

When you are developing your portfolio you should start to put a value on your time. This is essential in determining whether to have someone do the work for you. A plumber may charge you $75 per hour to fix a toilet that you can fix yourself, or if you have enough properties you may have a trained helper whom you pay $12 per hour and whom you can assign to the task. In time as you grow you can assess all the areas that either you can do or you have decided to sub out. Self-assessment in your business is important and ongoing.

We all have different skill levels. Some are more detailed and thorough than others. Assess your skill level, just like in any other business.

The areas of personal assessment are quite simple:

- Do you have a skill set for this type of work? Can you do any of the things that may be required? Can you paint? Do you know how to use a hammer? Best to be able to do something. If not then you need to be a fast learner and learn things trial by error.
- Can you communicate with people? If you are a likable person, have the gift of gab and are honest you may have one up on the introverted person who has a hard time talking to a stranger. I don't mind hunting someone down to collect rent. Some people don't like looking a tenant in the eye when they take them to court for non-payment of rent. Their traits will come out as time goes on with the development of your business.
- Can you handle the ups and downs of the business? It may be an unexpected repair or nonpayment of rent. I have had tenants who know the system and will work it hard on you. What happens when they get three or four months behind on the rent and there becomes a point of no pay? You still have to make the mortgage payment. The bank does not just say, "Sure, pay when you can." This is most stressful to people. Multiply that 2 or 3 times with some bad tenants.

CHAPTER 19: LANDLORDING

- Can you do basic bookkeeping? Mortgages as well as all the other expenses that must be tracked on a monthly basis. You don't need to be able to do a tax return but you've got to be able to present the financial information in some type of order that is accurate.

You can set your own hours, and that's an advantage to most people. Whether it be weekends or nights if you work a full time job or 24/7, you decide. Also the size of your portfolio will also dictate the amount of time you may have to put in. Obviously the more you take on yourself, the more personal time that you will have to put into your business.

Learn to be patient. Projects take time to do. Some go quicker than others. You may not see immediate results. You must be patient. Remember you are not going to hit homeruns every time. If you are impatient this may not be the business for you. Evaluate yourself and see how you fit in.

Tenants will take advantage of you if you are timid or weak. That will cost you money. You know your personality, so you should be able to decide what you can and cannot do.

The winner-take-all is an approach not for everyone. It is your goal either way to try to minimize your risks. As a landlord you become a target for those who don't mind rolling the dice for money, whether it's because of an injury, eviction, or a violation of the fair housing act. You always want to be careful.

Here are some ideas that may help you to minimize your risk or exposure:

- Deal with tenant complaints immediately, whatever they may be, especially repairs and maintenance. Document everything that you have done and make a file. Don't make a leaky faucet your undoing; you don't want a tenant to cite a leaky faucet as the reason for nonpayment of rent.
- Do surprise maintenance inspections on the property. Be prepared to do a few minor things that may get pointed out. You don't want to prolong a problem. Be sure to take a mental note of the property for the file.

- Be sure you have all the inspections on the property both building, zoning, as well as any code regulations.
- Be sure your taxes are paid.
- Be sure you have proper insurance coverage on the property. Obviously for the bank and your potential physical loss and exposure.
- Transfer risks to others by forming LLCs. This will minimize your exposure.
- Eliminate obvious risks and dangers on the property, including pools with diving boards, poorly functioning decks, cracked windows, accessible roofs.

Think about your rental property as your home. Take care of your investment.

CHAPTER 20

Marketing Your House, Either for Flipping or Renting

IF YOU BOUGHT THE HOUSE RIGHT AND IF THE MARKET IS RIGHT, YOU MAY BE ABLE TO SELL THAT PROPERTY WITHOUT DOING A THING. You can put a house under contract and then assign or sell the contract for a higher price, never taking ownership or paying any money. That is the best way to flip. If you have knowledge of people, buyers who are in the market to buy a particular type of house in a neighborhood, you may be able to bird dog the deal for the potential buyer. Perfect way to do a deal. A few of these a year and you'll be golden.

Marketing is the way you get the information out to the public. How do you get the message across to John Doe? Which vehicles do you use? What is the most effective tool in selling my product? What will work for me? Marketing is complex and can be very broad in nature. Many times the difference between success and failure is the marketing—how you communicate your product. I will condense some basic ideas and principles in this sector to apply to either selling or renting your home.

There are so many methods to market your home either to sell or rent. The biggest obstacle today is that the buying market has slowed down. People want to buy but just can't get the loans. This is a hurdle. There are many other creative ways to put families in homes, but how do you put them in *your* home? How do you reach that market?

In the old days, newspapers were the main vehicle to sell or rent your property. It's not that way anymore. Newspaper ads are expensive, and today it has become a dinosaur largely due to cost and distribution. The internet is cheap when it comes to getting your information out. The goal is to say hello, to introduce your product to the market place. This is the beginning step to making something happen with your property.

If you are flipping, this part of the process is essential: being able to sell the property. You have to have your property ready to go, marketable, and most important priced right to sell. Retail is not a dirty word but with market conditions as they are today it has become harder to sell a piece of property at market rate.

When pricing your property remember every deal is different, and even though you want top dollar for your property, remember that $2,000 either way can make or break a deal. Most people will start a little higher than what they want so they have some wiggle room—room for the realtor, the marketing expenses, and the heavy negotiations that may take place. You can get a good idea what is selling in the market when you do your research.

Marketing Plan

Here's a few ideas to consider for your marketing plan:

- ▶ What are you offering for sale? What piece of property are you going to market?
- ▶ What is your target market, who is your potential buyer? What are you selling and who can afford to pay the price you are asking for the property?
- ▶ Why should this potential buyer buy a property from you and not another flipper? What makes your deal so good? You know a flipper has got some profit built into the house. You may wonder why you cannot do the same thing and get the same deal. It's up to the flipper

CHAPTER 20: MARKETING YOUR HOUSE, EITHER FOR FLIPPING OR RENTING

to convince you as the buyer that this property is a great deal and you should buy from him.
- Where are your buyers? Do you know where your buyer is located? You have to be able to reach the people that may want to buy your property. Are they local buyers, state, or national? Are you selling to a wholesaler, a flipper, or a homeowner? There are different approaches to each type of buyer.
- What is my budget if any? Realtors will tend to want to have more money to promote the property than if you were trying to sell the property yourself.

Advertising

When you are about ready to rent or sell your property, it is important to be prepared so that you are ready to make a deal.

Use professional signs. I used to use the premade ones you by at a store and sometimes may still do that. However set yourself apart from the pack and have some nice ones made up. You can get a nice sign and frame from a local supplier. Of course you can add some extras to the sign like a flyer box and a place to hang balloons or banners. Some people will have an upscale wooden one made—wow. Although it's not necessary, you are identifying a brand—your brand, and that is important. Stay consistent with size, colors, name, phone number, so that people will start to identify with you. These are important tools to market your property and build a name for your company.

Be sure that whatever medium you use you put together professional-looking information: a flier, sign, or online advertising. It is important that you go out there first class.

Be sure you have the correct address with legal description on the property, along with good quality pictures. In today's environment you don't need a professional. There are great cameras with software to pull together some sharp fliers for marketing your property.

Make sure you list a number for a phone that you're often near, so callers can reach you. The worst thing in the world when you are advertising something is to miss the calls of prospective clients. It does not matter if you are using your main number or a secondary number—just answer the phone. If someone leaves a message, call him back. He may not buy now, but maybe later. I cannot tell you how many times someone has called about one property but, learning I had already rented it, ended up taking another property not on the original ad.

That is an advantage of having properties in the same area and priced around the same. You can capitalize on single shotgun marketing, which will give you greater results.

Keep track of people who call and may end up being someone you can rent to next month. They may not be ready to make a move today, however knowing that you will have an opening in 30-60 days may fit their needs. Look for opportunities and do all you can to benefit yourself as well as the customer.

Just Some Thoughts

When people come to me for advice, I'm always shocked at how unwilling they are to take it. You know where I stand; you know what my expectations are. I have set the bar high, so you can surpass your expectations toward excellence. Don't ask me to compromise my agenda because you refuse to put forth the effort. Once you become committed, the effort is actually effortless—*once you become committed*. You're the one that came to me, so you have a few choices to make.

You can adapt, conform, and succeed; you can become part of the winning team; so eliminate the complaining and whining. You decided to be a part of our mission; you made the commitment, so it is in your favor to follow it through. Succeed or fail.

Of course, you can leave. Truly it is a free world; you can quit and go somewhere else. But I don't want you to do that, so tighten it up and let's go. Running away from challenges and adversity could be a sign

CHAPTER 20: MARKETING YOUR HOUSE, EITHER FOR FLIPPING OR RENTING

Developing a pricing strategy is important to your success in selling a piece of property. If it is a wholesale market you are after, you must take a look at the people you are going to market the property to. In our REI investment group we may have several levels of wholesales. Entry-level wholesalers get one price, and mid-level wholesalers get another price, and a low-level scab may get an even lower price. You start where you want and go from there. An entry-level wholesaler may jump at the deal especially if the price is right. And he can make some money on the deal. Honestly, he may not know the game very well and pay the higher price. If you the seller bought the property right, you can sell at any level you want to. Pricing strategy is important since it will determine your profit.

---

of weakness. Remember you wanted in; you engaged me.

You can be stagnant and do nothing, hide in the corner and not be noticed, hope that the issue goes away. When you look again, the challenge and the opportunity are still there for you to succeed. Embrace the positive, so you can be an integral part of the team.

We have a mission a plan for success; our road map has been laid out. Don't be discouraged if we don't get from point A to B in one step. We must take all the necessary steps to build that solid foundation, so that we can move forward to success. No one said it was going to be easy.

No one said it was going to happen overnight.

Embrace the situation and become part of a winning team.

When J. C. Penney released their new ads in 2012, with a revamped marketing scheme, I thought it was just the change that the 600-unit retailer needed. They decided under the leadership of a new CEO that they would not have traditional sales but instead have everyday low prices—sale prices at a value all the time. The changes were initiated with colorful, cute, and catchy commercials. I thought it was clever—what do I

continued on page 236

Everyone will price his deal differently, depending on what he wants to accomplish. Decide your philosophy, but if it does not work, change it. There are no laws that dictate how much you must sell your property for.

For Sale By Owner or a Real-Estate Broker

How do I sell my home at the right time and the right price so it sells quickly and I can make some money? Price is a very important factor in selling your home. Do your homework so it is priced right. You don't want to list the property too high, so it sits there like a dead log. People will think that it is overpriced or that there is something wrong with the property. Either way that's not what you want. It is advisable to do some comparisons of similar

---

know? They appeared to be positioning themselves with the T.J. Maxx and Marshalls, who countered with commercials as well, the fashionista approach. Who would notice a war among apparel retailers? Not the average customer.

When earnings were reported later that summer, it became clear that the plan had not worked. JCP lost a record $176 million in one quarter and a huge portion of their customer base. A surprise to me! I never guessed that the plan with the catchy commercials would fall short of a winner. Now they have a real problem. What do they do?

Do they plow ahead and try to lure those customers back?

Do they modify their approach to marketing and alter their new mission?

Do they change it completely and go back to their old scheme?

The stock dropped 75 cents per share. Consumer acceptance and confidence is down. Someone has to make a move. Someone has some serious decisions to avert a crisis. But this is the entrepreneurial adventure. And although the goods and the customers are different, the adventure in the world of income property is exactly the same.

CHAPTER 20: MARKETING YOUR HOUSE, EITHER FOR FLIPPING OR RENTING

houses for sale in the neighborhood. Take special note of the prices of the ones that are selling and of the ones that aren't. Looking at both scenarios you will get a pretty good idea of the price you should sell your house for. Obviously, if you go in with a lower price than comparables around the area, you may indeed sell it quickly. A lot will depend on how much you have in the property and how much you want to make. It's not a bad idea to sell more houses for less than top dollar. Do you sell 10 houses per year at $10,000 profit or 5 houses at $15,000 per house profit? A lot of these decisions you will make based on your business plan.

If you have the marketing skills and ability to close a deal, then you may indeed want to consider selling the property yourself. You'll have to put up with a lot of the tire kickers, so you really need to be patient and willing to both work a deal and be rejected. The advantage of this is that you can market the property any way you want and you can save on real-estate commissions. An alternative is to pay agents to bring you a buyer, but you manage the sale. Without a realtor you will lack the personnel and marketing coverage, and you won't have access to the Multiple Listing Service. If you do retain a seller's agent, select one who will dedicate the time and energy your property deserves. Many times a seller will pick a real-estate agent who is a friend or acquaintance but is really not qualified to sell your property; this is a mistake. In the real-estate world, there are agents who specialize in certain aspects of the business. There are those for example that will do REOs, wholesale, short sales, high-end or low-end properties. In addition there are agents who will specialize in a certain type of seller or buyer, like a re-location specialist, a first-time homeowner, or an investor. So it is a little complicated to get the right real-estate agent to list, market, sell, and close on your property. You want a professional who specializes in your market, not your friend the realtor.

If the market is hot, and your property is great, and you have it priced right, you may sell it quickly without a real-estate agent. If, however, you are new at the game, it will be a little harder for you to grasp the complexity of what needs to be done. Also if you are flipping 10 properties per year, doing your own prospecting and a lot of your own rehabbing work, you just may not have the time to sell a property and therefore should work with a realtor. A strong realtor listing and selling your properties will be able to help you find the deals you need.

Many times a real-estate agent can market your property at a higher price. He works for you the seller and is ethically bound to protect your interests. A good real-estate agent will not give up the form and does not have to. He can play good cop/bad cop with the buyer.

A real-estate agent will help you formulate a price for your property. He will have greater access to information that can help make a business decision, most of this which will come from the MLS or the local board of realtors—information that you don't have access to.

A good realtor should know how to stage a property. He will know what furniture to put in a vacant property that will give it great eye appeal. He should be an expert in putting together an ad campaign or how to run a successful open house. You need traffic—a way that people will find out about your property.

It is essential to have someone—you or a realtor—that is versed in social media. In today's competitive marketplace where there is one deal better than another and there just seems to be an endless supply, you will need someone with the right talent and plan to get out there and grab a buyer.

Real-estate agents may sometimes do a better job in getting all those extras, those items that you may not remember or have the knowledge to get:

- ▶ A security deposit large or small—something substantial that they will put into escrow.
- ▶ All the paperwork, including mold and lead disclosure, buyer and seller rights, exclusive sales agreement, and fair housing disclosure.
- ▶ A proper closing, including possibly a closing agency.

- The best price for your property.
- An existing client list, even out-of-town buyers.
- Complete pre-qualification of potential buyers.

However many homeowners do try to sell their own homes and do a really good job in doing so.

- You can usually put a little more heart and soul into the sale. You have a vested interest in making a sale happen and may not allow a potential sale to pass.
- You can make a decision on the spot versus an agent who has to reduce the offer to writing. You as the seller can negotiate a deal right then and there with the potential buyer.
- You can hire your own title company and closing agency to consummate the deal.
- You may make more money since you won't have to pay a commission.
- Some real-estate agents will do a non-listing, putting your property on MLS for a fee, say $500; this is another great way to market your home.

The trend today is for the homeowner not to sell his own property but to use a real-estate agent. Your agent will have access to more prospective buyers than you as well as the skills to market and close on the property. There are always sensitive issues that will come up in a negotiation that a realtor will be able to guide you through.

It is vital that the process remain ethical and legal. Realtors are licensed and trained to go through the process. In addition realtors have to report to a licensed broker within their firm, so there are checks and balances on each deal. This is great for the investor selling his property.

Don't be stingy with commissions. Sometimes when I have made offers of $5,000 and the commission is $500 or less, I will write into the contract a bigger commission for the agent. When you do this, you send a positive message that you are going to pay for hard work, especially when they are successful. It's a win-win for everyone on board. You will be able to count on that real-estate agent working for you again and again. When a deal comes across that agent's desk you want the agent to call you first. Not the other guy.

Staging and Showing Properties

So you are ready to sell your flip property. You have done all your homework, your due diligence, and it is now show time. If you are selling distressed property you may not be motivated to put on the show. However anything above that you will want to really do it up right.

Staging your property is when you dress out or partially furnish the property so it looks like a real home, something your prospective buyers may be interested in. Some people just can't figure out how a home will look when it's furnished; you can show them. You don't need a lot, but you should have something in the property, so it sings out "Buy me, buy me."

Companies have popped up all over the place that specialize in staging homes. The higher the value of the property the more you may want to accent your property. They know exactly what type of items to put into a property to make it work for re-sale. As the owner, you pay a monthly rental fee for the furniture. This has been a growing business. If you can afford it and want to get the most out of your property, consider this extra as an option.

I talked about curb appeal: the few extra plants, a new front door, fresh mulch, trimmed bushes. It will not cost a lot of money, and it will help you sell your property. Before you splurge, drive around the neighborhood and just see your house as a drive-by. Compare your place to the others in the neighborhood and do an assessment. Think for a minute how prospective buyers would look at your property if they were driving by and shopping. Ask yourself what you would like in a house that you want to buy. You may be in great shape.

Keep your property looking crisp and simple. Let the buyer be the decorator. Yes, put out a new welcome mat. Put out a fresh plant and plant a few fresh plants near the front door or the walkway. A new screen door, nice mailbox. Don't overdo it, and be sure to take the junk out of the property.

Clean the property before you start to show it. If there are blinds on the windows be sure they look good and are not bent. The windows should be

CHAPTER 20: MARKETING YOUR HOUSE, EITHER FOR FLIPPING OR RENTING

clean inside and out. All the appliances must be new. Don't have smudges on the paint.

There are certain things prospective buyers and renters will focus on when they are previewing a house. For instance, if the family has children they may want a nice flat yard; if they don't have children they may not want a yard at all. If they are single they may not want a large kitchen. You need to appeal to the majority in an effort to sell your property. You want more bang for your buck. Little touches that may help you market your property:

- When staging a home, less is more, but you should add a few touches—simple but nice. A bedroom that is sparsely decorated will make the room look larger.
- I have usually kept a storage facility for items, things that I may need at different properties, and it has worked well. Those lawn ornaments that I take from one property may work somewhere else. Be creative.
- Put out a nice flier on the counter for people to take with them as they leave. Include pictures on the flier for lasting memories.
- Don't have things lying around: cleaning supplies, rags, unessential items. Take all these things out with you when you leave.
- Potential buyers will dissect the property, so you should do the same. Be sure the light works in the closet, check all cabinets, and be sure the basement is clean. Do a thorough walkthrough for all those areas that may turn someone off. You don't want any excuse for not selling the property.

Open houses work great when trying to market a property for sale. Most of the time they will be held on a weekend when most of the house buyers are off and can come by to take a look. Here are a couple of ideas that may help you do a nice open house for both the realtors and the buying public:

> **You need to appeal to the majority in an effort to sell your property.**

- Set certain hours that you will hold the open house. Provide a large window of opportunity to accommodate busy schedules.
- Showcase the property, with a well-manicured yard.
- Put out balloons and banners, a sign, things that look professional that will attract attention to the property. You want people to drive by and see the action.
- Soft music throughout the house will create ambience.
- Fresh flowers
- Maybe for the realtors offer a nice lunch and for the general public offer a drink and cookies. This always goes over well.
- Be sure to have all the fliers near the front door. Maybe a fish bowl for a drawing of visitors' business cards.
- Be sure that the lighting is right. Especially if there is real good accent lighting that you want to showcase. Use the dimmer switches for proper mood.
- Be sure that the basement and garage are cleaned.
- In short, the house has got to be clean; you want a fresh smell when people come in.

If you want to be one step ahead of the competition in an effort to sell your property this is the way to do it. Whatever your plan is do it just a little better than the other person.

Some more ideas to spruce up your yard:

- mow
- trim the bushes
- pull dandelions and weeds
- trim the border
- attend to the driveway, at least a patch and fresh seal to an asphalt driveway
- fresh flowers, annuals are good to put in, something maintenance-free
- get rid of dead plants and trees
- mulch

This will give you a new look to the landscaping of the house.

In review there are several items you can do that will make your place look great to sell:

- Do not have any window HVAC units in any of the windows.
- Fix broken windows and screens.
- Power-wash vinyl siding
- Replace old gutters and downspouts if necessary. At best consider cleaning them and be sure that they are hung properly. Pay close attention to the downspout, and water curbs.
- I love shutters. If you don't have them, add them; if they are broken, fix them; they will make a place stand out.
- Repainting the place ensures a fresh new look; change up the color to one that is contemporary. Also, re-seal wherever necessary and caulk. Take your time do it right.
- Look at your exterior lighting; for a little money you can really do a nice upgrade to the property. Include some security lights around the property.
- Trim. If you are good at colors, look at your trim and see if you can complement the base color with a nice accent color. Your house will stand out.
- Painting. Before you paint your house be sure you take a minute and detail the imperfections take out nails and hooks, caulk, replace rotten wood, scrape and prime peeling paint. Do the little extra thing that will make the property look really good. If you do a good job, the property will stand out when you are done.

Assessing and Accepting Offers

You know there are those easy decisions when someone comes and looks at your property and offers cash for it; it's a no-brainer. But then there are those where the buyer has no money and wants to make a deal. It will become complicated. That's when you have to take a hard look at the offers and evaluate each.

You are almost like an auctioneer, asking for the best deal. What do you do when you have several folks wanting your property?

I have found the simpler the deal, the better. Cash with no contingencies is good. Once you add contingencies or an out-clause in a contract you lose your edge. That person may walk away from the deal, and you will have lost another buyer. So it is important that you review all the offers and be smart about which one you accept; a realtor can help with this process. One thing is for sure: a realtor can do some background on the investor and see if he is for real. The realtor can also qualify a buyer, maybe not perfectly, but by reputation and track record.

Any deal can change dramatically if the buyer has to obtain financing. You may require a penalty clause if an offer is made on a piece of property and the bidder cannot come up with the money. The other worthwhile option is to charge a larger deposit.

You don't want to sign a contract during negotiations, unless you are sure that the buyer has financing in place or cash. If you are working with a realtor, he may be able to pre-approve a buyer for you. Many sellers will get excited when there is activity on their property and go with the highest offer, but that contract may not be the best contract in the long run for the seller.

Obtaining loans today is a little harder than it was in the early 2000s when property values were escalating and it was easy to obtain financing. Since the bubble burst it is harder.

You've got to love cash offers; it is easy for you or your agent to verify cash. All you need is to see a bank statement or have the buyer put the funds into escrow with the closing agent. Reputation plays a huge role in this process especially if you are in an area where people know each other. There is a network and investors will know each other in the network.

Is your buyer sincere, is he serious, and does he want to buy the property that you have for sale? This is what you need to be able to figure out. Especially if there are several offers, you need to be able to evaluate all of them. This is an act in itself.

They say you should get 1% of the purchase price as earnest money. As the seller, I want to aim for more. As the asking price gets lowered, be thinking of getting a higher percentage. If the buyer is serious he will have the additional funds for a deposit and will not mind putting it down. It is credited at closing, so it is ok either way. You want to minimize your potential losses as the seller, and if the contract falls apart you want to be protected against any losses.

If you are selling a rental property you may want to postpone a closing date to get the extra month's rent.

I like selling a property *as is*, however the buyer may negotiate a decrease in price for an *as is* sale.

How to Qualify a Buyer

You may get a lot of tire kickers and it could end up being a huge waste of time. Time is money; don't waste it. Truly if you have done a good job marketing your property and it is priced right, you could have a lot of people knocking at your door. This is good, but how do you qualify the right person to buy your property?

> ▶ What is your gut feeling of the prospective buyer at the first meeting or phone call? Before you set up an appointment to meet him, try to qualify him over the phone. You want to find out what property he is interested in, how eager he is to make a move, and whether he has the funds to do the deal. Can you determine if he is a serious buyer or a tire kicker? Tough to do; if he passes the test, then have him go by the property and do a drive-by to see if there is enough curb appeal to move forward. Then make an appointment to see the inside. There are exceptions to this rule. If he has the money

and wants to do a deal today, you should be able to tell and act accordingly.
- If the prospective buyer is interested don't let him leave without a negotiated contract ready to sign; you want to be prepared with all the back-up information that he may want, along with a contract ready for signatures. That way your prospective buyer either signs then or will have something to review, sign, and return to you. Very important to be prepared.
- Once the contract has been executed with signatures and consideration, you will want to bring the contract to your agreed-upon attorney or closing agency.
- After all the contingencies in the contract are done—inspections, financing, due diligence—move forward to a closing. Set the date for the closing, inform all parties that are involved in the purchase, go to the closing, and close. Be sure all is complete, signed, sealed, and recorded prior to taking possession.

How Long to Market Your Property

Holding on to a piece of property will cost you money and eat up any potential profit. While the property is off the market, you've got interest payments, marketing costs, management fees, lost profits, reduced price, additional taxes to be paid, and repair and maintenance, without moving forward in your grand plan. Put a time limit on the sale. Since 2012 the housing market has been so volatile, no one has been able to accurately predict when it will come back strong. The banks are much harder to deal with. The average person with a mediocre credit score is not able to get a loan. Therefore sellers have to target a different group of buyers as well as to be just a little more creative in their sales approach.

If properties that you are flipping are not selling in a reasonable time, you may have to either lower your price or consider renting the property.

Contracts

A unilateral contract is one in which only one party makes an express promise, or undertakes a performance without first securing a reciprocal agreement from the other party. In a unilateral—or one-sided—contract, one party, known as the offerer, makes a promise in exchange for an account by another party, known as the offeree. If the offeree acts on the offerer's promise, the offerer is legally obligated to fulfill the contract. An offerer is legally obligated to fulfill the contract, but an offeree cannot be forced to act or not act, because no return promise has been made to the offerer. This is one-sided, and you need to be careful if you are the offerer and not getting anything. This type of contract can be good if you are the offeree. There can be a reward if the requirements in the contract are met by the offeree.

> If properties that you are flipping are not selling in a reasonable time, you may have to either lower your price or consider renting the property.

A bilateral contract is a contract that binds two parties in some type of performance by each and involves some type of consideration for that performance—usually the exchange is money. This type of contract is distinguishable from a unilateral contract in that a unilateral contract involves a promise made by one party in exchange for the performance of some act by the other party: a person selling his home to a buyer, in exchange for money, called *consideration*. The party to a unilateral contract whose performance is sought is not obligated to act, but if he or she does, the party that made the promise is bound to comply with the terms of the agreement. In a bilateral contract both parties are bound by the exchange of promises that are outlined in the agreement.

Be careful of all the conditions that may be put into a contract. As the buyer you want conditions to get out of a contract without penalty or loss of deposit, but as the seller you want penalties, loss of deposit, and no conditions. When they put *as is* you are good to go, especially with cash.

Here are a couple of things to look for in a deal:

- Does financing need to be approved or is financing in place? You never know how long this process may take for the buyer.
- Cash talks; go for the cash deals.
- Is the sale contingent on another piece of property selling? You really may wait a long time for the one property to sell, so be very careful.
- The property must pass a commercial or home inspection. Home inspectors make money by finding things wrong with a property for sale; another potential delay.

Appraisals are usually required by the bank. You as the seller may want to get an appraisal. They do cost money—money that may be wasted. Banks will usually only lend a portion of the appraised value of the property; generally eighty percent. Does your buyer have the balance for your deal? Do you have verification?

Parts of a Contract

- Both parties of the contract must have legal capacity (be 18 years or older) and have the mental capacity to negotiate and comprehend the terms and conditions of the contract. Be careful if someone does not have the mental capacity to negotiate or sign a contract; it will become invalid and you could be liable. You need to exercise caution when entering into a contractual agreement.
- An offer is a written agreement communicated to the current owner or seller from a buyer for something specific, e.g., a piece of property for a specific price. There are terms and conditions that are met with an offer. It's wise to have an expiration date on an offer, and if there are performance issues in an offer, you want them spelled out in detail so there is no confusion.
- Acceptance. This is a timely written response to an offer that is made prior to the buyer giving legal notice to the seller with consideration.

If the acceptance has no changes to the offer then it is done: if the acceptance contains changes to the offer it is a counteroffer, which must be initialed by both parties and signed by both parties. If there are no further changes, the offer is accepted.

- Counteroffer. A rebuttal of the offer, because the seller wants some changes to its terms and conditions. The buyer and seller can go back and forth until both agree on the terms and conditions. I recommend both parties sign or initial and date the changes. With consideration, you have a fully binding contract.
- A written contract is a legally binding and enforceable instrument that transfers property from one person to another. A contract outlines the terms and conditions so there is no confusion over the property that is to be transferred, the amount to be paid, as well as any terms or conditions of the property and sale that must be adhered to. This is a legal instrument and can be enforced in a court of law.
- Terms and Conditions are usually found in a contract and spell out specifically the obligation of both the buyer and the seller. There is usually a list of items that need to be agreed upon as to be in compliance by both parties prior to conveyance of the property. They have to be signed and dated accordingly. When you are the seller, you don't want to talk about the questionable items that the buyer may use against you to negotiate a lower price.
- Identification of property. When selling a piece of real estate, it is best to use the physical address, the tax number, as well as (and most importantly), the legal description of the property. I always recommend that you cover all your bases so there is no discrepancy as to what you are selling.
- Oral agreement. Never make an oral agreement with someone. A handshake does not cut it anymore in the legal world. You want to get it in writing in the form of a contract that has in it all that you want to convey. The provisions, terms, and conditions need to be written.

- Earnest Money or Deposit. To make a transaction legal you must put down consideration: any amount of money that needs to be in the contract. I would suggest that the larger the deal the larger the amount. As a seller I want the earnest money to be nonrefundable because in a sense you are taking the property off the market; there should be a value to that. However, the buyer will want a lower, refundable deposit and contingencies in the contract, so he can get out during his due diligence period. Both parties to the contract generally want what's best for themselves. As a seller you must be careful. If I were selling a property and offering basically 100% financing, I would be sure that the buyer meet certain criteria: great credit, good work history, as well as a good reputation.

You could also do a wrap. This is where you would sell the house to the buyer contingent on the existing mortgage. The buyer pays you a monthly payment as per the amortization and agreement. You in turn pay the mortgage payment. You would usually put a time limit or term on the deal. I have done several deals like this, and it has worked out well. I was able to get the retail price I wanted. For several years now the buyers have been paying the mortgage payment which still is 90% interest. There is a little left over from the payment, which I have been putting toward the principal. The payoff down the road will be handsome.

If you are in a position to do some deferred deals, then do them. In this case the different payment will be in excess of $80,000 which was my profit on the property: that in turn will allow me to buy additional properties for the investment portfolio.

You do have to be careful that you have a good buyer, one that will pay you. If you finance a property in full you could later be in a position of having to foreclose on the property, and you don't want to do that if possible.

If you are selling a distressed property and finance it 100% to a buyer, the property probably needs a lot of work. Hypothetically the buyer puts in $20,000 in renovations into the property, making it very nice, salable, or rentable. In time, if he cannot make the payments, you are in a position to take the property

CHAPTER 20: MARKETING YOUR HOUSE, EITHER FOR FLIPPING OR RENTING

over! Not bad if you were able to get some payments on the property, then get the house back with all the improvements. I would consider that a way to double dip. As the seller you can now sell the property as an improved property.

Family

Our attitudes have huge effects on our lives—either positive or negative. When you meet a difficult challenge with a positive attitude, you are more likely to overcome it. If you go into that same challenge with a defeatist attitude, a negative one, you are much more likely to fail.

You don't want to hear a person always whining: that ladder is way too tall, that hole is too deep, this problem is too difficult. None of those things matter if you have a positive attitude and you want to succeed.

Misery deserves company. If you are unhappy for any reason then change your mindset. Ever met anyone who always seems miserable, who just can't seem ever to be happy? His attitude is negative; you just have to wonder how in the world will that person ever be able to succeed. Don't be miserable as well; it's like carrying around extra baggage on your quest to succeed. Sure you can always throw someone a lifeline to give him some hope for success, but at some point if that lifeline is pulling you down you must decide to let go.

You use your life experiences to find your path of success. Take a moment when you can to enjoy the fruits of your labor.

Enjoy yourself; you are a good person; it may not matter to the next person, but it truly matters to you.

You must trust yourself before you have the ability to trust someone else. You will find relationships that are built on trust: friends, family, a spouse, don't let anyone harm that trust.

When I was building the Macado's restaurants, there was trust between my brother Richard and me. We did everything together like we were kids. We made plans for our future on paper napkins while flying with our families on vacations. I trusted him. In the early days he trusted me too. What he wanted was the pot of gold that was under the rainbow—not part of it, but all of it. He wanted to fuel his ego. His answer was not to communicate with me, not to express his feelings as you would expect in a close relationship, whether in business, marriage, with family or friends.

Honesty has always been my policy. Maybe I have been too strong; many people just don't want to hear the truth. They want to be told what they want to hear, just to reinforce their behaviors. When I didn't get that honesty from my brother—when I didn't get any communication at all, sure, I was hurt; I was surprised as well as disappointed when he separated the companies. He basically fired me with a smile on his face. So many people in our business environment have had similar situations, and no one likes it. You think you have security, a comfort level. Especially with family.

If you are in a performance-type job, you are told straight up I am hiring you to coach my NFL team: you win the Super Bowl or you are fired. Ok I get that, so if I don't win the Super

Bowl, I will not be surprised if I get fired. I already know the fire's hot before I am able or willing to touch it. You won't put yourself at risk.

The two relationships are truly different. There is much more pressure when you have to win a Super Bowl. It's going to be tough to have a positive attitude with your people especially when you have lost a few games and your chances of a title become slimmer. But don't look at the downside; cherish the opportunity. We feel confident that you can do it, that you can succeed, and that no one will stop you. Don't forget that it is a huge task and every other coach out there is charged with the same instructions and the same pressure to succeed. There is only one winner every year. Is it going to be you?

You are who you are; embrace yourself; never sell yourself short. You are the person you are meant to be. So many of us discover this asset late in our lives. Being unique, different, special may be viewed as a negative to some, but to you it will be an asset, one that will set you apart from the rest. Don't disappoint yourself by thinking differently. Your day will come.

You are unique to the world, and you must embrace that about yourself. Do not allow the naysayers to make you feel unqualified or different. They should think of you as special, as a champion of men. Trust who you are. It's hard when you are young and you are trying to figure out your identity. As you get older this is something you can get your hands around. It will hit us all at different stages in our lives. It does help if you have a mentor to pave the way to full understanding.

You cannot be someone you are not and also be happy. I know when I was married, Margaret wanted me to be like her father. It is impossible for a spouse to replace either one of their parents. She needed to accept me for who I was, as I did her. Only at that point can you build a relationship.

Life is not easy for anyone. We all have trials and tribulations that we deal with every day. Many of those trials and tribulations form us. We will take many turns. Some learn from their experiences better than others. Others never learn. Maybe that person is you, still trying to figure out who's on first and who's on second.

As terrible as it may be, now that my mother has died I can move forward without restriction. I feel a huge burden off my shoulders. Although I now have a total financial mess to deal with—but being free has an immeasurable value. The humiliation of defeat, the stigma of a loser, and the perception of always being wrong—I can add many more to that list—these weights are lifted and I have a starting point from which to grow. And grow I will—that's the prize.

It won't take long to head into the direction of success and most importantly find that level of happiness that you deserve. We all have a way to figure it out. God has a plan and he gives us the strength to be successful with our plan. We work hard: some take on life's work with a great deal of pride and are responsible in fulfilling that mission; others do not. They do as little as they can to ride the coattails of their neighbors.

CHAPTER 21

Leasing

YOU MAY DECIDE THAT YOUR INVESTMENT PORTFOLIO WILL BE ONE OF RENTING PROPERTIES. If that is your direction you must understand your responsibility to the tenants, and theirs to you. It is not an easy task; not everyone can do it. You have to have the right personality and disposition to be successful. If you do not, then seriously consider hiring a property manager. Put the round peg in the round hole. This is important. Know your strengths and weaknesses so you can be successful.

Determining Market Rents

First of all, it is essential that your numbers are accurate. Never take risks. Everything must be done in a highly calculated manner. Gather the market rents for the houses on the block or in the vicinity if possible. If not, a comparable house very nearby.

I bought a duplex yesterday and searched craigslist for houses for rent nearby prior to purchase. I couldn't find any. I then went to rentometer.com; I don't know why I bother because it is not accurate. I then searched the local paper's online classifieds; nothing either. Finally I bought a Sunday paper, which is when most of the for-rent ads are listed. I got a few that were relatively close—a confirmation. Save your Sunday papers to review.

I then went to the house and knocked on other multifamilies around it. Fortunately there are many. I asked tenants how much they pay and how many bedrooms they have. I told them that I am thinking about buying the house down the road. In the process I found out quite a bit of information on the seller and stories of the various people who used to rent there. I also have confirmation now in two sources, the paper and the people. I always take what the surrounding people say with a grain of salt as they can be complete idiots but usually full of useful info. I now was positive that each of the two bedroom units will rent for $525. Do your research.

The amount of money that you can charge for rent is between you and the lessee. You can negotiate that amount as you would negotiate any contract. Property location is a key factor in determining the amount you should charge: what the market will bear. If all the properties around your property are renting for $500 per month and your particular property is larger, nicer, and has more amenities, you may be able to get $700 per month. What can the market bear? All those little extra things you did during the renovation will make a difference, the deck, the kitchen, the baths, the type of heat. All these and more will play an important part not only for potential resale but also leasing. Tenants will shop around for the nicest place on the street for the cheapest price. When they've found the perfect place, they should pay for it.

Since I have specialized in low-end properties in less-than-desirable areas of town, I use comparisons as well. I consider what the going rate is for properties in the area—I am not going to get $1000 for a property in an area where the highest rent today is $600. I try to make my properties some of the best in the area, so I can get the maximum rent in the block. By buying multiple properties in an area, I can control both the rents and the type of people that move into the area. I can change a street, and so can you; you create your own market. This is important if you are trying to make your property desirable for either lease or purchase. These thoughts become part of you action plan—your blueprint.

Owning real estate is a business; managing property is a profession—a profession of protecting your property. Nowhere in this book have I mentioned charity, although some people manage properties like that. If your tenant does not pay the rent, then where will you get the money to pay your mortgage and other bills? It is vital. It is much harder to manage property in depressed areas and from people on fixed incomes.

> Owning real estate is a business; managing property is a profession.

Sometimes a tenant who happens to do his own repairs pays the rent on time will give you an illusion that this work is easy. They are all not like that. You will get your share of people who don't care and won't pay the rent. A tenant asked me one time if he might paint. Reluctantly, I gave him permission. Well, he painted the room black and then moved out in a month. It was horrible trying to repaint black. Just do the work yourself.

Don't get upset. I usually give people a little wiggle room and allow them to hang themselves. I hate to do it, but at least that way you can sleep at night. Just don't give these people the entire rope because they will hang you for sure. When I strike, I usually strike hard. That's what the court system is for.

Leases

Leases are a legal contract that the property owner through his property manager or agent will enter into with a tenant or lessee. In a lease, the lessor is the landlord and the lessee is the tenant. With some type of consideration, it is a legal contract. Include any and all pertinent information in your lease, which will help you protect your property, your investment.

Any changes, modifications, terms—all agreements with the tenant should be in writing. If it is not in writing, it is not binding in court. You hate to think of divorce before you get married, but you must plan your exit strategy. Even the best tenant in the world may turn against you and create a stir of problems.

Go into each lease prepared and diligent. Most judges today are pro-tenant and anti-landlord. You may be right but still lose! The industry needs good landlords. In many cases it's not the landlord who is the problem; it is the non-paying tenant who spins a situation so that he is the victim. Judges have often been sympathetic to these tenant stories; sometimes it is just pathetic. It is a common misconception that landlords make a lot of money and exploit tenants, especially the poor ones. Prove that misconception wrong.

As a contract between two parties, the lease will spell out exactly what your responsibilities are as well as your rights. It will also talk about tenant rights and responsibilities. It is pretty clear cut. As a landlord, include everything you can to protect yourself. However, housing laws and regulations vary greatly by state: for instance, how much you can collect on late fees, who pays attorney fees, and how much can you charge for a deposit. Start with a standing lease and modify the lease to your particular state.

Verbal modifications to a lease are inadmissible in court. Again, put any changes or promises in writing, date the document, sign it with the lessee, and reference the original lease to which this change is an addendum.

The Lease Pays Off

I just had a tenant move into an upscale townhouse I have. He signed the lease and within the first 60 days he wrote a bad rent check for $600. He was notified that the check bounced and that there were fees associated with the bad check. During that initial period of time while he was moving in he wanted to do some things to the property. As in replace the kitchen cabinets and replace the carpet, which was new, with hardwood floors. I told him ok but at his own expense.

For the last seven months he has avoided the payment on the bad check. He occasionally has been behind on his rent and have worked with him on catching up. Now he is asking for credit for the work that

When you have a multiunit building you may decide to enforce some rules and regulations, including use of common areas, parking, yard, grilling. You must be sure that you are very clear about your expectations. Include it as a Rules and Regulations sheet in the lease or as an amendment and sign and date it.

Also there are other very important areas that you may want to consider: mold disclosure, the consumer protection act, disputed claims in writing, tenant assertion (rent money in escrow), lead disclosure, fees for damage. It does not and will not hurt you to over-inform your tenants.

Just remember when a potential tenant wants to rent a place, he usually is like a child at Christmas, all giddy; he wants the place bad. So many times he is so wrapped up in the moment he doesn't think about signing the additional amendments that you carefully go over with him. You as the lessor and property manager must be dutiful and go over all the areas, so there is no mistake that you disclosed everything to him and that he signed all the papers. Be honest; take the time to go over all the details. The new tenant is probably not listening and may just sign his car over to you.

---

was done on the property, i.e., hardwood floors, the cabinets, and a few minor repairs. Well in the lease it clearly states the tenant has to pay for the repairs. Easy. Nowhere in the lease does it allow for compensation or credit for the items he did do. There was no amendment to the lease that gave him any credit for this work. The bottom line is, clearly, that he gets no credit and he is obligated to pay the bad check and fees. You as the property owner don't have the luxury of taking the money off the mortgage payment or the property taxes. You still have to pay them. Therefore he still owes the $600 plus fees. It's not personal; it's simply business.

Most leases stipulate 30 days' written notice for termination. As the lessor you must demand that communication be done in writing so it is documented. Make no mistakes; it is important. And it is the law.

When a lease expires it will usually continue month to month, until notice is given by either party. The rent will not automatically go up unless it is specified in the lease. I usually keep the rent the same if I have a good tenant who pays the rent on time every month; there is nothing like the security of a good, paying tenant.

Disclosure requires the lessor to tell everything he knows about the property. There is nothing to hide: best to put it all in writing so everyone knows what is what. This will avoid erroneous expectations on anyone's part.

Leases are usually boiler-plate documents with some items that have been added. If you are the lessee, be sure you have read all the fine print so you are familiar with the terms and conditions of the lease. A good owner, property manager, or lessor will have some hidden items in this lease that pertain to his property directly and will also protect his interests. A strict pet policy is an example of such. Or care of carpet.

There is usually some argument over repairs and maintenance. Who really is responsible for the repair? The tenants never like to pay for a clogged toilet even if they clog it. You will fix it as the lessor and good luck getting your bill paid, unless you have a deposit and take the payment out of the deposit, which is exactly what you should to do.

As a lessor, you want your tenant to obtain renters' insurance. This is important in case something happens to the property for which they are responsible. That way their insurance will cover the cost to repair or replace. You can usually get a pretty good rate from your insurance agent as well. Some lessors will put this in their lease and actually chase the lessee each month to be sure it is paid. Always a good way to protect yourself.

How you structure your lease is important. Take a look at the one in the Appendix and use it as a starting point. You want to be sure you have covered all your bases just in case. Plan for the worst and expect the best.

Lease-to-Own

A lease-to-own is where a tenant enters into a lease to rent a piece of property and also enters into a separate contract to purchase that same property. The tenant and the owner negotiate a price. There is a limited amount of time for the tenant to purchase the property.

The tenant will usually pay a little extra each month on the lease that will be put towards the deposit on the purchase of the house. A smart seller will try to get a deposit in addition to the increased payments. A slick seller may market these types of deals during tax season when people are expecting their tax return. The clientele to target are average income families who may or may not have good credit. This could be an opportunity for a buyer to own a home again. They should know, although they probably don't, that they are paying a premium.

A seller may want to get as much up front as he can, knowing and maybe hoping the buyer will default. Some sellers will sell the same home over and over again.

There are some issues with lease-to-own deals that you should be aware of; here are a few of them:

- ▶ There may be a due-on-sale clause with the lender, who may force you to pay the balance in full. You will want to remain current with your payments. Don't give the lender an excuse to look at or review the note. Answer all correspondence from the lender.
- ▶ Your property may be reassessed for your property taxes. So be careful. It may not be worth arguing if you as the seller have built in a project structure.
- ▶ If the IRS views the lease purchase as a sale you could be open to any and all taxes. You may want to consult your tax accountant if you have many of these types of transactions.
- ▶ You may not be able to evict the tenant. So therefore I recommend some strong language that will protect your investment as well as your ability to evict the tenant for nonpayment. Get the appropriate language from your attorney and include it.

Several Rules for Leasing Property

1. Background check: You can do both a civil and criminal check. There are websites that you can go to that are free; see your state for specific details. You really want to check for sexual crimes, predator crimes, gun and assault crimes.

2. Credit rating: A lot of landlords will do credit checks on their prospective tenants.

3. Application Fee: Many landlords will charge a small application fee for running their credit application and lease processing

4. Visual: Many times you can look at a person and size him up: how neat he is, how he speaks, and how polite he is.

5. References: Ask for references and call one or two of them and see how these people are. Ask a few key questions and you can get a feel. See Appendices.

6. Site visitation: Some landlords will go by the place where they are living now to see how the yard looks. They may even ask to see inside.

7. Former landlords: Many tenants may not want you to call their old landlord but sometimes if you can talk to the previous landlord to see if the new people pay their rent on time and how they were as a tenant.

8. Get a security deposit. You may not collect more than 2 months' rent as a security deposit. Get at least one month's worth. In lower income areas, you may have to work with prospective tenants by

taking some payments on this. Usually a good idea to take the full security deposit and work with them on rent payments.

9. Don't pay for improvements made by your tenants. Do not let the tenant make improvements unless you are aware of what he plans to do. Some want to paint—dark colors are unacceptable.

10. The owner should not pay for any utilities. Let the tenant pay for power, water, and gas. Watch the utilities—some utility companies are looking to collect unpaid utilities from the owner of the property.

11. No lease is perfect. Try to put together a solid lease that includes attorney's fees. Each local court will demand different things in your lease. Each judge will have different thoughts. You may have to change your lease to adapt to the local judge's discretion.

State Laws and Judges

Most leases are boiler-plate forms, but it is vital that you know what the laws are in your state so you can make sure your lease is legal. As mentioned, judges also have particular things they want to see. The consumer, your tenant, may be protected by the Consumer Protection Act or the Landlord Tenant Act, and you must not violate any of those provisions. It is best to know what these provisions are and put them into your lease so both you and your tenant are protected. Aim for a good, solid lease—one that conforms to the law. Over time, you will both win and lose; when you lose, modify your lease so you don't make the same mistake again.

Leases can be double-edged swords. You must follow the letter of the lease as you expect your tenant to. What may get you mad is when the courts turn a cheek to the lease in favor of the tenant, no matter what the lease may say.

CREDIT

The nicer the neighborhood, the richer the tenant, and the better the credit. You will find that folks in poorer neighborhoods may not have the credit you would prefer. Get used to it. Poorer people tend to have not-so-good credit. You may have a tough time deciding what you want to do in these situations. Just remember to be fair. You may get one or two bad ones but for the most part people do need a place to live and will pay you their rent.

Evicting tenants is a process that is guided by the law through the courts, which they monitor very closely. It is important to follow the right procedure of the law in all evictions—the process will vary greatly by judge. Just remember to move quick.

Not fair, that's right, but welcome to the world of property management.

You cannot exceed the law for legal fees or attorney fees. You cannot get a criminal warrant for a bad check. These are clearly defined. You are best off protecting yourself in a lease. Don't over-extend the parameters of the lease so that you come across to the court like you are extorting monies from your tenants—like them or not, it does not make a difference. I personally have pushed the boundaries sometimes. There were many times I won and won big. But there were other times that I did not do so well and sooner or later paid the price.

In the town where I manage property, there are three general district judges, and each has his own opinions and interpretations of the law and how it applies to a lease. I have been concerned about my lease and have made modifications over the years to accommodate the different judges. Then they change their position; it may drive you crazy and right out of the leasing business.

One time, I did a repair statement on damage to a property, recording work that my crew and I did. There was an incredible amount of damage. Even though the statement was not contested (the tenant was a no-show), the judge wanted verification of hours and how much each person was paid. He asked why I made what I made and said I was not worth that wage. Whoa. I also had all my receipts for paint, materials, and the like. I thought I had them in order. The judge asked how much paint I used per room and what I did with the leftover paint and how much it was worth. Crazy. I got most of the labor and most of the materials. I just don't recommend putting yourself out there like I did a couple of times. Keep meticulous records.

Here are some questions the judge may ask you:

1. How old is the carpet, what is the depreciation?

2. Let me see receipt for the stove and refrigerator in the house.

3. How long ago did you paint?

4. What did the property look like prior to your tenants moving in?

5. Do you have a tenant move-in checklist?

6. Whose responsibility is the heating system?

7. Where did you buy the kitchen cabinets? Do you have the receipt?

8. Do you have W-2s for your employees?

9. Who prepared the quote for repair?

10. Do you have copies of canceled checks for payment?

11. Whose responsibilities are repairs and maintenance?

These are just a few of the questions that could be asked. Cross your t's and dot your i's. Don't put yourself in a position to fail. I want you to succeed.

Deposits

The best thing for you to do is to get a security deposit. The law will allow you only two months rent for security deposit. One thing that I know is that getting a high security deposit is very difficult. How does someone pay a month's rent say $800 plus $1600 in security deposit, then turn around and pay for all the hook-up fees for utilities and the like. It gets expensive.

It is much harder to get deposits in the poorer neighborhoods, which is ironic since these are the neighborhoods where they are most needed; I have rented to poor people for a long time. They struggle to get their rent together, let alone a deposit. So many times I don't get one and truly I am taking a chance and most of the time I lose big, in so much as they do not give a tinder about the condition of the property; when they leave, it is terrible, and I shake my head again and again and wonder why I did not get a deposit. Going after them for damages later is always harder to do.

When I don't get a deposit I try to get a premium rent. If a place rents for $600 market value, I usually try to get $650 or $700 which will cover some of the expected future losses.

What some people will do—and it is a great way to get your deposit—is to collect $600 and apply it to the deposit, and then let them make payments on the rent that is due. You sort of keep them at bay and are able to hold eviction possibilities over their heads. This works very well. It also gives you a deposit. So, remember that you do have options. Leases are put in place to protect both the lessor and the lessee. Residential leases are most certainly not very complicated, unlike commercial leases. Commercial leases usually have many, many more sections that have to be negotiated between the parties: insurance, taxes, property maintenance—all should be included and reviewed with a good commercial lease. One thing is for sure: they will almost always be one sided for the lessor. As a lessee, you do want your attorney to review the lease with you. This is very important.

As an owner, you need to be in touch with your investments; here are a few areas to be on top of:

CHAPTER 21: LEASING

- Monthly and yearly cash flow. Manage these numbers in your pro-forma to see how accurate your projections are. The closer the better. If you prepare a budget, be spot on.
- Prepare a balance sheet so you can control your expenses; again, match these numbers against your projects to see how accurate you have been.
- File tax returns.
- Work with local, state, and federal government to be sure that you are in compliance with the laws. This can range from building permits and housing inspections, to labor laws. It is a constant concern.
- Most states have a Consumer Protection Act and Landlord-Tenant Act to protect the rights of tenants. They are very clear as to what you may and may not do. The tenant is very well protected.
- When you negotiate a lease with a tenant, you have a responsibility to him and he to you. He is obligated to pay the rent. Repairs and maintenance issues should be described in the lease so all parties know who is responsible for what. A clogged toilet is usually on the tenant; a leaky roof is on the landlord.

Screening Your Tenants

You want to take every precaution with the references, credit checks, and verifications of jobs, to be sure your tenant is who he says he is. But there is no guarantee any of it means anything. You'll be amazed to see good prospective tenants turn out to be horrible and bad ones turn out to be great ones. It is a crapshoot.

Go as deep as necessary to protect your property; you do not have to rent to everyone. You must adhere to the fair housing laws, which is easy: just don't discriminate. Most important, do not be biased in your decision whom to rent to; be fair and equitable. Here are a few things to request when considering a prospective tenant:

- Take an application—one that gives you information about the prospect, including salary, a work history, credit information, criminal or civil action, as well as some rental history as well. Too much information is better than not enough; cover all your bases. See the Appendix.
- Ask for references on the application. You can call and get a feel for the person. References are also good if you have to collect money from a tenant who skips town. A reference can provide information on that person.
- Verify an income, so you can be sure he will pay. I am always concerned as to how long the applicant has had that job. The longer the better. If someone has had a job for a long time, he is less likely to quit it over a rental dispute. That way also if you have to garnish his wages for possible collection of rents or damages due you will be able to do so. You must think long term when you are interviewing a potential renter. You are counting on that income, the rent, for cash flow. In many cases it is needed to pay the mortgage. You have set up a pro-forma and considered the rent as income. You did not rent the property for the people to live in the house for free.
- You can always check the civil docket history and see what civil problems the person may have been involved in. Be very concerned about payments relating to landlords who have evicted the potential tenants. That information is crucial. Also if you are concerned about their criminal background as well. This information is public record. Most landlords will check both civil and criminal backgrounds. I don't do as good a job with that since some of the people in the neighborhoods I buy are criminals. If they are going to pay the rent, what's it to me if they're ex-cons? It's difficult to collect rent when a tenant doesn't want to pay.

Some tenants will get SSI or housing assistance. Just be careful with folks who get subsidized; they may be less likely to pay you and their money is not garnishable.

In the past I have had tenants do some work to help them with their rent; you can use unemployed people for your labor force—just be careful. You may be ok renting to two people in the household, if at least one has the full-time job. Repairs and maintenance in a low-cost neighborhood are going to cost you more money. Since the properties are old, you cannot increase the rent.

I have found that the tenants can be less respectful than those in better neighborhoods. If you are renting, your tenants, when they cannot pay the rent, will try to come up with every excuse under the sun. They may even turn the overflow valve on from the hot water heater purposefully to flood the basement and then call the city to complain. Many of your judges today are pro-tenant and will just about give all tenants credit for any repair and maintenance complaint. It is not fair and not reasonable. Just be prepared and aware.

My Arrow is Sharp

I've got a good arrow, a great target, and I have been sharpening that arrow head for years. The time has come. Even if the moment is not exactly right, the prize is huge, and that's what we want. I want to set the record straight to validate a career and profession.

Many of us live our lives, wanting to validate the work that we have done. How many ideas have you had that someone else stole or used, claiming they were his? More than you can count probably. How long till you get back and set the record straight. Are you afraid? Are you trapped by a mother or a wife or some social environment that is holding you hostage to a success that is rightfully yours?

There is a time and a place for every opportunity to take a shot. You will know when. Prepare for the opportunity. It will come.

CHAPTER 22

Land Trusts

FIRST OF ALL, I AM NOT A LAWYER AND NOT GIVING YOU LEGAL ADVICE. Just telling you a little information I have learned about land trusts. Consult your attorney before using one.

There are a number of reasons to use a land trust in your real-estate holdings. One primary purpose of a land trust is to help your loved ones avoid the headaches and costs of probate court and excessive taxation when you die.

Land trusts are also used to keep the owner of the property anonymous on public records. You may not be interested in tenants, lawyers, or others knowing your everyday business. Knowledge of how much property you own can help a lawyer determine if it's worthwhile to take a long shot and sue you with a weak case.

Land trusts don't give you liability protection like an LLC does, but they do give you a little protection from title claims. If you for some reason end up getting a judgment against you, it won't automatically attach to the property, since the title is not in your name. The same goes if your trust gets a lien against it. The lien will not be against you personally but rather against the trust.

Land trusts are also used for ease of changing owners and working with the requirements of most banks. Land trusts are assignable, so once the property is in a land trust, it is easy to change the beneficiary (owner) of the trust to the

Rejection

You can figure you will get rejected many times. Sometimes you may fail. You may feel helpless to the point of giving up. You may be hurt. You may get depressed because of your own self-pity. Remember if success were that easy, then everyone could do it and there would be no challenge, nothing to work for. When you get to the top, when you are successful, you have climbed the mountain; it is wonderful thing.

If you have failed to acknowledge those failures, to learn from your errors, and to move on to bigger and better things, you will get stuck in a cycle of failure, making the same mistakes. Rejection and failure are not easy for anyone to take. They may bring on depression. Try to remain strong. You are not the only one.

Don't get defensive; don't have a chip on your shoulder; remain positive in all that you do. Try not to second guess situations. If you have done your due diligence, evaluated both the positives and negatives, then you will succeed, because of the knowledge that you have gained.

new owner. The trust agreement is a private agreement that is kept by you in your file cabinet so no one really knows who the beneficiary of the trust is besides you. The only other part of a land trust besides the trust agreement is the deed that has to be changed and recorded at the courthouse into the name of the trust.

Trusts are also used to buy property subject to the existing mortgage. This can help avoid the due-on-sale clause that all mortgage loans have these days. But presently, for the most part, banks are not calling the loans due at this time, because interest rates are far too low to make it beneficial to do so. They are happy to get the money they are owed.

Another benefit of a land trust is if you are having your property managed by a property management company, a trust is beneficial in preventing code enforcement from taking you personally to court rather than the property management company because the beneficiary of the trust is anonymous.

The trustee of a land trust is usually an entity (LLC) or person other than the beneficiary (owner). A trustee holds the legal title to all trust property. The trustee signs, notarizes, and records documents in his own name, not in the name of the investor. In a land trust, the named beneficiaries retain the use of the property and the income it generates. The trustee can act only when he receives written instructions from the beneficiaries, who maintain control at all times. If the trustee lives in a different state or country, it will be difficult and expensive for creditors, lawyers, code enforcement, etc. to determine who the beneficiary is.

There are positives and negatives to putting your property into a living trust. Some of the advantages are that you can avoid probate court, you can save on estate taxes, and you can save on income taxes—as well as possibly shielding your home from any creditor attack. You always want to consult the experts on this move, possibly your lawyer and accountant.

The disadvantages can be that you will have the cost of hiring an attorney to help you; it can be complicated from state to state. The end result will net a little advantage.

A living trust is created when the homeowner is still alive. It is generally set up as a revocable trust, permitting the grantors, also often the trustees and beneficiaries, to change the terms of the trust or dissolve it entirely. The trust takes title to the home and transfers control of the property to the trustee. When the grantor dies, the trust becomes an irrevocable trust, prohibiting future changes to the terms. Most living trusts are structured to avoid probate and its costs. While some states have streamlined their probate processes, many still require cost, time, and attendance at multiple hearings. This is a huge burden for the family. Many homeowners wishing to avoid probate and transfer title to their home to their heirs quickly find avoiding probate through a trust to be a strong advantage.

Should you ever become ill, disabled, or unable to manage your property or finances, another trustee can be selected to manage your trust to protect your home and your finances.

While placing your home in a trust can generate no extra favorable tax treatment, you may save some estate taxes if your trust is designed properly; consult an expert.

Never Say Never

There is always hope if you believe. It's hard sometimes to believe when you are constantly bombarded by negatives and problems—sickness, death, finances, a boyfriend or a girlfriend; it may never end.

You might feel like you are living with a cloud over you, but that may not be the case. They say that the good Lord only gives people what they can handle, that there is a reason for everything, that your day will come.

I ask myself, "When?"; you may ask the same question. It may have happened, and you did not realize it. The truth of the matter is that your time has come, and you have been blessed. You should recognize this and continue to grow. We sometimes want to give up, but we should not. There is light at the end of the tunnel, and that light is not too far away.

You may have to make some tough decisions, and you must work through all the positives and negatives to try to achieve the right answer for yourself. It matters how that answer may affect others in your life; however, most important are how it affects you today and how it will affect you tomorrow. If that decision does not work then try, try again. Never say never.

CHAPTER 23

Insurance

BE SURE YOU PROTECT YOUR ASSETS BY HAVING INSURANCE. It is important. A basic policy with fire and liability may be sufficient, but a comprehensive package on each property is ideal. Look into an umbrella package. If you get into property management, it's a good idea to require your tenants to have renters' insurance with you listed by name as an insured. This covers you in case they do damage to the property. You really must have some type of coverage, and in order to apply for it, you will need to know the basics of your property to include: construction, heat source, year of roof, electric and plumbing update.

Be honest when you apply: you could get jammed up if you don't tell them the truth; aim for full disclosure. You may lose in two different ways: Actual cash value, which is what it would cost to put the building back in same order. You may get more money for a repair than you would the cost of the property itself. Remember the actual cash value will deduct any depreciation from its value. Replacement cost is replacing the damaged property without the depreciation cost.

As a homeowner or investor you want to evaluate each option. Your personal home will be insured differently than an investment property. And then again you may evaluate how much you have paid for a property as to how much

Minimum Coverage

▷ flood
▷ earthquake
▷ mold
▷ acts of war
▷ lightning
▷ fire
▷ wind
▷ hail
▷ theft
▷ tenant damage
▷ personal property
▷ foundation or structure
▷ roof

you will insure it for. If you have a mortgage on the property, the bank will require certain limits of coverage.

Renters' insurance is important to require your tenants to have. It's tough to make them place it on themselves: they usually do not see a value to it. However what they usually don't realize is that it costs only pennies to get. It is money well spent if you are a renter. Good luck enforcing renters' insurance.

The basic goal of any type of insurance is to make you financially secure following any potential loss. Basically you agree to pay a small fee for protection against loss to your property whether it is the brick and mortar or if it is personal injury to a person or persons. Many homeowners will increase their coverage to include an umbrella policy. You want to protect yourself against the large catastrophic loss; the little ones you may be able to handle.

We all need insurance; we all need to protect ourselves, so that we are never in a position where one loss can cost everything.

Remember to be careful and thorough when employing your agent, who may be representing multiple companies; you want him to get the best rate for the best coverage. Review your policy annually. What they sell you today may go up in price; watch this very closely.

CHAPTER 24

Recordkeeping

IF YOU ARE JUST STARTING OUT, you will not have an organization and most likely be like the one-armed paper-hanger: you will have to do it all. One of the most important aspects of the business is being sure you are able to count the nuts and the bolts. You will need accurate records not only for reporting for taxes but also for borrowing money, as well as developing your profit and loss statement. Banks are going to want to see up-to-date financials and tax returns in order to lend you money.

Most people would rather mow a yard or paint a building than do paperwork. Everyone will have their own method of paperwork. I never did it on a day-to-day basis. It is either quarterly or yearly. And unfortunately I did it the old-fashioned way of handwritten ledgers, which was not necessary. Today there are so many programs that make recordkeeping a piece of cake. Whatever your method is, what you don't want is to get too far behind that you cannot remember what goes where. Each property should have its own analysis, so you can see what the cash flow will be like on each property. You may be fooled when you see what it is in black and white. What matters is that you have data, so you can make responsible decisions.

Always keep your files organized, whether for tenants, or specific projects, or city code information. Remember to put paper somewhere rather than letting it sit there: file it, mail it, or throw it away, but always deal with paper. Don't let it stack up.

Many people are using e-files to manage their life and their work. Do what works for you. You should keep all your records for a minimum of 3-5 years.

I usually do a lot of cross-reference filing. As an example, a repair to a property would go into a paid bill file but also it would either go into a tenant file, especially if it is a collectible repair, or a file for a particular property. If you go to court with a tenant, you will need the actual invoice for the repair. As you document your income and expenses, you will be able to develop a history. Whether you put it on a paper spreadsheet or a computer, you will be able to project a cash flow. You need to know if you are making money or losing money.

From the cash-flow analysis you will be able to formulate a budget that should include short- and long-term plans, either capital improvements or just repairs. As previously mentioned when you stair-step repairs to improve a property, you can do some of the repairs this year and some repairs next year. That way you are able to manage your cash flow properly, as well as continually making improvements to your priority portfolio. When you make improvements to a property generally you can increase the rent. It's nice, especially if you are in it for the long haul.

There are advantages and disadvantages to doing your bookkeeping manually or with an up-to-date software. In the beginning you may do it by hand, with a sharp pencil and a ledger sheet. I have been doing it that way for years; it is how I was trained. It's ok when you are small. Many younger people who have grown up with computers may think that system is archaic and jump right into some current software. Certainly, if set up right, from the beginning you can get all kinds of great information that will help you analyze your property. Most software can give you spreadsheets on things you didn't even know about. They have a lot of bells and whistles which is nice, especially for the banks, your partners, and any audits. Good complete and accurate information.

PART IV

Evaluation

IT'S A GOOD IDEA TO STEP OUT OF THE BOX REGULARLY TO SEE WHAT YOU ARE DOING AND HOW VIBRANT IS YOUR PORTFOLIO. Be realistic: if it's good, praise yourself; reward winners, encourage good work and routine results. If it is bad or broken and can't be fixed, it is time to discard it and move on. Don't get bogged down with losers. So many times I personally have chased the tail of a cat I could not catch. It is no fun and usually very costly. Sometimes it's best to cut your losses and move on to something more profitable and rewarding.

There is always going to be a plumbing leak, an unhappy tenant, or an annoyed building inspector. It is what it is. At the end of the day, take your mate out to dinner and catch a movie.

For each property, check your expenses. If you are renting it, do a projection for the year to see if your cash flow will be what you want it to be. If you flipped the property and have closed, evaluate the results with real numbers. Are you happy with the results?

We tend not to put a value on our time. So, you must think about whether or not those 1000 hours spent were worth a $10,000 profit. Does $10 an hour fit your budget?

Profit and Loss

When evaluating your work, you will want to look at the money. At the end of the flip, the sale, or even the monthly rental income, see if you made any money. Let's face it, you are not doing this for free; you want to make a profit. You need to be able to evaluate your success by the money, the profit, that you make. I have enclosed a Profit and Loss Statement of some properties that I owned a few years ago; you can see how I did. Evaluate the different areas that may be of some concern to you as well, like net profit, repairs and maintenance, management fees, utilities, collectability of rent, servicing any loans.

So how well do you think you are doing today, yesterday, and what are your plans for the future? Well, the proof, as they say, is in the money, the statistics, the numbers. That's your report card. If you see on your financial statements that you are not making any money, you must dissect those statements and see what is wrong and then put a plan together to fix it. It may be in the repairs and the maintenance; it may be in uncollected rent or in professional fees, but whatever it is, find the solution to reduce the costs and turn your negative cash flow into a positive cash flow. It is important to look at each and every area of concern. Even in the areas of no concern, you may be able to find room for improvement.

So many people think that this is easy; let me remind you once again: it is not. You may think you are playing a game of Monopoly, but remember the stakes are high and the money is real. If you are managing other people's property, the stakes are higher in so much as the owner will want results; he will want you to make him money and manage his property successfully. If you are flipping, it's a little different story: if you make money or lose money you will know right away. Be sure to keep accurate records of your expenses.

Setting and Managing Controls

This is important for every organization and business that you set up or are involved in. Sure if you are a one-man band—doing all the work yourself—then maybe this will not be as important. But as soon as you grow and hire someone to help you, whether it is a property manager, a maintenance person, or even an administrative assistant, there are several cardinal rules:

- Do not break the law.
- Do everything right. By this I mean, Do not take any short cuts.
- Hold your people responsible.
- Don't allow one person to do everything.
- Divide and conquer: divide the workload and hold people accountable.
- Two people must manage the money. One can deposit it and the other can manage it.
- You are the bottom line to all activity.

So when I suggest controls, I am talking about having a system of checks and balances on your operations. You may have someone who picks up the rent, then someone else has to manage it and make sure that the person who is picking up the rent is either putting it in the bank or giving it to the person who makes the deposits. Even though we are in the property rental business, we are in the business of making deposits. The more deposits, the more money we know we are paying. Paying a lot of taxes is ok, in that you know at that point you are making money. You want the right hand to know what the left hand is doing. Promote open communication; have a paper trail. It's these checks and balances that will keep your organization organized and professional. Many managers will put incentives in place to reward great work.

The bottom line is you. All information should be organized and passed down to you in a way that you get either a snapshot of what is going on or all the details, the *who's, what's,* and *when's* of what is happening in your company, from rentals to deposits to sales. You want controls. Don't be naïve: if you feel it needs to be in place then do it, and organize it more and more each day.

Remember that you cannot do it alone. Be smart about your business. Don't provide a venue for anyone to take liberties. People are generally honest; keep them honest.

The Exit Strategy

As you determine your entry level, think about your exit plan. You will want to structure your portfolio so that you have a plan to get out—and I don't mean that in a negative way. You want it to be a positive exit.

Shoulda's

We sometimes allow ourselves to fall in a trap of "shoulda coulda": what we could have done and should have done to make things a little better. It's easy to get stuck in a pattern of regret, to become frozen by mistakes we have made in the past. Don't live your life in the past, worried about how things might have turned out better if you had made a better decision in the past. Learn from experience and better equip yourself to make the decisions of the future—but don't get sucked into regret. You will be smarter and wiser in what you do next.

Don't dwell on what you might have done in your past. You made some decisions; at the time they seemed like good decisions, even though they may have turned out for the worst. Don't live your life in regret or disappointment. You have to look at the past as a learning experience that can make you a better person today. But then put it aside, so you can continue to grow.

If you don't let these shoulda couldas go, they will pile up on you, and you will develop a negative attitude, which will make future decisions difficult. Trust your instincts, and move forward in your efforts to reach your goals in life.

I bought real estate when my children were young. I did not have a lot of money, but I was able to buy some property which I turned into rental property. I found it easier to work on the properties when they were babies and did not need me to coach their soccer teams. When they got older, I bought fewer properties and did coach the soccer teams. The idea was that by the time they went to college the properties would be paid for, and I could supplement their college education with the income from the properties; it worked well. After college it gave me the opportunity to give them money as they needed. When the time comes, I can give them each a property, which they can use as collateral to buy their first homes.

A supplemental income stream can support all your needs. Remember the longer you hold on to a piece of property, the easier the management, the fewer the repairs, the better the income as the rents go up (hopefully the mortgage payment stays about the same). As time goes on, the equity and wealth of your own portfolio will grow; there are options here for you to expand, and you should seriously consider seeking legal advice to understand your options.

Despite these benefits of long-term ownership, it is important that you have an exit strategy. In order to have an exit strategy, you must have an entry strategy. What you buy, when you buy it, how much you invest, both in purchasing and renovating, will all be major factors in forming your exit strategy. You want to think of and use multiple strategies when going into a buy: a Plan A and a Plan B. Develop clearly stated goals; these goals will build your own individual blueprint for success. The first one or two will be a little more difficult until your road map, your blueprint, is totally developed. Remember that there is not an actual formula that works for everyone. There is direction and guidance in education and experience; these will be your best teachers as you develop your own plan. But this will take a little time. Be patient, work hard, be diligent and forthright, use caution, but continue to move forward in developing your plan which will give you the opportunity to build substantial wealth.

Here are some areas that you want to consider and evaluate when forming your exit strategy. I have mentioned most of these before, but they come into play here too:

1. What are your short- and long-term goals? Are you looking for income today? Income that you can live on? This may be your full-time job, and you need the income. Or do you want to supplement your income and are looking for short-term gains? Thinking long term will affect your strategy in that you are looking for steady and even deferred income. Your long-term goals may give you greater financial gains, but you have to wait and wait and continue to be patient.

2. Experience level. How many times have you asked someone if he wants to work? Of course he answers *Yes*, and you ask him what can he do. Always I hear the same thing: I can paint and I can do landscaping. Neither is easy and both require experience and expertise in order to do it right. Think of what you know and what you need to learn over the next few months and years in order to be successful. It will take time, and you will make many mistakes, which is fine as long as you learn from them. It's wise to try new things, learn new things; and when you make a mistake, you adjust, and take the corrective action so you end up with the result you are looking for. If you are new at this, then recognize that fact and don't pretend you are an expert at it. Remember that a little knowledge can be worse than no knowledge at all. Continue to learn and listen. Take in others' knowledge to better yourself.

3. Timing is everything when you buy and when you sell. How long will you hold on to a property? This is an essential consideration to maintain good cash flow and great credit.

4. Purchase price. What you pay for your new property is important as it will reflect what you see in the property for your exit plan. Remember that you may have renovation costs, carrying costs, and other costs that will also have an effect on your exit price on this property.

5   Terms of the Deal. Wow this is big; this is where you will learn to negotiate your deal. You may not have a lot of latitude with the bank, but you will have some latitude if you are doing seller financing. The interest rate you pay—the cost of money—will play a major role in your costs. Many times in a new construction the bank will do a construction loan, and the builder will draw on the loan during construction. This loan incurs carrying charges, which must be a factor in the selling price. So what you look at is time. Time is of the essence; once you commit and get your money you want to move quickly to use that money and have the property work for you. Developing a timeline for this is part of your exit strategy.

6   Property Value. What is your property worth, either in its current condition or more important in its condition after you renovate it? What will you have to put into the property in order to make some money? It is essential that you buy this property at the best price. Remember the $5,000 rule. Why start high when you can start low? The lower the better; don't be afraid to put in a ridiculous offer; you may be lucky and get the property.

7   Condition of the property. You can use the checklists provided in the Appendices to review the house. What do you think you can sell this house for in its current condition and what will you have to do to make the property either rentable or salable? The exit strategy on this property will include the property's needs and the costs to address them. You have to evaluate these numbers very closely. Be honest with yourself as you don't want to get into a losing deal.

8   Market conditions. I look at the hot areas in our investment strategy, and I look at the not-so-hot areas too, where you may be able to get a deal. Sometimes you can make a move and go to the area that is hot, before everyone else realizes it's hot. I fell into a deal in Danville, Va., and bought over 20 homes in less than 6 months. No

one wants to invest there, and this has created such an open door of opportunity for me.

9. Supply and demand are as old as the beginning of time. Define your niche, where you want to be, where your entry point is. I have specialized in mid- to low-income areas, and there is a great opportunity. I feel as though everyone deserves a nice home and opportunity to live in a palace—their palace. It's the workers of the world who don't make a lot of money that need affordable housing and a chance. I give them that chance. I have to be careful what I pay for the house and what I put into the house so I can rent the house at a rate that these folks can pay. I don't want to rent to them and then kick them out: I want to rent to them for the long term. I want them to eventually buy the property—part of the long-term strategy that I have. I create the supply and I constantly evaluate the demand. I create the supply by keeping the properties in great shape, making them desirable to rent and buy, as well as keeping the price fair.

10. Cost of money. How much are you going to pay for your deal? If you can do cash, that's surely the best way to go. But if you are using a conventional lender, private lender, or owner financing, there is usually an interest rate that you have to pay. It's related to the cost of doing business.

11. Profit. This is what we are all working for, isn't it? With your exit strategy in place, you ask yourself if you are in it for the short term (profit today) or the long term (profit over a period of time). You want to make a profit for sure. Don't be greedy. Some wholesalers want as much as they can get and will end up holding a property longer than they should; some will sell it cheaper and make less but end up doing more deals and having fewer costs. There is a balance in becoming successful. You must be able to assess this

balance and see what works for you at the time of your purchase and keeping in mind the other variables that will have an influence on the overall deal.

12. Location, location, and location. An important element in successful real-estate and business ventures. No one I spun the Danville deals to was interested. It was not the best location: run-down properties in what I would call working-class neighborhoods; some would call them the hood or the ghetto. I call it the suburbs of downtown Danville. The best location in town, close to everything; nice homes with great yards, a place where families can own a piece of their American Dream. So I think it's a great location, many would disagree.

13. Cost of renovations. What you estimate may not be the final bill when the work is done. As you get more and more experience you will get better at this. A contractor's price is going to be higher than your price. If you want to keep your costs down, shop right, think smart, and do as much of the work as you can yourself. Be sure to get several quotes on jobs that you cannot do. Be aware of your money and how much you are spending. This will affect your exit strategy.

14. Tax consequences. When you get a little bigger and you feel the crunch always stay on top of your tax situation. You should pay your taxes. But you also should put together the best strategy to minimize your overall exposure. You can read up on this, but also seek advice from a CPA or a financial planner. Be smart and make some smart decisions that will drive your business to greater success. Your long-term and short-term strategy will come into play here.

Each of these factors that I have outlined for you will have an effect on your exit strategy. It is important to evaluate each and every one of them before you get into your purchase; before going in, know your strategy for getting out. You may have some strengths and then there will be some weaknesses as you do your evaluation: like winners and losers. You want to have more winners than losers. Try to follow your blueprint of success as close as you can, keeping in mind the variables that will affect your deal.

When working your exit strategy, have a Plan A, which is your ultimate goal of success. But as life will have it, there will be things that have a negative effect on your Plan A and you may start thinking of what your Plan B will be. Don't be afraid to deviate from Plan A and go to Plan B or even Plan C.

Here are some things that may affect your Plan A exit strategy:

1. Unexpected renovation costs due to something not disclosed, something you overlooked, something behind a wall, something you dug up. A change of plans, in layout or design: it could be one of a hundred different things.

2. A building or code inspector's edicts to make you do something you did not plan on.

3. Cost of money. The market changed and your rates changed through a variable rate.

4. Tenants who have not paid and you have to come out of pocket.

5. Poor management: boy, can I tell you about that. I've had some of the worst ever.

PART V

The Emotion

OUR ATTITUDES WILL REFLECT THE WAY WE LIVE OUR LIVES, both at home and at work. Successful workers clearly distinguish themselves from other employees. They may have a skip to their step, show a little energy, and put in extra time to complete a job correctly. Sometimes it is also the little extra that will make a negative person or situation into a positive.

Make smart decisions based on statistics, numbers, facts—not on emotions. To be successful, always move forward. When facing a decision, make a list of the pro's and con's as they arise; be honest with yourself and list them all, even if they are not important or appear to be insignificant. You may find out later the least important item may end up being the most important. See where it comes out: do you have more pros than cons or more cons than pros? Then make a decision, but try hard to take the emotion out of the decision.

Take this new venture seriously because I am about to change your life into a life that you have never seen before. I will put you on the path to be a real-estate millionaire with greater wealth, stability, personal growth, sense of achievement, security, and accomplishment.

Personality

This is an important element to your success. When you are thinking about a business to get into, in this case the real-estate business, and then narrow that down to a segment of that business (a property manager, a flipper, a rehabber, or even a contractor of sorts), you really need to take a look at yourself, your personality, your style, you as a person. Try to decide what specialty will be the best fit for your personality. Not everyone can sell a house, not everyone can be tough and do property management, not everyone has the skills to rehab. Not everyone can be a bottom feeder like me. It takes a skill set. You may not have the skill set today when you start but you may have the personality, the

SUCCESS

You never want to go into life, a project, a job, a family, with a defeatist attitude. Don't be a loser when you are winner. Winners don't quit. They maintain a positive attitude of success; they stay focused on their mission. It is important to embrace the task at hand, even if it seems insurmountable. You have the ability to accomplish this.

You must not drop the ball when the going gets tough; you must tighten your belt and keep on going. That last mile, when you want to give up, is exactly the point when you must not give up. You must have the inner strength to succeed and the belief that God has provided you the guidance, the love, the talents, and the faith to succeed. Be patient and allow him to do his work. Your time will come, and when it does you must be ready. You will be prepared, and your family will praise and glorify you in your success.

There is a time and place for everything. If your situation is not one that you should embrace, you will get the calling to move on; you will know. Don't look for a voice to respond in prayer. It certainly will not happen that way. But remember, the message will be clear!

backbone, the traits that it takes to be a bottom feeder. It's hard. Just as hard as it is to do high-end rental or sales of properties. What is important is to see where you would be best suited. I have bought a lot of properties from people who thought that they could do low-end properties, found it was way too hard for them and ended up selling them (to me!)—usually at a lower price just because they want to get out of it.

It's like being able to put the round peg in the round hole and not trying to put that round peg in the square hole. You have to look at this hard.

I suggest that you do one or the other. It's even harder to mix it up. Pick a segment and be the best at it. The best realtor in the market may think that he has all the tools to do property management or relocation sales, but at the end of the day he may be disappointed to learn that he doesn't and that he doesn't have the time required to learn that segment of the trade.

Take your time: you can learn it and be really good at it. But when you start, start with baby steps and specialize in a specific segment that you feel comfortable with.

Think about going swimming in cold water. It takes a brave soul just to jump in no matter the weather or how cold the water is. I suggest putting your toe in the water and checking it out. Same principle here, test the waters before you jump in. Read up on the different avenues, the options that you can take and see what is the right fit for you.

If you pick the wrong one, no harm, no foul: just change; alter your direction and stay on course.

What you don't want to do is pick a specialty and not like it and not have an option to get out of that segment. You want to be sure that, if you get in, you can get out as well.

The bottom line is that you want to be happy with your choices and you also want to be successful. Let me help you.

Work Ethic

No matter the situation, always be professional and courteous; put yourself in the seller's place. I am not suggesting that you should be weak; however, you don't want to be mean or rude. I make every effort to remain civil, cordial.

> When my brother, Richard, separated the restaurants that I founded, he spent the next few years taking everything he could get his hands on. Here was going to be a long-term negative after-effect. He did not care that he was ruining lives. People can be selfish, self-absorbed. Even today my family is still feeling the ripple effect of those negative decisions.

Create a positive reputation for yourself; don't be a liar—it does not work. Build a reputation as a fair, honest seller; a good reputation increases your value.

Your buyers and your tenants are your customers; treat them that way. Make wise business decisions; you don't have to agree always, but be firm and fair. Get your deal and make it work. You want good paying tenants and repeat customers who will buy more property from you and refer their friends to you. Once the word gets out that you are a good investor, people will come to you. You can establish this reputation by being honest and fair, doing a good job. Through real-estate investment groups, fliers, business cards, business affiliates, your city and neighborhood groups and others, you will get your name out. Cherish that reward.

A person with a negative attitude has the same power to influence others just as much as a person with a positive attitude. Plus, people with positive attitudes tend to be happier. They perform better, are able to set and reach goals, and boost both morale and productivity. It sure is nicer to work in an environment where there are many people with positive attitudes.

As a leader you need to be able to keep your people focused on their goals. You don't want too much deviation. Those with a negative attitude will bring the morale down. They will have a negative impact on production and prevent goals from being reached. They just don't care and will transfer that opinion to others.

I have always tried to have a positive attitude even in days of gloom, knowing that having a negative attitude was not going to help me succeed; it was all up to me. Sure I faced rejection and failure; those speed bumps will tempt you with a negative attitude, but you can work through them.

No matter how depressed or discouraged I was, due to problems that I had or frustrations from family and business, I tried very hard to maintain a positive attitude. There were times I was negative, but I tried to keep those thoughts to myself. It's almost like you are portraying a positive attitude without letting your people know what you really feel. It could be contagious, and that would be very bad. So lift up your spirits and turn that attitude around.

When you want to go out and be with friends for the evening, do you pick a friend who is down and out, someone with a bad attitude, or do you pick one who has a skip in his step? I think the choice is clear. Of course, there have been many times I've wanted to lift up a friend with a bad attitude; it's not always easy, but it sure is worth a try.

Stay consistent; keep your attitude as positive as you can. It's tough to have a positive attitude at work and then when something negative happens take out your frustration or anger on your loved ones. But it sure is hard to leave the problems at work. Find the good in everything.

No matter how bad my weeks or days were I always tried to project a positive attitude at home. When I was married, I tried so hard to shelter my wife from any of the negatives that would worry her. Sometimes I would share things with her and probably should have shared more. Often she would try to provide solutions, which I sometimes received well but many times not so well. I could have done better. I was looking for solutions so I could resolve the problem, but I was always pleasanter to be around when I had a positive attitude.

You always have control over your attitude. You need to be able to look outside the box and evaluate your attitude, good or bad. Also listen to what other people say, how they perceive you. I have had many bad attitudes—probably well deserved—and have used that negative attitude as a strength to get something done, to accomplish another goal.

We all have a way of processing both our negative and positive attitudes no matter what they are. Can you get out of a funk? We all know a lot of people who find that negative attitude and just can never seem to shake it. Negative, totally unhappy people are around all the time.

There are ways you can handle your attitude, good and bad.

1. Know your stress level. Some people can get stressed over losing money in the market as well as others may stress out because they cannot mow their grass when they need too. We all have different stress levels; know yours. Also, any high stress will have both an emotional and physical toll on you. It will affect your personal relationship and may also affect your health, giving rise to eating disorders or high blood pressure.

    Having different ways to release that stress is good as well: physical exercise is a great hobby; playing a musical instrument, getting together with a group of friends unrelated to your job—anything to get your mind off what is bothering you. You should always go into the new activity with a positive attitude so you can balance the negative one. Balance is important.

    Continue to focus on the positive things around you. You may never eliminate all the stress from your life, but you sure can work to *minimize* the stress, which is important. Finding balance is an individual process. Look for activities that will counter the stress. Always being in a stressful environment without balance will soon take its toll. Surround yourself with people you can connect to and avoid those that give you stress. Don't hang around people whom you don't get along with.

2. Be aware of what is negative and what is positive in your life. Before you tackle any problem it is always best just to see what you are up against, so you can make a plan. Got to have a course of action, a game plan. You can make two lists—one list of all the negative influences and a list of the positive ones. You are best eliminating as many of the negatives that you can. I always try to take care of a few of the easy ones so the list is not so long and I have less to focus

on: four out of eight done is easier to wrap your arms around. Even if you leave the big ones to do, at least you don't have a lot of them. Doing a few of the easier ones first will give you some immediate satisfaction.

3. Personal Feelings: Whatever you do in life affects other people, especially the ones that are close to you or directly affected by the situation. Don't let feelings fester; they will eventually anger you. I have always been one to let people know how I feel about something, especially if it affects me. If you ask me a question, I will give you as honest an answer as I can. If you don't want to hear the answer, don't ask the question.

4. Stop blaming someone else for what you are directly responsible for. You can walk away, but you can also solve any problem once you identify it. You must be able to recognize what you want to solve. You will feel good about what you have accomplished. It is always important to put the past behind you. During your success you should stay professional. There is no sense in hurting people along the way; it's just not worth it.

5. Like *It's a Wonderful Life* with Jimmy Stewart, we all have a value in life. We don't realize how much our lives affect others or how instrumental we are. You always need a support system, someone to provide you encouragement to move forward. Sure if you have a huge negative attitude—"Waa, waa, woe is me"—and the world is coming to an end, maybe you should really get out of the rain; you put yourself there, so now get out. You can do it if you want to, but you really have got to want to. Some people thrive on being miserable; they really do. So align yourself with positive people who will provide reinforcement and positive feedback for you to succeed. Success is paramount for you—nothing less will do. It is important to have a positive attitude to reach that goal.

Athletes don't prepare all week for the big game on Friday night thinking, "Hey I am ready for this game and I am going to lose." You must have a positive attitude to succeed. Rudy never gave up his dream when he set out to play for Notre Dame, and so he did. He got to play. He succeeded despite all the hard work and negativism that constantly bombarded him. Try to filter out the negative and to focus on the positive; that way you will succeed. You don't want to be the one to put a damp cloth over someone's head. It's always important to have a support system that you can depend on. Wives and trusted business associates are great for that.

6   Seek out a solution. You may know the answer but just won't execute it. How many times did I know the answer but due to the external constraints I just did not act like I should have. Sure there are some regrets; sure it gave me some negative attitudes, and I could not solve problems that I had to live with. Slowly you can solve all problems; it does make you feel a lot better when you can. If your plan is to solve a problem tomorrow, then tomorrow it is.

7   But be sure to address the problem; don't let it sit there like I did for so many years and allow it to fester. It does not go away; you have to make it go away. Best to tackle the problem you face daily. I recommend doing it right then and there; that way it is done. Today if someone is frustrated with someone, he may say "Can I have a word with you?" "Grab a coke and let's talk," "Hey, need a minute," and go to a private area and just talk about the problem. You may be able to solve it quickly.

8   How many times has there been just a small problem that has been allowed to snowball into a big one? Soon it is out of control. It's like a divorce; in order for both spouses to move on with their lives it is important to put all the chips on the table and deal with all of them.

Sure you may need a mediator or a judge to handle the issues. Once it is broken down to its minute detail then you can build on what is left.

You are your attitude. People gravitate to successful people with positive attitudes; no one wants to be around someone who kicks the dirt in disgust all the time, and has nothing nice to say about anything or anyone. Or even the person who has all the answers to everything and every situation—the one who has been there and has got the answers. You can only take that attitude for so long until you just get fed up with it.

You therefore have a choice: embrace a positive attitude that will help you succeed or have a negative attitude that will simply act as a weight or an anchor and bring you down. You have choices to make. It's time to make the right ones.

Experience

Over the years you may have the opportunity to take free classes relating to real estate. Many of them are offered through your city or their extensions and are very informative: building codes in your state, housing enforcement agencies and laws, fair housing, tax evaluation, the court system, economic development projects and incentives. Although they may not seem relevant at the time, not only will they provide knowledge, they will also allow you to network with other investors who are trying to do what you are doing. So interact, talk, exchange ideas; this is a great way to learn.

If you are a realtor, you will be required to take continuing education classes on an ongoing basis, which will further your education and understanding of real estate. Take first the ones that actually interest you, and then take the other classes. Laws change, the rules and regulations of the industry also change, making the knowledgeable investor more likely to succeed. It's difficult to win if you don't know what you are doing. In order to obtain a real-estate license, most states will require you to have taken several business classes at a college. Many community colleges offer such classes. On top of that there is a basic real-estate fundamentals class you can take to prep for the licensing exam. Very worthwhile. Companies in your area offer these programs.

This will provide you not only the knowledge that you may need to be successful, it will give you a financial incentive and marketing advantage as well. It can also be a career builder as well and will open more doors to new buyers. I personally found that so many more contracts could develop by being a realtor. In most areas the realtors are active in all areas: education, marketing, trends, lobbying for laws, and promoting good will and organizations and causes in need. They do a great job and hold themselves in high esteem as professionals in their field. If you decide this is not the route for you, then at least consider the classes and programs that they offer. Support them as much as you can.

The other educational route is vocational training. If you aren't versed in electrical, plumbing, or construction, look into programs or classes at

SUCCESS

Evaluate each person on the merit of his own ability and what he can achieve. We must not assume everyone will get an A in class, but we must not forget that a C or B student has the ability to get an A. We must teach those students how to get that A.

We are all different in the world and that's what makes us all so very special. You are special unto yourself for being you, and you must embrace yourself.

Don't allow people you love and respect to try to change who you are. I allowed that to happen to me, and I was wrong. I spent many years thereafter working through the consequences of those times when I had made the wrong decisions despite knowing better.

We all make choices, some good and some bad. You are influenced by your environment—your family, business associates, colleagues, and friends—in making those decisions, but the decisions are not theirs to make—the decisions are yours. I should have taken my own advice 20 years ago; had I known then what I know now I could have avoided many mistakes.

the local community college or vocational/tech school. Be one up on your subcontractors; if the job is complicated you will be able to talk to them intelligently. You will have enough knowledge to be able to understand the work and the estimate.

You may get to the point where you can do small jobs and repairs. This will indeed save you a great deal of money, and in addition you will be able to estimate a price for any work to be done. If you have not purchased a property yet and are trying to produce a plan for possible purchase, being able to pull the appropriate numbers together is necessary. Estimators may talk so much per foot as a cost estimate; you should be able to really tie down a more accurate price, a bare bones price due to your extended knowledge.

Sure you have regrets, and it's those regrets that you live with constantly, always running through your mind: why did I give in, why didn't I do what I knew was right? I messed up, and now I have to live with it.

Will there ever be a day of redemption? God will provide the guidance that you need to move on. If we forgive those who have hurt us, we will be stronger to tackle life's next task. Then, maybe, it was not our time. God knows your time and will reveal it.

Living your life as a good person from the heart and soul will work wonders for your success. Although as people we do tend to judge others, we should be careful not to. It is simply not our place. Those who have hurt you and others will get their day of judgment. People will certainly judge you though. Many people, including my mother and my ex-wife Margaret, have been very judgmental of me over the years, and it took its toll. No one put you or them on earth to judge, to criticize to the point of humiliation and degradation. It's discouraging and dehumanizing.

Of course it is up to you to raise yourself above those people, to stand

continued on page 300

Never feel like you know all the answers and don't need any more knowledge. The advantage of this book is that it offers another perspective on how to be successful. If you are committed to this new endeavor, make the total commitment. There are many classes you can take. I took the real-estate path, always taking the free seminars offered by the real-estate association, the city, anyone willing to teach a class; I was there. Your local real-estate association can provide details; keep up with your local paper too.

In the longer term, community colleges offer business and real-estate degrees as well, which you may want to consider. Work towards obtaining your real-estate license and then associate yourself with a company. You could then have access to information before most people get it. Sort of like getting info hot off the press.

Ambition

As a manager of several people I can compare employees right on the spot. There are those that can hit the floor running and others who cannot get it going after months of transition. Clearly as a manager you must distinguish between the two.

The big football game is tonight and the home team is favored to win. All the players run out on the field. Some warm up, some joke around, some walk over to the bench. Everyone on the team has a different way of getting ready for the game. Then they lose. Reflecting back to when the team ran out on the

strong in your convictions and beliefs even if they are wrong. Do not waver, for your strength will carry you through the trials and tribulations—although it will feel like hell.

Where is the light at the end of the tunnel when we look so desperately for it? Keep moving forward taking those steps, secure and bold to make enough progress that you will indeed see light at the end of the tunnel. Never give up.

field, some of the players ran out hard and fast, warmed up prior to the game, and played their hearts out, while others fooled around or hung out at the bench; these hurt the team. After the game they had a lackadaisical attitude toward the results of the game. Had they had a better attitude, just maybe they could have done better. You just cannot take anything for granted. But you can go out and earn it. It's not such a bad thing to pay your dues to achieve your goals—we all did it.

No matter how much pressure I was under in the restaurant business with that snow ball getting bigger and bigger each day, I had to remember that there would probably be yet another problem today to deal with, maybe something catastrophic that would change the entire direction of our company and me. There was not a lot of positive reinforcement coming from my mother and partner or from my wife; it was all negative, reflective of their attitudes toward me. Maybe it made them feel better about themselves to find fault in all that I did. It's not nice but people do it all the time. Nothing I can say will really inspire you to be a better person or do well; only you have that power. No man is ever an island even if sometimes you may really feel that way. Even if you invite friends, no one wants to take that trip.

So there you are. You get up each morning knowing what you have to deal with. Trying to put together some change so tomorrow will be better and of course it will. You have a great attitude and you will make a difference today despite any of the road blocks that anyone has decided to put in your way.

Today the work ethic is different than it was a few years back. Years ago you saw more high achievers. People needed and wanted to be motivated. There were sales seminars to ensure growth and stability with a company. Companies grew, people grew; it was a prosperous time. Today's environment is more survival mode. People are losing their jobs. Companies are closing. Families have lost their life savings. Now the focus is on damage control. Let's keep everyone focused and calm. Everything will be ok.

Our economy has become unstable. You and your company have to work harder for fewer rewards and in many cases for mere survival. If you had a job in 2012, you kept it. You may have hated it, but you didn't have much choice. Everyone's day will come and rewards will come as well, but you must remain diligent and faithful. Continue to be loyal and work hard. Try to maintain a positive attitude as much as you can. There is someone outside your workplace who does not have a job and who I am sure will take yours.

It's really hard for management to work with negative attitudes in the workplace. If you have one you may want to mask it so no one knows. Go out of your way to be involved with your company. Take on extra work where you can. Come in early and stay late from time to time. Take on different responsibilities in the job; get some cross training. You can always learn more skills. Advance yourself with self-help programs and educational classes. You will get noticed and you may get compared to other employees who are not doing their jobs.

You are in the process of taking a negative and turning it into a positive; someone will notice that you have a good attitude. You will become successful.

It is very difficult dealing with anyone with a negative attitude; there is usually no initiative to do much—a lack of drive, lack of motivation. It's hard to get someone off first base. You see it in many families as well as in business. You used to get an allowance for doing chores around the house when you were growing up: taking out the trash, doing dishes. Some parents made their kids do that work for no allowance. And others especially in today's home and workplace would rather text, watch video games, or just do as little as possible.

Speed Bumps in the Road

If you are not used to making mistakes, welcome to the real-estate business. You will make mistakes, probably more than you have ever made before. Thankfully, the real-estate market moves slower than the stock market, so you do have time to recover. To recover you must continually evaluate your options as well as the decisions that you have made. I have put too much money into rehabbing certain properties and have had to say enough was enough—stop doing the fun stuff. That happens; there will be another day to finish.

There are several key things to remember when doing deals.

- ▶ Don't be afraid to think outside your box. Talk to other investors, get opinions, look, and evaluate what other people are doing. Maybe you are doing it all wrong. Think through all your options which includes looking into other opportunities. Be progressive in your thinking. Your blueprint of success is your road map; sometimes you have to decide whether or not you should take the high road or the low road.

- Mistakes can hurt you financially; try to cut your losses when you can. In the late 2000s the real-estate bubble hit so quick that many of us were too slow to react and took huge losses. Even when I knew what to do I could not do it. It hurt, but as easy as you made a mistake and lost some money, you can recoup those losses fairly quickly—a few good deals and you can be running again.
- As a buyer, avoid deals that allow for 100%+ financing; this will restrict your projected cash flow. You will get hurt somewhere along the line if indeed you do too many of them and there is a little speed bump in the road. Do you have the back-up to weather the storm or are you totally leveraged out?
- Remember you are in the real-estate business, not in any other business. There are a lot of reports available that can help you analyze trends; both on a local and national level, the board of realtors will publish trends and statistics. Your local government will also provide information as well. If you are a member of an investment group, they too will provide information that can direct you to make routine decisions.
- Raw land. I had a piece of raw land that was primed for development and took a huge hit on it. Be careful with raw land. You have got to have money to support this potential opportunity. Raw land can be a time killer.
- Time is on your side. You don't have to move it today, but don't waste your time either: when it is time, make the move.
- Check and double check. Don't be afraid to talk to people, friends, family, competitors, members of your real-estate group, even contractors who know a little about property and your ideas. You may find that they can give you a different angle on something that you

want to do, whether it is a purchase, a renovation, or a buy-and-hold leasing situation. Some members of our REI group are contractors and architects who when you talk to them casually will give you some great advice. Keep the creative juices flowing in all that you do. You may be doing a great job; just remember that there is always more to learn or a better way to do something.
- Swindled. Been there and done that. Watch out for the fly-by-night broker wannabe who says he can work a deal. I have seen those deals. These are the types of guys that work the courthouse steps and slit their friends' throats. You know what they say, Don't dance with the devil.

Learn from your mistakes, so you don't do them again. Don't let your ego be your worst enemy. Don't make the same mistake twice. You will make mistakes, and that's understandable since you are learning a new business. Just be sure you have done all that you can to avoid any mistakes. Every deal is different, so you must do your due diligence on each one of them. You may easily pay too much for a piece of property, or you may not analyze the repairs properly and put too much in the property. When remodeling, how many times have I done the work wrong and had to do it all over again. Way too many times. Mind you, it was rarely that I made the same mistake twice. Three times, never.

Just when you think all is going to the cleaners a disaster may happen that may cause a moment of angst but in the long run may prove to be ok. I had a friend who owned an art gallery, and when the flood of 1985 hit our town it washed him out. He had a lot of insurance and was able to pay his building off and open a second location. He came out ok.

Just be honest with whatever you do. You never know what may be around the corner.

Patience

I recommend that you don't stay up all night worrying yourself to death on how you can make a million dollars with no money down. You just need to move forward on your road to success; follow your blueprint. The infomercials will blast you with every idea in the book to entice you to buy into their idea, whatever it may be, to be the next Henry Ford or Donald Trump. Don't pay attention to them. Save your money and try to get a good night's sleep.

Once you follow the plan that I have laid out for you, you will find your path to success. It is easier than you may think. You will not need a huge hype, just the self-assurance that you can do it: you can do it yourself, and you can start today.

Giving your properties some time will create greater value. The trick is that you have to be able to hang in there for the duration. Time will push the values of your properties up. Rents will go up as will your income. The greater the rents, the more disposable income for you, which is what you want. As you do, more properties will gain more appearance and be able not only to find better deals but also make more money. Take your time; don't get anxious; make smart decisions.

PART VI

Four Case Studies

Case Study #1: Prospecting

I am working on a property on Gilmer in Roanoke, Virginia. It's an ok property and for weeks I have been prospecting the neighborhood. The end of the block towards 5th Street is a little rough, and I may want to stay away from that end. There are two properties across the street that are looking great—right in line with my portfolio.

The one is boarded up tight as a drum but appears to be solid. In checking around the neighborhood I am told that the property has been in the family name for many years and that the family took care of the house. This could be ideal for me. I go to the city's CSI and find out a little more about the property, zoning or code violations, any issues that may be associated with the property. I obtain the name and address of the property owners and write them a letter, letting them know that I am interested in their property. In my letter I share with them only the negatives which include the code violations (mostly maintenance and mowing violations). The people that own it probably don't even know what the city has done to them. The owners may be willing to move the property cheap in an effort to minimize their potential losses. The lady has not called or written back yet.

The house next door is owned by Harold, a nice older fellow, on dialysis, who inherited the house from his grandmother and lives there for free. He does not have the money to turn the heat on and uses portable heaters instead. I made an offer of $13,000 last year: $2,000 down and the rest financed over a three-year period of time. He turned it down, as he was talking to a realtor who said he could get $20-$30,000. So he listed it. Went back six months later and offered $5,000 which was rejected, but we settled for $7,500. Title work revealed that it had a cloud on the title, so it could not be transferred correctly. The person on the title, Harold's brother, was dead, so we could not get a clear title. That's ok I went back and offered Harold $1,000 and settled for $2,500 cash—we take the house as is. Ok that's fine. On a defective title in transfer, after ten years with new owners the title defects are lifted, and the title becomes clear. If no claims to the house surface over the next 10 years, I just acquired this house for $2,500—what a great deal. The plan is to clean out the property really well. Scrape, repair wood damage, caulk and paint outside.

I don't think I will have $6,000 in the property with the basic curb appeal that I will do to address a potential code violation on the exterior. That will keep city off my back, which is good. Repaired, this property could be sold for $50-$70,000 total, with anywhere between $3,000 and $5,000 down and a monthly payment that the buyers could afford—with a five-year balloon note. Now if they make it a home and put in $5,000 to $10,000 and then default, I would then obtain a renovated house that could be sold for $60-$70,000 total with the same amount down. Not bad.

I will sell this property under a land contract, so the new owners will take ownership but not title. They won't know about the title defect and during the process I can either clean it up or sell as is. With a 30-year mortgage at 8% on $50,000 their payments are going to be around $400 per month. Or when we change title in the period of time to pay off, it's not so bad that they would take a blemished title. If I have done due diligence on trying to clear up the title and am unable to, I can disclose this to the owners. If no one has come forward in the 3-5 years that they have lived there, I would say that no one will. The original owner is dead.

This is a bit riskier than your conventional deal but remember you don't have a lot of money in the deal. You received a reasonable deposit, and for whatever period of time until the note is paid off, you are getting $3600 per year in interest and principle—most of the money is interest. So by the time they pay off the note it will be about what they originally borrowed. Not a bad little arrangement.

Some people make a living just doing deals like this. One after another. This is great way to get some cash flow without overextending yourself.

This is a good example of building relationships in a distinct geographical area when you are prospecting for investment opportunities. You are working yourself into an area where people will like what you are doing to the properties in their neighborhood; you are honest and doing what you have promised. You are trying to provide opportunities to all people, enabling them to get a hold of the American dream. This is one example of how you can buy into a property.

Case Study #2: Multiple-Purchase Deal

I love this deal. Ten years ago you may not have been able to get a deal like this, but in the post-recession real-estate environment you can.

Several months ago I was looking at a property on Patterson Ave in Roanoke and had it all worked out. I wanted to convert this large duplex into a single-family home. It was $12,000—not bad. So I called the seller, Jason, whom I liked right away. He was making a lot of money as a software consultant as well as in real estate in Northern Va. with a friend of his, a guy named Randy. Then in a short period of time the real-estate market crashed; his home, which he paid $1.4 million for, was now worth $450,000 with a hefty $5,000 per month mortgage payment. He and Randy took a beating in the Northern Va. market. So as an out to rebuild himself, he came to Roanoke and purchased ten properties real quick for the sole purpose of trying to save face and recoup his losses, make up for money lost. But Jason convinced Randy and a few friends to buy in on the deal, to try to build a portfolio of $500,000 in less than a year.

Every one of the properties was in a different part of town; there was no coordination of the purchases at all. He was not trying to change a neighborhood, and he definitely did not have a blueprint. He had something; maybe he figured he could get rich quick in real estate. Make a lot of money with zero cash in months. Wrong.

So I talked to him. I liked him. I got to a point where I found the ten other properties, through my own efforts as well as him telling me.

He had two other properties that were paid off in full and others with mortgages. What he did, which is dangerous, was over-leverage the properties to include the rehab monies. Three properties on Marshall, two of which I used to own were worth at best $100,000. He packaged rehab money for his other properties together with those properties and mortgaged the farm in total for $275,000. Randy bought in on it and signed away. He had no idea of the neighborhood these properties were in or the extent of the renovation of the properties.

Jason had gone through several contractors who took him down hard. Each time they would start over with yet another plan. Money could not be spent fast enough. If Jason did not take it from the loan, he got it from Randy or his family. Even I may have lent him money; he was easy to believe. And he was getting in over his head. Randy had not caught on but was getting mad. Jason's wife filed for divorce—they had a couple of young kids—and Jason got transferred from DC area to West Virginia. Basically from an hour commute to a three hours each way. He had to get an apartment during the week for his job, because he couldn't quit: he was depending on that income to keep his properties afloat.

Then he was putting band aids on the properties in Roanoke. Supplies were everywhere. He hired a management company to manage his rental. He was at a 50% occupancy rate on the few rentable properties. The code enforcement folks were on him bad, calling every other day and putting him on notice to do or die. They are good at that. They have a way of bringing you to your knees.

Jason broke under pressure and filed for reorganization bankruptcy Chapter 11. He did not tell all his people, only a few. It took a while for me to find out, but I finally did—thanks, Randy. You see I saw an opportunity to prey on the weak. Not that I was secure. By no means was I going to borrow any money pretending I had cash to purchase. I worked with him on a few deal combinations for the properties. During the negotiations I discovered that he had another lender—not the bank, but a hard-money lender that was foreclosing on two of the properties for $50,000 and $60,000. Now I ask, Why didn't Jason share that with me? I had to read about it in the paper. That changes the rules somewhat.

He tried to put a deal together without total knowledge and endorsement of Randy his partner or the bankruptcy court. Randy and I are developing a relationship. I am being told of some interesting things from Randy: that Jason has no authority to sell, that Randy is making the mortgage payments, that there may be some allegations of bankruptcy fraud on Jason's part. Talk about walking into a hornet nest. So I tell Randy my situation and already have put together a team with Kevin and Dallas. Dallas is the foundation guy, the radical libertarian, and Kevin truly is a deal maker. Kevin had been in the mortgage business for years as well as the double-wide trailer business and did well. His business dried up and was looking to move into something else. He needs inventory and he needs the expertise of people like Dallas and me. So there you go, three talented people.

Quickly I brought Kevin up to speed and put him in touch with Jason and Randy. Both guys liked Kevin, and soon Kevin was looking at contract options, which he shared with me. Kevin tends to chase a deal. Not Dallas or I—we let the deal come to us.

Randy found out a lot more information about Jason and what he was doing and not doing in his partnership. Randy felt as though he had been cheated by Jason and opened up a can of worms; he contacted the bankruptcy court. Kevin put the puzzle together. The deal got bigger and crazier and still too expensive for Dallas and me, the kings of bottom feeders.

Kevin kept working hard to put together a multi-property deal. He was close. It would be for all ten properties. The hard-money lender wanted too much personal information from us—no that's not going to happen. He did not realize at this point he could double dip easy and have all kinds of people on the hook. We won't give him all that he wants. Randy got madder and madder; he hired a consultant and paid him $12,000 to interview and investigate Jason for fraud. This deal sounded better and better for us each day. But I always have to remind Kevin and Dallas to chill out. Kevin put the brakes on.

I told Kevin not to chase this deal any further. By walking away from this one we leave in a position of strength. Kevin told Randy to work through the bankruptcy issues with Jason, to conclude his investigation and see how the chips fall. Two months later Kevin got a call from Randy.

The bankruptcy court filed charges on Jason for fraud and awarded Randy full ownership of the properties. Immediately Kevin positioned himself to put together a package deal for all ten properties. The objective: to spin off the ones that have high-interest loans (i.e., the hard-money guy), wholesale a couple of them, and maybe keep a few of them for rental and leverage for the group. All this seems possible and doable. Dallas will review each property to see what they need for either sale or rental. He can get the price right and all the work done. For the most part the work is almost complete—just a few cosmetic touches left. Jason spent all the money that needed to be spent; all we need to do is complete it.

I hate to prey on the disadvantaged or the foolish. There are two lessons here to remember. First getting rich quick does not happen. Second, beware of building a portfolio on dominoes. It can work during good times and effective management. But there are also times that it may not work. When one domino falls, they all may fall. If you are going to take that risk, be sure that you have a strong management structure in place and the time to do a great job. It's always good to have some back-up financial reserves too. That's the smart way to go. During the late 2000s a lot of people lost a great deal of money not having financial reserves.

This turned out to be a great deal; we were able to purchase all the properties on a land contract and have relieved Randy of the headache which has overwhelmed his time and his cash reserves. He is happy, and we are happy. At this time Kevin is working his magic to liquidate and consolidate. This case study is also a lesson in the value of developing relationships with folks;

Kevin, Dallas, and I contributed our resources and talents and accomplished something that we could not have accomplished alone.

As a new investor, it is going to take you some time to put together the knowledge to make a deal like this work, but you have time. You will not find the "millionaire deal" in a week. It does take time. This one deal was not a million-dollar deal either. Take the steps necessary to succeed, but very rarely will they be giant steps. Firm baby steps are just fine. Think the deal through. If a deal is too big or complicated for you at this moment, bring in that partner or two that you can trust to make a nice deal happen. Obviously you want someone you can trust and after you gain that trust, work hard to keep it. In the case of Jason and Randy, initially they were friends and had a great idea. They made some money. One saw an opportunity to take advantage of the other and he did. Avoid temptation either in a real-estate deal, a financial arrangement, or a partnership.

Case Study #3: Turning Around a Bad Neighborhood, and Making a Difference

On Marshall Ave, in an historic area of Roanoke, I owned three properties twenty years ago. Other investors came in and bought property there, and together we turned it around a little at a time. We all put lots of money into the properties, but we never got the tenant mix just right: the middle- to upper-class tenants we sought never moved into the neighborhood. Instead, we continued to get lower-income families. Then in a flash they changed nationalities and went down to even a lower income. Hard to believe. People who had real nice homes with serious investments could not give those homes away but ended up selling those properties at a loss and losing their investments. Even over a period of twenty years and with some serious investors, we were not able to turn the neighborhood around.

So thinking down the road, what do you do next? There was another street near Marshall: Day Ave. The housing authority bought all but four of the properties on this street and put together a great plan. Now this street was bad: the properties had lots of units in them and they were full of very low-income people. It was real bad. The housing authority renovated these properties into single-family homes and made them upscale. They sold most of them. As of today there are a couple more to be sold. They were able to turn an entire street around. They did a great job. It did increase the value of some of the surrounding properties. I happen to own one of those properties, and it has more than doubled in value. Not bad off someone else's idea and hard work. That does not happen often, but when it does happen it is nice.

So even though you may have the pulse of a neighborhood or street, you may be wrong about the effect you can have on its direction. If it goes bad, you may have a problem recouping your investment. When you set out to turn around a neighborhood, you will have a larger amount of exposure. Of course, if you got into the area cheap, you will be better off. A flipper should aim to get into a market or neighborhood early and get out right before he hits the top of the market. Learn to read the business lifecycle and aim to get out before the decline.

Case Study #4: Prospecting

I purchased an 80-acre tract of land on a popular lake for the purposes of developing a sub-division. I thought I had purchased it right; I had put some money down and financed the rest—didn't even have to go to a bank. It was great. I did my due diligence on the property and formulated my business plan: put in 74 patio homes. I even got lucky (which happens sometimes) when the county put in a 12-inch water line, which saved me $800,000 in water development costs. The project was moving along just fine: the water development took about two years to get approved by the Board of Supervisors and then finally installed. But then the real-estate bubble burst: I had not yet broken ground on the project, but I was ready to build and sell. The only problem was that there were no buyers: no one could get financing. People were losing their properties, their homes, their investments. I had to put a hold on the project: I paid only interest on the property until my cash reserves ran out, and then I lost the property.

I did not have liquid reserves to sustain me through this tough time. Initially like most people I thought the repercussions of the crisis were not going to last long, that I could weather the storm and bounce back. You can prospect, you can hedge a bet, you can extend yourself on a big project, but you must be careful.

I was doing this project with my mother, who passed away in 2009. When she died, it went awry because the trustee of her estate did not want to protect our investment as well as the improvements to the property, which included the water development by the county, as well as the design and plan of the project. She let it go. This was such a terrible mistake.

I had a builder who was willing to do all the building for the development and was even willing to do this with his own money. So to an extent we had a financial partner who was a partner but not really a partner: he was, however, willing to share the risk. The upside for him was that he was going to be involved in a great project: I had taken care of the soft costs of the project and the big one, the water, was already on site. The sewer was taken care of, as well as septic tanks—perfect; and the land was perked for all 74 lots. The builder had a lock for 74 building lots with no investment. This was a win-win for both of us.

We both were going to make some money. We were also in a position to do some financing for the buyers as well.

Well, time went on and I personally did not have the money to make the interest payment that was required. The trustee of the estate was not approachable. This was such a good deal for everyone. It is a shame that she let the property go contrary to my mother's intentions before her death. This cost us about $500,000 and left many unpaid bills.

So you always want to be careful on your partnerships. What if something happens? You must be prepared. Err on the side of caution. Protect your interests. I did not and lost a lot of money. I still have the plans for the project; I never got paid for any of my work or ideas. You lose time and money when a project or a dream does not work out.

Glossary

AAA Tenants These tenants will have the best credit ratings. This is based on a national credit rating service.

Abandonment The release of a property without giving it to anyone else; terminates ownership.

Abatement A decrease in the amount that is owed.

Abnormal Sale A sale that does not fit the criteria of a normal sale. The terms of the contract may be a little unconventional. This could involve an out-of-state deal, a possible foreclosure, or a person who just cannot afford the property.

Absentee Ownership An arrangement in which a property owner is not involved in the leasing and maintenance of his property. You may see this with out-of-state owners.

Absorption Rate The total space in a property that can be sold or leased in a particular market.

Abstract of Title The history of the ownership of a piece of property, available from the local circuit court.

Accelerated Depreciation A method of depreciation that increases the write-off at a faster rate.

Acceleration Clause A clause in a mortgage stipulating that the amount owed be paid back quicker. The total may be due immediately. Usually invoked when a loan is in default.

Access Entry by a property owner into a leased area of his property; it is customary to give the tenant 24 hours' notice.

Accessibility The ease with which one can gain access to a property. It is best to spell this out in a lease and not have to go through the courts.

Accrue To accumulate.

Acquisition Costs The cost of purchasing a piece of property. It is best to have a contract in writing with consideration. These include the cost of the property and building, the title, repairs and renovations, recording, legal fees.

Acquisition The process of acquiring or purchasing a piece of property from someone else.

Acre 43,560 square feet of land.

Actual Eviction This is a violation or a breach of an agreement or a lease. To obtain an eviction, you need to go through the courts and obtain a writ of possession, which is customarily served by the sheriff.

Adjustable Rate Mortgage (ARM) A mortgage whose interest rates will change from time to time.

Adjustments Changes to a price that was previously negotiated through a contract.

Aesthetic value The value given to property by appearance alone. Do not let this term fool you; it is you as the investor who must create the aesthetic value.

Affidavit of Title This is a sworn statement by the seller to the buyer that there are no defects in the title or the deed. It is in your best interest to have an attorney or title company check this prior to closing.

Agency The authority of a person to act as the principal party's representative in negotiating sales transactions with third parties.

Agent One who acts on behalf of another. This is helpful in real-estate transactions when someone wants to work through a third party.

Agreement of Sale A written agreement, with consideration, between two parties, a purchaser and a seller, which they must sign.

Agreement Either verbal or written statement of facts between two parties. The best advice is to put it in writing with consideration.

Amortization Dividing an amount of money over a period of time. The mortgage company spells out the amount of principal over a period of years at an interest rate.

Appraisal Estimating the value of a piece of property by a person who specializes in doing so.

As Is A phrase used in contracts to indicate that the property will change hands in its current condition. In other words, What you see is what you get. Let the buyer beware. *Caveat emptor.* This is the time to do your homework.

Assignment This is a great way for a starter or an experienced investor to buy or sell property. You find a deal or have a deal and you transfer the rights to that deal to someone else for a fee. So if you are a good prospector and can find great opportunities, you can put them under contract and then assign, or transfer, that contract to someone else. This is especially convenient if you need money for your long-term projects.

Assignor The person who transfers the right or benefit of the transaction.

Assumable Loan A loan in the seller's name that can be taken over by the purchaser, who then becomes responsible for the debt and continues to make payments to the institution as the seller did. Years ago, assumable loans were the way to go for investors. Today you must gain approval from the lender to assume the debt.

Bait n' Switch A method that prospectors use to drive a price down once they find a house to make an offer on. My associate who has no interest in the property will make a low-lowball offer, below what I am willing to pay. Of course they know that offer will be rejected but it does establish a benchmark, a potential of the house's marketability. So the house is listed at $17,000; my associate offers $3,000, which is generous. I come in and offer $5,000—my line. The buyer usually will think that he has done well, gotten $2,000 more than what the market will bear.

Balloon Mortgage A loan with a repayment schedule that includes smaller payments at the beginning of the loan and larger payments at the end. These payments include principal and interest. Be careful that if you do one of these you don't wait until the last minute to refinance or secure the funds; be sure you have an avenue for these funds. Commonly used for flip type properties to give the flipper some wiggle room.

Balloon Payment The balance of the mortgage that is due in full on a specific date. Sometimes a lender will structure a debit on a 30-year amortization with a five-year balloon. That would make the balance due in full in five years.

Bankruptcy There are several types: Chapters 7, 11, and 13. I share these with you in two lights. If indeed you have extended yourself with loans and mortgages and need time to reorganize your portfolio, then bankruptcy can help you. Today, it is harder to be granted bankruptcy than it was yesterday, but it does give you time, especially in a Chapter 11 bankruptcy of reorganization. You must have a plan to pay off pressing debts to keep your portfolio in place.

On the other side, bankruptcy offers opportunities for prospecting, if you can work with a bankruptcy trustee to obtain properties cheap. Sometimes they are auctioned, but at times they are listed with real-estate agents. To save money spent on commissions, have your funding in place and make a deal with the trustee. Most trustees want to close the file, liquidate the assets, and move to the next case. Oh yeah, it's about their fees.

Beneficiary The lender under the terms and conditions of the trust.

Bill of Sale A written contract from one party to another transferring ownership of property.

Bird Dog To prospect or provide leads for another person. In a team effort a property that does not fit my portfolio I can give to my associate, and likewise he can "bird dog" for me. **Bird dog.** Someone who goes out and finds the deals and brings them back to the investor there is usually a fee that is charged, like a commission.

Bleeding a Project: Excessive spending. Be careful of partners, yes, but also of borrowing money for the property and the rehab; you don't want to start robbing Peter to pay Paul. Full-time rehabbers who need an income may take money from a rehab for their income, but this will bleed you dry. You build a house of cards, which can collapse quickly. It's the domino effect. Give your portfolio time to mature. Be patient; there will be a time to get a paycheck.

As a prospector, watch for bleeders. We've purchased many a property from investors who started out smart but grew so fast that they could never stop the bleeding. As a re-investor you can pick up multiple properties from a bleeder, especially when he fears the ultimate danger of collapse. You will need liquidity, cash on hand; move in quick—act quick, close quick.

Blueprint Your roadmap to success. Contractors use it to build houses and buildings; you use it to plan your portfolio. Follow your course of action.

Bottom Feeders Prospectors who pick up the scraps; they buy usually what no one wants. They tend to purchase distressed or condemned properties. This is a good business because most people are afraid of what they may or may not see in a property. Usually you can offer low prices for these properties. By the time a property is at the low end for a bottom feeder, everyone is anxious to get rid of it: the city wants someone to buy it, and the owners want to move on. Limit your exposure and potential failure, and start as a bottom feeder.

Bottom Line The number at the bottom of your financial statement: it's either profit or loss.

Breach of Contract The breaking of the terms of a contract by one or more parties. Be sure you read your contract twice. Protect yourself if there is a breach; you want to be sure there are provisions for penalties paid to you if the other person defaults on the contract. There are remedies for default; pay particular attention to these details. Monetary remedies work well.

Break-Even Point The point at which income and expenses are equal. Be realistic: do not hedge. Don't forget your vacancy rate. Don't kid yourself or the bank. This is your rule, your report card. A measure of success can be determined by your break-even point.

Broker A person who acts as an intermediary from one person to another, similar to an agent. A broker may run a real-estate company and have real-estate agents working for him.

GLOSSARY

Bubble I have to mention this only because of where the economy is today. This occurs usually after a rapid amount of expansion and price increases followed by a sharp slowdown.

Building Codes Rules and regulations governing new constructions and renovations. The national code is called BOCA.

Buy-Sell Agreement An agreement between co-owners or partners in a real-estate investment, especially laying down the rules for an easy liquidation. Become familiar with this term. You can purchase premade buy-sell agreements from an office store. This will protect you and your partner if something were to happen. And it may—a death, a divorce, or just a falling out. Plan the out before you go in.

Capital Wealth, such as money or property (excluding properties with liens), which you may use to obtain property and fund projects.

Cash Flow The movement of cash through a business; income less expenses. You are working towards a positive cash flow.

Checkerboard Development Controlling a development area in a checkerboard fashion, sometimes used in developing new subdivisions. A developer may refer to it as angles and straight lines. I like domination and control of an area. Also I use vertical development, preferring to buy an entire street.

Clear Title A title with no encumbrances, no liens, and no mortgages, which makes the title marketable.

Closing Costs All costs relating to the purchase and transfer of property, including deed preparation, title insurance, taxes, attorneys' fees, etc. Be sure you budget funds for these expenses, which could be $500 to $3,000, depending on the property. Shop your closing costs.

Closing Date The date the property transfers from the seller to the buyer; it must be recorded.

Closing The transfer of a property from the buyer to the seller, also called settlement or close of escrow.

Cloud on Title A defect in the title or claim against the property. This can be cleared up; you can purchase a property with a cloud.

Cluster Development Developing or purchasing properties that are arranged in a cluster.

Code A systematic set of rules and regulations that cities develop to maintain properties within an area in the city.

Compound Interest Interest that accumulates based on the amount of unpaid interest as well as principal.

Condemnation The determination, obtained through court action, that a building is unfit for occupancy.

Conditional Offer: An offer or contract that specifies terms that must be met (for instance a zoning issue or a financing issue) before the offer can be accepted.

Consideration Some form of payment, or the promise of payment, to finalize a contract.

Contingency A clause that will allow the buyer or seller out of a contract, if certain conditions have not been met.

Contract An enforceable agreement between two or more parties that includes the following:
- consideration
- competent parties
- legal description of what you intend to accomplish
- agreed-upon terms

Cosigner Someone other than you who will sign on a promissory note, thus guaranteeing it. If you are just starting out this may be necessary. It's good to have someone capable of helping you.

Cost Approach A method of valuing of a piece of property that assesses the cost of renovating the project.

Cost Basis The value of the property usually used for accounting purposes.

Counteroffer Start low in your offer. The art of negotiation may prompt the seller to make you an offer; you may go back and forth before you reach an agreement.

Credit Your ability to borrow money. This is important. Initially you may not need credit, but as you grow, you will. Your credit score is calculated by credit institutions and credit companies, and it matters. A high number is important. Even if you have a good credit score, continue to work on your credit. If you have bad credit, you can improve your credit score; I will give you some guidance to build good credit. Even with bad credit and zero dollars it is possible build a portfolio; you just need integrity and a blueprint.

Curb Appeal The subjective evaluation of your property from the outside. Usually a good coat of paint, mulch, and flowers will enhance the property and give it good curb appeal.

Debt The amount one person owes to another.

Deed In Lieu of Foreclosure The transfer of a property by the mortgage company from one person to another, precluding foreclosure. This process can save all parties a lot of money and may be helpful when prospecting for properties.

Deed A written document recorded by the buyer and certified and recorded in court; it lists the legal owner and description of the property.

Default This is one's failure to perform specific duties or obligations outlined in a contract.

Depreciation Decrease in value due to the deterioration of the item.

GLOSSARY

Development Loan Like a construction loan a development loan may be disbursed in parts as the job or development progresses. Usually you pay interest only on this loan. Upon completion of the project the loan is converted to a long-term commercial loan.

Down Payment Earnest money put into escrow for the purchase of a property, per a written and fully executed contract.

Due Diligence Moving forward on a commitment, usually contractual, in a timely and professional manner, often relating to financial, zoning, laws, or conditions stipulated in the contract. **OR** Doing your homework to see if the deal or contract will work for you, to be sure you are doing the right thing, making the right choices.

Due-on-Sale Clause A clause in a mortgage requiring the borrower to pay off the mortgage in full prior to transferring title. Found especially in mortgages on new properties. There is usually a due-on-sale clause upon someone's death. This is important in your deal; banks are hesitant to work around these clauses.

Earnest Money on Deposit Monies tendered upon the execution of a contract. Often required.

Eminent Domain The right of a government to take property for the good of the public.

Equity Stripping Leveraging, or borrowing against, all equity in your properties for the purpose of buying additional property. Refinancing, second mortgages, and borrowing from hard-money lenders are all possible methods of equity stripping. I share this term with you as a precaution. It may seem tempting, but you will end up with a larger or additional payment that has to be figured into your cash flow. If you do this enough you can put yourself in a tenuous situation and could cause the house of cards to fall. If you have good cash flow, then this is yet another way to raise cash and grow.

Equity The difference between the value of the property and what is owed on it. The value of the property that belongs to the owner. As you build your portfolio you want to build equity in your properties. It is the equity, the value, that will enable you to borrow money for future projects. Keep the mortgages low; look to enhance the property values through your improvements and rehab, thus creating equity.

Escrow Money or property put into the custody of a third party and paid to the grantee upon fulfillment of conditions. Sometimes used for purchases and/or disputes.

Fair Market Value The value of a property based on marketability, including neighborhood, area, condition, financing, This is the amount you are willing to sell a property for and what the buyer is willing to pay. This is regulated by marketability of the property based on many factors, for example, neighborhood, area, condition, financing, all play a part.

Feasibility Study An analysis of a property or project you may be considering doing. It covers the development, the cost, the financing, the marketability, the project—all aspects of the project. And it allows you to determine whether you should undertake the project.

First Lien The lien of a mortgage, which has seniority over other liens on a property.

First Mortgage A loan made on a piece of property wherein the lender has a first lien position; this is recorded in the deed books.

First Right of Refusal A provision that gives a party the opportunity before any other party to turn down an opportunity to purchase a property.

Fixed Assets Tangible assets, property that you have acquired. The more you have that are paid for, the better you are.

Fixed Expenses As opposed to variable expenses. The amount of these expenses will not vary from month to month. An example is a mortgage payment. You need to recognize on your profit and loss statement what you can and cannot control. And whether you are satisfied with your cash flow.

Flip To purchase a property, usually at wholesale, with the sole intention of turning around and immediately selling it again at retail, perhaps after making renovations and updates.

Foreclosure The process whereby a mortgage holder, after a borrower has defaulted, takes possession of a property and sells it to satisfy the debt; this is a legal procedure that involves the courts.

General Partners Partners who are involved in the running of the partnership.

Ghetto The low end of town, usually where poorer people live. Holds opportunities for prospectors. This can be a gold mine for a bottom feeder.

Golden Rule A pre-determined limit on what you want to spend on all initial offers.

Gone Fishing A term I like to use when asking for rent. I have a house that I have been renting for $600. Maybe not the Hilton, but it's nice. So I market this property for $800 instead; I am fishing, trolling to see if I get someone to bite. Better than 50-50 someone will fall in love with the property and rent it for $800. Remember, next time you may not get that amount, but you got it now. It's ok to start a little high and then back off.

I have had some tenants call me after month of paying $800 and tell me that the previous tenant paid $600. It's none of their business really. I tell them that I made a lot of repairs to the property, and that it is a tight market. In today's economy the tenant must beware; the landlord is in charge. So get what you can when you can. Be fair, up front. You are in business to make money.

Good Faith An agreement guaranteed by the word of the parties; honesty.

GLOSSARY

Grantee The person who receives the title to the property; the buyer.

Grantor The person who gives up the title to the property; the seller.

Gross Profit Profit less goods, like mortgages, but before deducting variable expenses.

Handyman Special Common term that is used to market properties that need work. It is a catch phrase—look at this property very carefully. It may have serious flaws that are out of budget to repair.

Housing Codes Codes that are enforced on a local level to protect both the landlord and the tenant.

HUD A government agency. This will outline your closing statement. And give you a line by line breakdown of purchases and expenses in your sale or purchase.

Income Approach Using the income or rent from a property to place a value on that property. In other words, net operating income over the period of life of the property. This approach will give you a higher value than the cost, or "brick and mortar," approach. Consider using this approach to develop a higher balance sheet.

Inner City Usually refers to densely populated areas inside city limits. Like ghettos, these neighborhoods are good for prospectors and bottom feeders.

Joint Ownership Ownership of a property by two or more people.

Joint Venture A legal entity, very similar to a partnership, whose sole purpose is one deal. It is great if you find that perfect project and need an asset partner.

Land Poor The condition of owning lots of land with mortgages and expenses, without enough cash flow. A lot of new investors can become land poor; I have been there myself. Be careful: balance your operation; consider the downsides of development or the economy; don't cash strip your portfolio. Remember those with cash can make a quick deal today versus tomorrow.

Landlord The person who owns the rental property.

Lease Option The option, written in to a lease, giving the lessee first option of refusal to purchase the property. This is not my favorite thing for sure. It is a good hook if marketed properly. Especially to a cliffhanger. If you are the lessee, you want to specify the terms and conditions of the buy. If you are the lessor, you may not want to commit to a price in a futures market.

Lease Purchase Also not my favorite; I do not recommend it, although it is a great way for an investor to double dip. You buy a piece of property and depreciate it; pay off the mortgage and take all the tax advantages of the property. This works great with folks with bad credit and not a lot of cash who cannot get a loan. If it feels like you are taking advantage of someone, you are; don't kid yourself.

I just did one the other day. The property, if sold for cash, would sell for $49,000. I wrote a lease purchase for $79,900. They pay $650 per month, which is the market rent. In February when they get their taxes they pay $5,000 and thus the deal is done. Eighty percent of lease purchases end up back with the mortgage holder who with a properly written contract can take the property back quickly. You can set up a 30-year amortization with a 5-year balloon payment. Chances are they will not make all the payments on time over the next 60 months. All they are paying at this point is interest. At the end of the 5 years you are getting almost full price $79,900 minus $5,000. About $75,000; not bad especially with an 80% default rate.

Do the math on that deal. Some people do just that for a living. Sure I would take the $5,000 and buy another house using my $5,000 rule. Thank you for my purchase money.

Lease A legal document that allows one party (the "lessee") legal access and use of a property while another party (the "lessor") retains ownership. A lease must be signed and is binding in a court of law. It specifies a term, rent, as well as other rules and conditions.

In the past I have found that different courts, judges, and municipalities require different things be included in a lease. Start with a good lease. As you move forward, take note what you may want to change in your lease to make it better and protect your investment. Don't be afraid to make changes. You need to protect your interests.

Lessee The tenant

Lessor The landlord, or the owner of the property.

Liability Your debt or financial obligations. These should all be governed by notes.

Lien A legal right to repossess and/or sell a property as security for monies loaned; an enforceable claim on the property as a result of an agreed-upon debt or obligation.

Limited Partnerships A partnership consisting of two or more people where one person acts as the general partner. It works well if you have several investors and you plan to do the work. Your role, as well as your compensation, is defined. Also best to have an operating agreement drawn up on the limited partnership.

Line of Credit An amount of money, granted by a bank, that the borrower may draw upon as needed. Requires good credit.

Liquidity (Depth): Cash on hand. To have cash is to be able to secure deals and is more important than good credit.

Location The most important element in buying or selling property. "Location, location, location." It defines the piece of property.

Mortgage A written document that is recorded by a deed of trust for a sum of money usually in the amount of the value or portion of a piece of property. The lender then holds a lien on the property, and the borrower has to repay the amount plus interest.

Net Profit Gross profit less variable expenses. This is the money that you can take home, what is left over after all the income has been brought in and the expenses have been paid. The bottom line. Hopefully it's positive.

Net Worth The larger the number, the better. This is the total sum of all assets less all liabilities.

Notice to Quit Three days' written posted by certified mail notifying a tenant of default.

Occupancy The physical taking over of a property. Physical possession. You may need a date for this.

Offer One party tenders a deal, a promise to another to make something happen.

Opportunity Cost You should think through what $5,000 can do for you today. Do you take or give up an opportunity? A deal today or tomorrow? A bird in hand is worth two in the bush.

Option The right of a person to buy a piece of property at will; to exercise the purchase at a certain time and place.

Owner Financing: Financing provided by the seller. When you don't have good credit, when you have no money, focus your prospecting on FSBO (for sale by owner), which opens the door to owner financing. In a depressed economy when people are not building and must sell, these types of deals are available. Don't be afraid to make an offer and insist on owner financing. Be careful: review the contract and do your due diligence; the seller is looking out for himself, not you.

Passive Investor An investor who provides funding for your projects and does not participate in the operation of the company. I like this type of investor. (An **active investor** is a general partner and takes an active role in the company.) It is important to have an operating agreement in place, outlining duties and responsibilities, so no one is overstepping his areas of responsibility; you don't want an active partner putting the company or you in a compromising situation (accessing accounts, dissolving assets, overbuying).

An operating agreement can put all your concerns on paper so that you have a blueprint on how to run your business. If a dispute arises you will have the outline to manage it. Self-discipline and management are good. Also important is to implement a system of checks and balances, which preserves integrity, honesty, and growth.

Pass-through Transactions This is when a deal will pass from one investor to another. A lot of active investors will work together one investor will go one place and the other in another place so they can double their exposure.

Payback Period The time it will take to pay back your mortgage.

I like the stair-step method to pay back mortgages. You vary the amortization schedule so you pay back 5, 7, 10, 15, 20 years. It's hard on the 5-year payback; do a small loan at the 5-year and the larger on the 20-year. This enables you to obtain available cash when you need it. Remember, in 5-7 years you may be thinking of some renovation work on your properties. This does not work for all people. I don't recommend interest only loans because by never paying principal you never work your loan down; at some point you have got to pay back the money that you borrowed. Look at your cash flow and determine your payback. Remember payback amount ties directly into your payback period.

Penalty A fine levied for defaulting on the terms of a contract.

Personal Property Items that belong to the seller and do not convey at sale, unless they are itemized in the sales agreement.

Portfolio All your properties.

Possession Occupancy of a property. Usually, the time of closing, before which the buyer does not have free access to the property. Sometimes if you are a risk-taker you can get a possession date prior to closing for a continued feasibility study, demo, or renovation. I am guilty of jumping the gun on a contract or sale. I like stipulating in the contract for the allowance to start work. The seller will insist that you do this at your own financial risk. It gives you a leg up to start. I have at times completed the house rehab before I closed on the property. It's risky.

Predatory Lending The loaning of money in hope and expectation that the buyer will default and the owner can and will repossess the property. Some aggressive lenders will make a living lending in this fashion. Be careful if you are the borrower.

Prepayment Clause A clause in a mortgage governing prepayment (whether it is allowed, whether it carries a penalty).

Presale Selling a property before you close or before you finish the rehab. There are advantages to the buyer, who can make recommendations and changes, and for the seller, in so much as he moves his product. In a foreclosure the buyer can be the seller and never take possession. This is a real flip and can be very profitable when you buy the property right. In today's market you sell wholesale for a quick sale. Years ago you could discount retail and come out strong.

GLOSSARY

Profit The available cash after all expenses have been paid.

Promissory Note A written agreement between two parties for a specific amount of money to be paid back in a period of time with a certain amount of interest.

Quit Claim Deed I have used this a lot and it does allow for an easy conveyance of property. Usually seen within family or a prior recent sale. There are no warrants on a clouded title.

Rate of Return If you take the $5,000 you make on the lease purchase and buy stock versus buying that home for $5,000, which will make you the most money? The yard stick of success measures only one thing: profit.

Redemption Period The period of time that a person has to make a bad situation right, usually when a loan is in default and the mortgagee must get the loan current.

Refinance A new mortgage on remaining principal. Lowers monthly payments but extends the total term of repayment and increases total interest. You won't do this for awhile; however, if the situation is right and you need cash to expand, refinance. Refinancing a property can be a valuable tool for growth, but be careful not to exceed your ability to retire debt and create cash flow.

Let's say you have a small mortgage on a property and completed the rehab; you have a considerable amount of equity. You can take out a second mortgage, which may have a negative effect on your cash flow, or you can refinance the property to pay off your first mortgage and give you cash. If for instance you get $10,000 out of the refinance, you can then buy two houses for $5,000 each. Seeking greater opportunities by parlaying your existing equity to build your portfolio. I recommend that you try to double up. Split the equity and do a two-for-one versus just one property.

Rehab Renovation of property from any state to occupancy.

Rent Money paid for leased space either commercial or residential, as governed by a lease.

Repossession The taking back of a property by a lien holder, as a result of default on a note or deed of trust. This is not a good situation if you are the borrower. You can lose a great deal of equity in a property if you allow it to happen. There are remedies outlined by state laws that the lien holder needs to follow. Be on top of it when you get notice and do all you can to remedy the situation.

On the flip side of the coin if you are prospecting and know of lenders, private but also hard-money lenders, make a deal; they may sell you the note either before or after they repossess the property. If the lender knows he has a good solid payer to back up his primary he could make a deal and pre-sell his note. Great way to make extra money and as a prospector this is a great way to get into properties with equity and no cash.

Reverse Mortgage A mortgage in which the homeowner acts as lender and seller and the mortgage company acts as borrower and buyer. During the term of the loan the "lender" retains occupancy of the property. This is usually used by the elderly, who will receive monthly payments, while selling their house over a period of years. I am not going to explore reverse mortgages in this book of investing. Note that reverse mortgages are a financial tool that allows homeowners to take money from the equity of their homes. Watch this type of financing closely to see if there are opportunities for prospecting.

Sales Comparison Approach This method is a great tool in marketing your property on a flip or resale, retail or wholesale. You get to have a basis. You can use the MLS to see what properties are selling for in the area. You can see what actual sales values have been. And finally you can look at tax values, which are consistent throughout an area, and make a determination. Even still, in determining your sales price you always factor in what the market will bear. Financing also is an important element in the sales formula.

Sales Contract An agreement of sale that requires signatures and consideration. It is legally binding.

Sales Price The price that is put on a piece of property for sale.

Sandwich Contract Great way for a prospector to obtain properties by using the original person to the contract; you are the third party.

Sandwich Lease A lease that exists between a tenant and a subtenant. Do not allow this.

Security Deposit A deposit made by the lessee, and held by the lessor in escrow against property damage or unpaid rent.

Seller Financing See **Owner Financing**

Short Sale A sale orchestrated through the bank for an amount that is less than the present mortgage. It gives the buyer a reduced price.

Slumlord A person who does not take care of his property; one who puts anyone in any property and allows it to run down. When you start and you buy in an area (say, the inner city), and you do a nice job with the renovation and put a nice family in the property, which they take care of like it is their castle, people may refer to you as a slumlord—it's ok, your cash flow will probably be better than theirs.

Special Warranty Deed A deed that provides special warranties against consequences of action by the grantor within the realm of defects in the title.

Starter Castle A large house on a small lot. These lots were previously large, but over the years have been sold from around the house. They look funny from the street. They're usually seen in areas that have experienced shifts in demographic. You can put apartments in these old, large homes, but it's a tough sale and tougher resale.

Supply and Demand The basic business principle in retail goods, services, and housing. In an economy like today's economy, the housing market is so bad that people with good credit cannot get loans, and properties that were selling for retail are now selling for wholesale. Foreclosures are at an all time high; construction has almost stopped. People who owned homes are now renting; people working are now unemployed. Investors are in the driver's seat: if you want to flip and can do owner financing, you can almost name your terms. You can put anyone in a home, thinking that you will be taking the home back in a short time.

There is a supply of properties; how big do you want to get? What is your management and financial capacity?

Tax Base The assessed value of a piece of property (land and buildings) based on valuations performed by a city government. A tax rate is charged to the homeowner based on the tax evaluation. Over 60% of a local government's revenues come from taxable property. Cities will spend a great deal of money to collect these taxes. Especially in a down market.

Tax Lien A lien placed on a property for failure to pay taxes. Should taxes remain unpaid, the property will end up in a judicial tax sale. Know this well. As a prospector, going to tax sales is a great way to acquire property. You sometimes can get a bargain; the property will be sold, the city gets its money, the buyer gets an unencumbered property, and most important you get to have cash and close in 10 days or so. Good deal most of the time, but do your due diligence: these properties tend to need a lot of rehab.

Teaser Have fun with your new career. Enjoy yourself. Stay positive. When you are prospecting, it's ok to be ridiculous—a teaser. Test the market; it's a great way to learn. If you don't try you will never know.

Tenant The person who takes temporary occupancy of a property; lessee.

Throw-In You buy a house in an area and sometimes they will have a lot next door that belongs to them. Don't talk about the lot when negotiating your deal. When you write the offer of purchase, the contract, put the lot into the deal. It's not worth anything today—just throw it in; the seller will go for it.

Title The evidence of a person's right to take ownership of a piece of property. It is the history of the property which usually can be found in the circuit court in your area. You can do this yourself or you can hire a title company to do the work of you.

Unlawful Detainer Notice by the owner to the tenant of his intention to seek possession of property through the court.

Unsecured Loan A loan made with no exchange of collateral. Get all you can. A good deal for you. Just be sure you pay the lender back, and don't burn this bridge: Having a source for unsecured loans is valuable.

Vacancy Rate It will vary from company to company. If you include non-payers as well as vacancy a great rate is 10%; in somewhat poorer neighborhoods it will be 20%. In your pro-forma use 20%. If you can reach 10%, this is a variable expense a property manager can control.

Variable Expenses Expenses (such as a water bill, repairs and maintenance issues, and payroll) that you as the property manager/owner can control, as opposed to fixed expenses (such as a mortgage payment) which will not change.

Variable Mortgage Rate An interest rate on a mortgage that will change as the consumer price index changes. Something to be aware of when you start to get a mortgage.

Venture Capital A method of raising a great deal of money from many people for generally high risk projects that tend to give a great rate of return. Just starting out I would stay away unless you are fortunate enough to land a big deal. Do your due diligence repeatedly on this.

Verbal When it comes to contracts and arrangements, do yourself a favor: put it in writing in the form of a contract.

Vertical Development Development of properties in a linear arrangement, as opposed to checkerboard development. In my sense of development I would consider buying a street. By doing this you are able to change the scope of the street. You can control the tenant mix, the rents, the resale over the years. I have also found that it is easier to manage: When you collect rents or money you just walk down the street. I have done this several times, and it works great.

Warranty An assurance that there are no defects on the title.

Wraparound Mortgage A second mortgage that covers the first mortgage. It is most helpful when you purchase a property with an existing mortgage and you enter into a new mortgage while keeping the old one in place, so you don't need new financing. In essence you "wrap" the existing mortgage. Many investors use this method to take over properties whose owners are under water and need capital.

You will like this; learn it well and understand it, especially now with little or no cash. Now that opportunities are abundant since the housing market crumbled, wraps are common.

Zoning A regulation within locales to govern the use of land in certain areas of a city. Zoning regulates structure, size, lot size, type of businesses, etc.

Appendices

The following appendices are provided as resources. Before applying them to your own needs, do a little research to ensure that they do not contradict any state or local laws and ordinances.

- A **Condition Checklist**
- B **Property Evaluation Form**
- C **Common Rehabbing Costs**
- D **Lease**
- E **Memorandum of Option**
- F **Prescreening Questions**
- G **Residential Rental Application**
- H **Maintenance Agreement**
- I **Lead Disclosure Statement**
- J **Mold Addendum**
- K **Thirty-Day-Notice Acknowledgement**
- L **Ten-Day Notice**
- M **Five-Day Notice**
- N **Standard Vacating Checklist**

A. Condition Checklist

Whether you are buying, selling, renting, or investing, review the checklist below and see if there are any problems with the property that you want to buy. There will be some negatives and some positives. Be able to evaluate both and decide which are important to you; put a dollar value on each of them. You may have the experience to estimate this yourself, or you may have to hire a home inspector or a contractor to help you. There is a lot to check and double check to be sure that you are doing the right thing, when you put in a contract to buy this home.

APPLIANCE/ SYSTEM/ SERVICE	N/A	YES	NO	UNKNOWN	ESTIMATED REPAIR COST	NOTES
sprinkler system						only in commercial property
swimming pool						high-end; be careful
hot tub/spa						may not increase property value
water heater						___ electric ___ gas ___ solar
water purifier						
water softener						___ leased ___ owned
sump pump						
plumbing						what type? leaks? shut-off valves?
whirlpool tub						
sewer system						___ public ___ septic
air conditioning						___ electric ___ gas ___ heat pump
window air conditioners						usually will not pass on purchase
attic fan						
fireplaces						when was chimney last cleaned
heating system						type? Look at service records
humidifier						usually high-end homes only
gas supply						___ public ___ propane ___ butane
propane tank						___ leased ___ owned
ceiling fans						look at light kit
electric air purifier						

CHAPTER 24: RECORDKEEPING

APPLIANCE/ SYSTEM/ SERVICE	IS THE ITEM IN WORKING ORDER? N/A	YES	NO	UNKNOWN	ESTIMATED REPAIR COST	NOTES
garage door opener						
intercom						
central vacuum						not in low-end; be sure it works
security system						___ rent ___ own ___ monitored
smoke detectors						in bedrooms; hardwired or battery
dishwasher						
electrical wiring						updated? size of panel
garbage disposal						
gas grill						will not pass unless built in
vent hood						
microwave oven						
built-in oven/range						
kitchen stove						
trash compactor						
household water source						___ public ___ private ___ well
Other						
Other						
Other						

Property is zoned: (Check one.)

___ residential ___ commercial ___ historical ___ agricultural ___ industrial

___ office ___ urban ___ conservation ___ other ___ unknown

	YES	NO	UNKNOWN	NOTES
Are you aware of any flood insurance requirements?				Are you in a flood zone?
Do you have flood insurance on the property?				
Has the property been damaged or affected by flood, storm run-off, sewer backup, drainage, or grading problems?				Look for stains or mold; look in crawlspaces and closets.
Are you aware of any surface or ground water drainage systems which assist in draining the property, e.g., French drains?				Walk around home; check grading.
Are you aware of any water seepage, leakage, or other drainage problems in any of the improvements on the property?				Look at the below-grade block inside the house.
Have any additions or alterations been made without required permits?				Go to the city or CIS and look what permits have been pulled.
Are you aware of previous foundation repairs?				Is the house sinking?
Are you aware of any alterations or repairs to correct defects or problems?				
Is the siding intact, has it been properly installed?				Does it need repairs?
Is the insulation sufficient?				Check basement / attic.
Does the yard need extensive work?				
Are the windows new? Do they work?				Are they insulated?
Are there outbuildings?				Condition?
Are you aware of any defect or condition affecting the interior of exterior walls, ceilings, slab/foundation, basement/storm cellar, floors, windows, doors, fences, or garage?				Inspect all areas closely for signs of deterioration.
Has the roof ever been repaired or replaced during your ownership of the property?				Look at moving, torn, or worn-out shingles.
Do you know the age of the roof? Layers of shingles?				Specify:
Do you know of any current problems with the roof?				Inspect the roof carefully.

CHAPTER 24: RECORDKEEPING

	YES	NO	UNKNOWN	NOTES
Are you aware of treatment for termite or wood-destroying organism infestation?				
Do you have a termite bait system installed on the property?				Look for traps.
Are you aware of any damage caused by termites or wood-destroying organisms?				Go into basement and look at floor joists.
Are you aware of major fire, tornado, or wind damage?				
Are you aware of the presence of asbestos?				Do not disturb.
Are you aware of the presence of radon gas?				
Have you tested for radon gas?				Get a copy of the report.
Are you aware of any lead-based paint?				Disclose. There are federal programs.
Have you tested for lead-based paint?				
Are you aware of any underground storage tanks?				hot issue today
Are you aware of a landfill on the property?				
Are you aware of hazardous or regulated materials or other conditions having an environmental impact?				
Are you aware of prior manufacturing of methamphetamine?				Check with local law enforcement.
Have you had the property inspected for mold?				
Have you had any remedial treatment for mold on the property?				
Are you aware of any condition on the property that would impair the health or safety of the occupants?				
Are you aware of features of the property shared in common with adjoining landowners, such as fences, driveways, and roads, whose use or responsibility has an effect on the property?				

	YES	NO	UNKNOWN	NOTES
Other than utility easements serving the property, are you aware of easements or rights-of-way affecting the property?				
Are you aware of encroachments on the property?				
Are you aware of a mandatory homeowners association?				Specify amounts of dues and special assessments.
Are there unpaid dues or assessments for the property?				Specify past-due amount and payee.
Are you aware of any zoning, building code, or setback requirement violations?				
Are you aware of any notices from any government or government-sponsored agencies or any other entities affecting the property?				
Are you aware of any threatened or existing litigation or suit directly or indirectly affecting the property?				
Is the property located in a private utility district?				water, garbage, sewer, etc
Are you aware of any other defects affecting the property, not disclosed above?				

B. Property Evaluation Form

You may put in 15 contracts a week or even every day. You have to make a decision based on the condition of each property, which will inform the cost estimates for all renovations. Here is a checklist to evaluate a prospective purchase

GENERAL APPEARANCE

Year built:	Structure:
Condition of yard and driveway:	
Condition of the property in summer	Condition of the property in winter
Adverse effects of weather or the environment:	

FOUNDATION

Exterior foundation	**Interior foundation**
Porches and Decks: Structurally sound? Painted or finished? Condition:	**NOTES**

ROOF

Roof: Inspect closely Old or new? Type of roof: How many layers of shingles?	**Soffits**: Condition Historic?
Gutters: Type: (inside / seamless) Materials: Downspouts: Check on a rainy day.	**NOTES**:

SIDING AND TRIM

Materials	Damage
Is the trim complete?	
Soffits and fascia	Windows

GARAGE, CARPORT, SHEDS

Condition	Size

LANDSCAPING

Condition	Are improvements necessary?

WINDOWS AND DOORS

Exterior doors	Interior doors
Windows: Type Materials Condition Single- or Double-Pane	**NOTES**

BASEMENT AND ATTIC

You may get dirty, but these areas can tell a true story of your potential investment.

Basement Type Ventilation Damage Accessibility	**Attic** Access Insulation Check electrical Check for leaks and holes in the roof

ELECTRICAL

Service size Panel size (old houses often need an upgrade) Ground	Age and type of wiring Disconnects Subpanels

CHAPTER 24: RECORDKEEPING

HEAT

Fuel Furnace Age of system	Distribution method Adequate supply to rooms

INTERIOR

Walls and ceilings: Condition Repairs (Check basement and attic) Trim	**Floors**: Are they solid? What are they made of? If there is carpet, what is under it? Condition of carpet?
Appliances: Condition	**Fixtures**: Condition
Cabinets: Condition	**NOTES**:

These are some areas to look at; surely it's not every area, but it is a good start. Put some estimates on each area as you go through and, if you can, figure out what your costs may be to renovate. This will be important to determine your resale price and/or rental.

C. Common Rehabbing Costs

(The cost ranges listed are for materials only, unless indicated by the word *installed*.)

JOB	COST	PER UNIT
GUTTERS	$2.50 - $3.50	linear foot (LF), installed
LEAF GUARDS	$1.50	LF, installed
RAIN LEADER	$16.00	each, installed
LANDSCAPING	$300 - $600	
DECKS	$15 - $30	square foot (SF), installed
STORM WINDOWS	$125	each, installed
REPLACEMENT WINDOWS	$250 - $300	each, installed
STORM DOOR	$115 - $225	each, installed
FRONT DOOR	$150 - $300	each, installed
ENTRY LOCK	$100	each, installed
EXTERIOR PAINTING	$1,500	3-bedroom 2-story
VINYL SIDING	$2.05	SF, installed
ROOF		
25-YEAR SHINGLE	$105	square
35-YEAR SHINGLE	$134	square
SHINGLE INSTALLATION	$45 - $150	square
SOFFIT	$3.00	LF
FLOORS		
BUFF WOOD FLOORS	$100 - $125	
REFINISH WOOD FLOORS	$150 - $200	
CARPET WITH PAD	$2.00 - $6.50	SF, installed
VINYL	$4.00 - $6.00	SF, installed

CHAPTER 24: RECORDKEEPING

JOB	COST	PER UNIT
KITCHEN		
PAINT CABINETS,	$250	
USED CABINETS	$750	
NEW COUNTER AND HARDWARE	$22 - $35	LF
NEW CABINETS,	$1,500	
NEW COUNTER AND HARDWARE	$50 - $75	LF
KITCHEN CABINET LABOR	$100	LF
KITCHEN SINK	$100 - $200	each, installed
APPLIANCES	$1,600 (new), $300 (used)	each
INTERIOR PAINTING	$150	room
INTERIOR DOORS, PAINT	$25	each
INTERIOR DOORS, REPLACE	$50 (new), $15 (used)	each, installed
DOOR KNOBS	$25	each, installed
BATHROOM		
TUB, SURROUND	$150 - $225	each, installed
TILE, SURROUND	$500 - $600	each, installed
TUB, PAINT	$200	each
TUB, REPLACE	$300 - $500	each, installed
VANITY	$200 - $500 (new), $50 (used)	each, installed
SHOWERHEAD	up to $100	each
TOILET	$50 - $100	each, installed
TOILET SEAT	$30	each
MEDICINE CABINET	$100 - $150	each, installed
LIGHTS		
BEDROOM	$30 - $60	each, installed
KITCHEN AND BATH	$50 - $100	each, installed
OUTSIDE LIGHTS	$200	
DINING ROOM	$75 - $225	each, installed
CEILING FAN	$90 - $200	each, installed

JOB	COST	PER UNIT
ELECTRIC PANEL, NEW	$1,000 - $3,000	each, installed
HVAC		
AIR CONDITIONING, ADD-ON	$2,500 - $3,500	each, installed
HEAT AND AIR CONDITIONING	$3,00 - $5,000	each, installed
WATER HEATER	$400 - $800	each, installed
SWITCH COVERS	$1.50	each, installed
DOORSTOPS	$2.50	each, installed
WINDOW BLINDS	$15	each, installed
RENTAL REHAB, GENERAL	$5.00 - $10.00	SF
FLIPPER REHAB, GENERAL	$15.00 - $30.00	SF

Thanks to architect Andy Stowasser for providing some of the information above.

D. Virginia Residential Lease Agreement

This is a legally binding document. If you don't understand it, get competent legal advice.

This lease is dated _____ and is established by and between _____ "agent" (through an owner, MACHER PROPERTIES LLC, RLPJ PROPERTIES LLC, SOUTHSIDE EQUITY LLC, the owner of this property that you are going to rent) AND _____ "TENANT" (referred to as TENANT, even if more than one). As used in this lease, unless the context implies otherwise, LANDLORD means owner or agent as it applies to this property. It is our intent to rent the property located at _____.

List any and all occupants, including children, who will be living in this property.

_____ _____

_____ _____

_____ _____

I. Rental of Property:
   A. DESCRIPTION: The owner rents to TENANT the property located at _____ (street number and name) in _____ (city), Virginia. The rental unit shall be rented to only the people listed in the lease either as the TENANT or occupants of the TENANT.
   B. TERM: The term of this lease is twelve months and thereafter occupancy will continue month-to-month
      1. It begins _____
      2. It ends _____
   C. RENT: TENANT will pay the rent of _____ dollars per month, payable in advance to the owner/agent the first of each month

beginning _____ . If the rent is paid on or after the 2nd day of the month, the TENANT may be subject to a $50.00 late fee and will be noticed with a 5-day "Pay or Quit" notice for eviction of said property. All rent will be paid to MACHER PROPERTIES LLC/ROLAND MACHER, at 1925 Salem Ave, Roanoke, Va 24016.

D. APPLIANCES AND UTILITIES
   1. LANDLORD will furnish the following appliances: refrigerator and stove.
   2. LANDLORD will furnish the following utilities: _____.
   3. TENANT will furnish the following utilities: _____.
   4. LANDLORD and TENANT will maintain and pay for all the utilities that they are to provide under the terms of the lease (electric, gas, water). It will constitute a default of this lease if a utility is disconnected for non-payment. TENANT agrees to use all utilities in a reasonable manner and not to engage in any conduct that will waste the energy or resource or increase the cost of providing such utility. In the event utility service cannot be provided or is temporarily disconnected due to circumstances beyond either LANDLORD's or TENANT's control (other than non-payment) and the appropriate party is diligently attempting to correct the problem causing this disruption, then neither LANDLORD or TENANT shall have a claim against the other.
   5. In the property where LANDLORD pays the water bill, LANDLORD will pay the average adult water usage of $25.00 per adult per month, and the average child water usage of $15 per month, for the TENANT and authorized occupants of the unit. Water usage over this will be the sole responsibility of the TENANT. LANDLORD will bill TENANT for additional water usage while TENANT occupies the rental unit, and if the TENANT does not pay within fifteen (15) days, LANDLORD may deduct that amount from TENANT's security deposit or obtain an unlawful detainer for potential eviction

from the property for nonpayment. TENANT will be in default and in violation of this lease. It is the TENANT'S responsibility to immediately notify LANDLORD of any water leaks including running toilet, sink, or faucet that does not turn off correctly, or other leaks under the sink, under the toilet, around the bathtub, faucets, broken pipe, etc., in writing and verified received by the LANDLORD. The only overages the TENANT will not be responsible for are those that cannot be seen outside and those underground, under the house, or inside a wall where the water does not run out into a visible area. In a single-family home, the LANDLORD will have no responsibility for any water issues. In case of a multifamily building: upon receiving a water utility bill that is over the average, LANDLORD will investigate upon notification, to determine if there are any unreported leaks or leaks that the TENANT is not responsible for as explained above. If an unreported leak is found in one unit only, the TENANT of that unit will be responsible for the ENTIRE overage of the utility bill. If there are unreported leaks found in multiple units, each unit will pay an EQUAL share to cover the overage of the utility bill. If it is found the overage is due to an additional unauthorized occupant, the TENANT of that unit will be responsible for the ENTIRE overage.

6. TENANT authorizes LANDLORD to request all utility companies (particularly gas and electric) to report any default of TENANT'S account, disconnect notices, or other service termination, and TENANT gives up any claim he might have against such utility company for any reports they may give LANDLORD in good faith. A photocopy of this lease may be given to the appropriate utility to indicate TENANT'S permission to give information about TENANT'S account.

7. KEYS, LOCKOUT CHARGES: LANDLORD will provide TENANT with one key to the unit. TENANT is responsible for making additional copies for other occupants. The key must be returned when

TENANT vacates the property. If it is not returned, there is a cost of $200.00 to replace the locks on the unit.

II. SECURITY DEPOSIT, LATE FEES, AND OTHER CHARGES; APPLICATION OF PAYMENT
   A. SECURITY DEPOSIT: The security deposit is $200.00 and may earn interest that will be credited to TENANT in accordance with Virginia Law. TENANT grants LANDLORD a possessory security interest in such deposit. The deposit, with interest if applicable, will be refunded to TENANT upon written request by the TENANT directed to the LANDLORD within 5 days of leaving the property. Otherwise they will forfeit their total deposit. The deposit will be refunded to the TENANT after 1) this lease is terminated, 2) TENANT vacates the unit, removes all his property and delivers to LANDLORD all keys to the unit, AND 3) deduction of any damages, unpaid rent or other lawful charges then owed to the LANDLORD by TENANT. TENANT agrees to the fee schedule of repairs, damages, and maintenance. If the TENANT does not allow LANDLORD to do an inspection upon vacating the property, the TENANT then forfeits any rights of the security deposit.
   B. LATE FEES: If the rent is not received by the Agent or Owner before the first day of the month, when the rent is due, then the rent will be considered late and will be subject to a late charge of $50.00. Rent will be considered timely if received by the OWNER by 9:00am on the 2nd day of the month, but not a moment after. EVICTION PROCEEDINGS will begin on the 6th of that month, after the 5-day notice has been sent to pay or quit. LANDLORD may accept any type of payment plan by the TENANT that is in writing and approved by the signature of the LANDLORD. However, in that case if one payment is late by a day the entire month is considered late and a charge of $50.00 will apply.
   C. MONIES OWED. If the entire rent is not paid for any given month and a late fee charged, any new rents paid will be applied first to the outstanding monies, and the current month's rent will be considered late.

D. ATTORNEY FEES. If the LANDLORD files legal proceedings, the TENANT will be responsible for any and all Attorney fees, twenty-five percent (25%) of the total amount awarded by the Court. In addition the TENANT will be responsible for any and all Court costs, filing fees, witnesses and other costs associated with the collection of monies due to the LANDLORD. The TENANT agrees to pay attorney fees as well for Interrogatories, Warrants in Debt, Writs of Possession, and collection of any other monies due from the TENANT to the LANDLORD, assessing the TENANT twenty-five percent (25%) of monies received or a stated fee that is reasonable by the attorney.

E. CHECK. The LANDLORD does not take checks, but in the event of receiving one that doesn't clear, there is a $100.00 fee for any and all returned checks.

F. OTHER CHARGES. The TENANT agrees to pay any and all charges imposed by the LANDLORD that are not prohibited but reasonable and that have not already been imposed on the TENANT.

G. The TENANT agrees that if there is any litigation on this lease or any counterclaim related to this lease and the TENANT obtains an attorney, either private or through legal aid, that the TENANT—win, lose, or draw—will pay any and all fees charged. If legal aid submits a bill of time to the Court, the Court will recognize that this TENANT will personally pay his fees and hold the LANDLORD and AGENT HARMLESS of any and all actions against them.

H. APPLICATION OF PAYMENTS. All money paid by the TENANT to the LANDLORD will be applied in the following order: FIRST to any amounts due to LANDLORD for security deposit; SECOND to any unpaid charges, other than rent, due to LANDLORD under the lease; THIRD to rents due under this lease; FOURTH to payment of court costs, attorney's fees, accrued interest, and principal in that order. If LANDLORD has obtained a judgment against the TENANT, then any and all deposits, security, etc. will not be returned if the TENANT decides not to rent the property.

III. CONDITION OF PROPERTY: MAINTENANCE AND REPAIR BY TENANT AND LANDLORD; ACCESS
   A. CONDITION OF PROPERTY; RIGHT TO NOTIFY OF DEFECT. TENANT has inspected the property where is, as is. TENANT understands that nothing will be done to the property unless approved in writing by the LANDLORD. It is the obligation of the TENANT under the Landlord Tenant Act to have 10 days to provide a written list of any and all defects and irregularities that exist as of the date of possession. Text messages are not an acceptable means of communication. If the TENANT has not put in writing a list of any of these irregularities and/or, without giving the LANDLORD ample time to make repairs, calls the Code Inspector instead, then the lease can be terminated immediately and an Unlawful Detainer can be obtained for possession of property. The Landlord Tenant Act provides for due notice to the LANDLORD on issues with the property.
   B. SMOKE DETECTORS. TENANT acknowledges that there are at least six (6) working smoke detectors in the property. It is the TENANT's responsibility to replace the batteries when necessary and make sure that they are maintained in working manner. If the LANDLORD has to replace or maintain them, then there is a charge of $50.00 per smoke detector. The TENANT will replace the batteries every six months at the TENANT'S sole expense. The LANDLORD suggests that they be changed in the spring and fall of each year.
   C. FIREPLACES AND WOOD-BURNING STOVES. Any open flame is not permitted in any part of the house unless it is approved by the LANDLORD or AGENT. If the rental unit covered by this lease has fireplaces or wood-burning stoves, the TENANT is to call the governmental authority, e.g., the Fire Marshall etc., and have the flues and appliances checked prior to using. TENANT is to maintain the flue and appliances in a safe operating condition throughout the term of the lease. The TENANT must also provide the LANDLORD proof of insurance for that property as well. This includes any and all gas appliances.

D. LEAD PAINT. The rental unit covered by this lease was built prior to 1978. Attached to this lease and made part hereof is owner's disclosure of information and acknowledgement of lead-based paint and/or other lead-based hazards to the extent known by the owner.

E. LANDLORD AND EMERGENCY ACCESS TO UNIT. In case of emergency or if TENANT requests repairs or maintenance to the rental unit, LANDLORD has the right to enter the rental unit without notice and at any hour to inspect the property and make necessary maintenance and repairs. LANDLORD may permit any person named in the Emergency Access Authorization section of the application or other individual designated in writing by TENANT to have access to the rental unit in case of a bona fide emergency. If for any reason the LANDLORD is denied access to the property this lease will be in default immediately, and without notice the LANDLORD may obtain an Unlawful Detainer to protect his interests in the property. If the TENANT feels as though the LANDLORD, given written notice of repair and ample time does not make the repair, then the TENANT understands that he may assert his rights under the Landlord Tenant Act and put all rent in escrow with the court. If TENANT fails to do so, then TENANT loses all rights to rent the property or any counter claim on their complaint. This is outlined in the Landlord Tenant Act, and the TENANT acknowledges that he is aware of that provision and rule of law.

F. LANDLORD TO MAINTAIN. Unless otherwise agreed in writing, LANDLORD will maintain any common areas. LANDLORD will also maintain those components of the rental unit that require repair due to ordinary wear and tear, and will comply with all requirements imposed on property owners by applicable laws and regulations, including building and maintenance codes. These areas must be cleaned by the TENANTS on a weekly and daily basis. If the LANDLORD cleans these areas he may impose a $25.00 fee to each TENANT occupying the property.

G. TENANT TO MAINTAIN. Throughout the term of this lease TENANT will keep the rental unit clean and in good order and repair as it is today, the day the lease is executed (reasonable wear and tear is expected) and will comply with all building and housing codes and regulations.

1. TENANT will keep his part of the dwelling unit and the part of the premises that he occupies free from insects and pests. The TENANT is responsible for any and all pest control from the day of signing of the lease. The TENANT verifies that there are no pests in the property at the signing of the lease and that any pests thereafter are due to the TENANT and therefore he will be held responsible for their eradication from the property.

2. TENANT will place refuse and trash in the appropriate receptacles on the proper day. If the trash is tagged and the LANDLORD has to remove the tagged trash there will be a $100.00 service charge.

3. The TENANT is responsible for keeping the yard clean of any trash and excess toys on the property. They agree to mow the yard in accordance with the ordinances of the city. If the LANDLORD has to mow the grass for any reason there will be a $100.00 service fee for the mowing of that grass. The TENANT is not responsible for any brush or hedgerows.

4. At no time will the TENANT have any illegal vehicles on the property. All vehicles must be licensed and tagged appropriately in accordance with applicable laws. The LANDLORD without notice may remove illegal vehicles and put them in his storage facility at the cost to the TENANT. The address is 1925 Salem Ave, Roanoke, Va. 24016

H. TENANT TO REPAIR DAMAGES. The TENANT will repair at his own expense any damage that TENANT causes to the rental unit (including plumbing and rain or sewer line stoppages, appliances, and furnishings) and will not deliberately or negligently destroy, deface, damage, impair, or remove any portion of the rental unit or its fixtures nor permit any other person to do so. They will be charged according to fees charged by contractor.

I. NO ALTERATIONS. TENANT may make no alterations, additions, improvements, or repairs to the rental unit without LANDLORD's written consent. This includes ceiling fans, telephones, window air conditioners, wall-mount TVs, satellites, and anything nailed or attached to the walls, except pictures or mirrors weighing less than 5 pounds. The TENANT is responsible for any and all repairs of nail holes upon vacating the property. The TENANT will hold the LANDLORD harmless for all damages and claims resulting from TENANT's alterations, additions, improvements, or repairs, whether authorized or unauthorized.

J. PAYMENT FOR REPAIRS BY TENANT. If LANDLORD bills TENANT for damages while TENANT occupies the rental unit and TENANT does not pay within fifteen (15) days, LANDLORD may deduct that amount from TENANT's security deposit. TENANT will then have ten (10) days to replace the money in security deposit or TENANT will be in default and in violation of this lease. In the absence of a security deposit, the cost of any damage will be added to the next month's rent and if that payment is not made, TENANT will be in default and in violation of this lease.

IV. PROHIBITED MATERIALS, PERSONS, AND ACTIVITIES

A. PETS AND ANIMALS OF ANY KIND. No animals including household pets (reptiles, birds, mammals) are allowed at any time. [This clause may be waived by LANDLORD's signature here: _____. If waived, all pets/animals will be the responsibility of the TENANT, who will be responsible for any claim or damages caused. The LANDLORD will not be held liable. Note that the animal (usually) has to be put up and secure in order to do any repairs and maintenance to the property. There can be no poop in the yard ever. If the LANDLORD has to pick up poop there will be a charge of $50.00 per visit to the property.]

B. ASSIGNMENT AND SUBLETTING. TENANT may not sublet or assign the lease to anyone else for any reason or allow anyone not approved in writing by LANDLORD to occupy the premises.

C. SIGNS. The TENANT will not post signs on the front of the property for any reason. There will be a charge of $100.00 if any signs are found and removed.
D. DO NOT DISTURB. TENANT will not disturb other tenants or neighbors at any time or violate any laws, ordinances, or codes that affect the health, safety, or domestic tranquility of the rental unit or surrounding neighborhood or area. No person whether known to TENANT or not may cause disturbances or commit illegal acts on the rental property. This may even apply to too much in-and-out activity to the property. Any illegal activity or disruptive behavior on or around these premises committed by TENANT or TENANT's associates and identified by law enforcement will be considered a breach of this lease. When other tenants' complaints become known to the LANDLORD or his agent and these concerns continue, this lease will be considered breached.
E. PROBATION. It is now the opportunity for the TENANT to inform the LANDLORD if anyone in the property is on probation, either supervised or on an ankle bracelet. If the TENANT does not identify any and all parties under the state's supervision, it will be cause for termination of this lease.
F. NO OTHER RESIDENTS ALLOWED; GUESTS LIMITED. TENANT will not allow any other individuals except those listed in this lease to reside in the unit, unless authorized in writing by the LANDLORD. TENANT may have temporary overnight visitors provided 1) any such visitors do not stay overnight more than three (3) days total in any three-month period and 2) there are not more than two overnight visitors at any one time. If TENANT violates this paragraph, then in addition to all other remedies provided by the LANDLORD, TENANT agrees to pay LANDLORD as additional rent to compensate for the added wear and tear of the unit, use of utilities and common areas provided by LANDLORD, $25.00 per person per day that such person is in the rental unit. Payment by TENANT and acceptance by LANDLORD of the sums specified herein is not a waiver of default or acceptance by the LANDLORD, and such sums will be accepted with reservation of

all rights of LANDLORD. If TENANT asks in advance, LANDLORD may, in his sole discretion, give written permission regarding overnight visitors and the terms of such written permission will be binding under the lease.

G. The TENANT understands that if he indeed has a complaint with the LANDLORD with repairs and maintenance of the property that according to the Landlord Tenant Act of Virginia he is required to file a tenant's assertion and complaint with the court, which requires him to put any and all rent due into escrow with the Court. A true copy must be sent to the LANDLORD as notice of said complaint. Failure to do so should result in the Court given possession of property as well as disregarding any and all claims by the TENANT.

H. The TENANT agrees to the fee schedule for damage, repairs, and maintenance to the property. If the TENANT moves out of the property and does damage then the fee schedule will automatically apply.

I. The TENANT is required to have renters' insurance and to show proof to the LANDLORD or agent of said property. This is for the protection of both the TENANT and the LANDLORD/owner.

J. The TENANT is responsible for having all the utilities turned on in his name as outlined by the lease. Failure to do so is a violation of code issues. Therefore, the lease can be terminated immediately. The LANDLORD can take possession through abandonment immediately, with the standard twenty-four (24) hour notice.

K. ABANDONMENT/INCARCERATION/DEATH. The TENANT names the person below to be contacted if the property is abandoned or if the TENANT is incarcerated or dies. Notice will be put on the door of the property and mailed to the TENANT and person named. Either party has 24 hours to move, secure, or make arrangements in writing with the LANDLORD for protection of their property. If indeed there is no contact, then the LANDLORD has every right and authorization from the TENANT to move their property into storage. The LANDLORD will notify the person designated as to where the property is and will charge $25.00 per day for storage of property. The property will be stored for sixty days. If the TENANT does not give any notice to the LANDLORD, then the LANDLORD can move quickly to terminate lease as well as the items left. The LANDLORD will give notice to the TENANT at the last known address and the designated person that they have identified. The LANDLORD can consider such property abandoned and may dispose of it in any reasonable manner, including discarding it or donating it to charity. TENANT waives any claim against the LANDLORD for property the TENANT has abandoned as stated above.

Name of person designated and address:

_____

_____

_____

L. The TENANT agrees that under any type of dispute against the LANDLORD or his agents by an outside attorney or legal aid, the TENANT will be responsible for any and all costs, legal fees, filing fees, and the like incurred by their attorney and sanctioned by the court. These costs will be costs that the TENANT has agreed to pay no matter what the outcome with the LANDLORD or the agent involved in the case

V. TERMINATION AND RENEWAL OF LEASE
   A. NOTICE OF TERMINATION. TENANT and LANDLORD may terminate this lease by giving the other party written notice of termination at least sixty (60) days before the date this lease is to end. The effective date of termination is given, unless a later date, which shall be the last day of a calendar month, is stated in the notice. Time is of the essence in this agreement.

B. The LANDLORD may terminate lease with a ten (10) day notice for any violation that the TENANT causes and given notice thereof.
C. SHOWING PROPERTY. With 24-hours' notice to the tenant, the LANDLORD may show the rental unit to anyone for purposes of rental or sale, or for any other lawful purpose. After either party gives notice terminating this agreement, LANDLORD will have the right to show the rental unit to prospective purchasers or renters, between 8am and 7pm on any day, without further notice.

VI. DEFAULT, EVICTION, AND ATTORNEY'S FEES
A. TENANT DEFAULT. TENANT will be in default if TENANT moves out before the end of this lease, including renewals, or if TENANT doesn't pay rent or other charges under this lease when due, or if TENANT violates any of the terms of this lease of the rules adopted pursuant to this lease.
B. EVICTION. If TENANT defaults, LANDLORD may evict TENANT by applicable Virginia law.
C. The TENANT is still responsible for rent, if TENANT moves from the unit before the end of this lease, or is evicted by LANDLORD because of TENANT default, TENANT will continue to owe rent until the end of this lease or the renting of the unit to others, whichever is earlier.
D. MOTION TO REHEAR. If the TENANT decides to play games with the court and ask for a Motion to Rehear and loses the case, the TENANT will pay the LANDLORD a $500 fee for time and effort and losses that he has incurred due to TENANT.
E. TENANT will still be responsible for all utilities, gas, electricity, water costs incurred after vacating these premises and will make the utility or LANDLORD whole for any and all charges. If the TENANT puts any utilities in another person's name without authorization of the LANDLORD, then the TENANT will be responsible to pay the LANDLORD a $500.00 fine for fraudulently obtaining utilities under false pretenses.

F. RE-RENTAL FEES. If TENANT moves from the unit without cause or because of eviction due to TENANT's default under this lease, LANDLORD will attempt to re-rent the unit. The reasonable costs of re-rental will be at TENANT's expense. LANDLORD may, in addition to all rents and costs due through the effective date of a new tenant's lease, charge TENANT the reasonable clerical costs of $100 for obtaining the rental, including a $100 processing fee and advertising expense required to re-rent the property.

G. ATTORNEY FEES. The TENANT agrees to pay any and all Attorney fees as outlined in a previous section, which is 25% of awarded costs, plus costs for interrogatories, filing fees, witnesses, warrants in debt, and the like, as well as any of the fees awarded to the TENANT by the court for their attorney on any cross claim action.

H. LANDLORD DEFAULT. If the LANDLORD does not provide services or repairs as required by law or under this lease, TENANT will notify LANDLORD in writing, not text message. If LANDLORD does not respond within 10 days, which is considered reasonable time from notice, then the TENANT has every right to put any and all rent into an escrow account with the court, so the court can decide the proper action (in accordance with law 55-248-25:1), and must inform LANDLORD with proper action through the District Court.

VII. CERTIFICATION, LIABILITY, AND WAIVER

A. APPLICATION TRUE AND CORRECT. TENANT certifies that all information and representations TENANT gave in the application and other forms are correct, and those forms and representation are incorporated into this lease. If there are any materials misstatements in such application or other forms which, if truthfully disclosed, would have resulted in LANDLORD refusing to rent to TENANT, they will be considered a non-remedial breach of this lease, and LANDLORD can terminate this lease on thirty (30) days' notice to the TENANT.

B. JOINT AND SEVERAL LIABILITY. TENANT, including all persons who sign this lease whether as TENANT, guarantor, or cosigner are responsible, together and individually, joint and several for all payments contracted in this lease and all other payments which TENANT might lawfully owe LANDLORD, and by signing this lease, they waive benefit of the Homestead Exemption as to the payment of these debts.

C. LANDLORD LIABILITY LIMITED. LANDLORD is not and will not be responsible for damages and injuries that TENANT causes to any person or property at anytime. TENANT hereby agrees to assume liability for and to hold harmless from any claims against LANDLORD for damages or losses that TENANT causes to any other person or property. In addition, LANDLORD is not responsible for any loss to TENANT's property, unless directly caused by LANDLORD. TENANT is required by this lease to carry rental insurance to insure TENANT's property.

VIII. MISCELLANEOUS PROVISIONS; GOVERNING LAW

A. RULES AND REGULATIONS. LANDLORD may adopt rules and regulations from time to time that affect all tenants equally and intend to promote the peaceful and beneficial use of the rental unit by all other tenants in the rental community. LANDLORD will give TENANT reasonable notice of any rules before they are in effect. TENANT agrees to comply with those rules, whether in effect now or after the date of this lease. If TENANT violates these rules, TENANT will be in default of lease.

B. EMINENT DOMAIN. In the case that governmental authority acquires the rental unit by eminent domain, this lease will automatically terminate upon the taking. If the rental unit is destroyed or substantially damaged by fire or other catastrophe, 55-248.24 of the Code of Virginia will apply.

C. SUBORDINATION OF LEASE TO MORTGAGES. TENANT agrees that this lease is subordinate to any mortgages, deed of trust, or liens that owners place on the rental unit, whether such mortgage, deed of trust, or lien is now against the rental unit or may be placed against the rental unit in the future. If the rental unit is foreclosed in enforcement of any such lien, the purchaser at foreclosure may terminate this lease.

D. GOVERNING LAW AND INTERPRETATION. This lease is to be governed, construed, and enforced according to the applicable laws of the Commonwealth of Virginia. If any provision is declared illegal by a tribunal of competent jurisdiction, only such provision shall be stricken from this lease and all remaining terms and provisions shall remain in full force and effect. Section and Paragraph headings are for convenience only and not part of the lease. This lease may be signed in multiple counterparts, and signatures on one copy might not be on others; the parties agree that all copies, however signed, constitute only one lease agreement.

E. MEGAN'S LAW DISCLOSURE. TENANT should exercise whatever due diligence TENANT deems necessary with respect to the information on any sexual offenders registered under Chapter 23, 19.2-387 et seq of title 19.2 Code of Virginia, whether LANDLORD precedes under subdivision 1 or 2 of subsection A of 55-519. Such information may be obtained by contacting your local police department or the Virginia State Police, Central Records Exchange.

F. CONDITIONS THAT MAY EXIST. In the event that all or a portion of the rental unit are below ground, that portion of the rental unit is subject to flooding during heavy rain and may be in a flood plain. There may be radon gas, fungus, or mold in the rental unit.

_____   _____
TENANT signature   LANDLORD/agent signature

_____   Macher Properties, LLC
TENANT name   RLPJ Properties, LLC
                                  Southside Equity, LLC

_____   _____
date   date

E. Memorandum of Option

On this date, the following parties entered into an agreement in which
_____
acquired an option to purchase an interest in property owned by
_____.

The property is described as:
_____ (address)
_____ (city, state, zip)

Legal Description: (Needs to be attached.)

1. The term of this agreement is TEN (10) years, running through midnight _____.

2. As part of this agreement, _____ agree(s) not to further encumber the property, nor sell any interest in the property during the term of this agreement. Any encumbrance placed on the property after this agreement is properly executed and recorded, including leases, will be subordinate to this agreement and will be extinguished by the proper execution of this contract.

3. This agreement will bind heirs, executors, administrators, successors, legal representatives, and assigns of each party to this agreement.

4. In the event of foreclosure, the owner's equity at the sale and any right of redemption shall transfer to the Optionee without further compensation and this contract shall serve as conveyance without further action.

Signed and sealed this _____ day of _____ 20____.

_____ _____
SELLER   BUYER

State of _____ County of _____

The foregoing instrument was acknowledged before me this _____ day of _____, 20_____.by _____, who is/are personally known to me or who has/have produced _____ as identification.

_____
Notary

My commission expires: _____

F. Phone Questions to Prescreen Tenants

My name is _____. To whom am I speaking? _____

1 How did you hear about my property?
   _____

2 What size rental are you looking for? How many people will be living in the property? (Note: Federal fair housing laws state that a rental should allow minimum of two people per bedroom, plus one.)
   _____

3 Is the monthly rent a price that will work for you?
   _____

4 What is your present occupation? Are the other applicants also employed
   _____

5 Where are you currently living?
   _____

6 Is there any particular reason you've decided to move?
   _____

7 When will you need to move in? Do you have a specific date
   _____

8 Do you have any pets? If so, what kinds and sizes? (Be sure to get some details about the pets and ask if they would be able to provide references for them.)
   _____

9 Are you comfortable that the first month's rent and the security deposit are due in full prior to moving in?
___

10 Have you driven by the property? (Always ask that the current residents not be disturbed.)
___

11 When can we meet? (Get full name and phone number of the person whom you will meet.)
___

G. Residential Rental Application

Name of Applicant _____ Telephone _____

Present Address _____

City, State, Zip Code _____

Social Security Number _____ Spouse's SSN _____

Credit Cards (issuer and acct #) _____

How many in your family?

Adults _____ Children _____ Pets? _____

Number of Occupants _____

How long have you been at your present address? _____

Present Landlord _____ Telephone _____

Prior Landlord _____ Telephone _____

Employer _____ Your Position _____

How long? _____ Contact _____ Telephone _____

Salary _____ Amount and Sources of additional income _____

Name of Bank _____

Checking account # _____ Savings account # _____

365

Additional Personal/Credit References

     Name   Relationship   Telephone

1. _____

2. _____

3. _____

I represent that the information provided in this application is true to the best of my knowledge. You are hereby authorized to verify my credit and employment references in connection with the processing of this application. I acknowledge receipt of a copy of this application.

_____ _____
Applicant   *Date*

H. Maintaining Your Rental Unit

We have provided you with a rental unit that is clean; everything is in working order, and it is pest free. Below are tips that will allow you to avoid costly fees from calling maintenance for issues that you are required to resolve. If you don't attempt to resolve these issues before calling maintenance, there will be a minimum $50.00 charge from maintenance. If you have attempted to fix the problem yourself according to the instructions below and were unable to resolve the issue, please call maintenance at _____.

Pest Control: As the Virginia Landlord Tenant Act states, tenants are responsible for pest control in their apartments; landlords are responsible for pest control only in shared areas. At the first sign of a cockroach, to prevent them from getting worse, immediately purchase a clear roach gel bait available at stores such as Wal-Mart, Target, Lowe's, or The Home Depot. Apply it according to the instructions on the package. These gel baits work much better than anything else but they may take some time. Reapply it every 2 weeks until you see no more cockroaches. If you let them live and breed, then they will get bad enough that you will be required to hire a pest control company, which can be expensive.

Stopped-Up Toilet: Before calling maintenance, please plunge the toilet; use a quality plunger with a very large head, allowing for the maximum amount of air to be pushed through the toilet. Small dollar-store plungers do not work well. We provided you with a toilet that is in working order. If you stop it up you will have to pay maintenance to have it unclogged. Try to unclog it yourself first to avoid fees. Be sure to never put anything other than toilet paper in the toilet. Tampons etc will stop up the lines.

Stopped-Up Bathtub: Bathtubs typically get clogged by hair, which is in an easy fix. In order to solve this problem purchase a product such as Drano from a retail store. Do not call maintenance unless you have tried hair-removal products at least 2 times.

Drain Leaking Under Sink: Leaks in the trap under the sink typically are a result of accidentally bumping into the pipe something that you are storing in the cabinet. To stop the leak, tighten the plastic or metal nuts that hold the pipes together under the sink.

Electrical Outlet Doesn't Work: If you have an electrical outlet that is not working, you need to first check your breaker to see if any of them are flipped before calling maintenance. Please also check the electrical panel outside to see if your power has been turned off by the power company. If it has a green tag, you're good. If it has no tag or a red tag, they shut off your power.

Light Doesn't Work: If your light doesn't work, the first thing you need to do is to replace the light bulb with a new one. If that doesn't resolve the issue, then check for flipped breakers; also make sure that the power company didn't turn your power off.

Power is not on: If your whole house doesn't have power, first check to see if the power company turned your power off. Second, check to see if other houses around you have power. If they don't, then call the power company rather than maintenance.

Noise from other tenants: If you are hearing too much noise from neighbors or other residents in the same house, please call the police (911). If it is happening on a regular basis the police will resolve the issue.

Picking Up Trash: The city picks up what they call bulk trash on one week and the next week they pick up brush. Call the city at _____ to inquire what the schedule is. You may not put out a pile of brush more than 4 feet wide by 4 feet tall by 4 feet long. Regarding bulk items, you may not put out more than 6 items every other week. That means 6 garbage bags that didn't fit in the trash can or 6 couches or 6 chairs etc. No more than 6 items. You must put these items out the night before the trash people come. If you put them out early there will be a fine. If the landlord receives the fine, you will be responsible for payment.

Appropriate Placement for the Trash Can: The city requires trash cans to be placed behind the "principal structure" of the house. They want you to bring it out at night and put it back behind the principal structure in the morning. It may not be put next to the porch. It needs to be placed next to the house. They do not consider the porch to be the principal structure. If the landlord gets fined for improper placement of your trash can you will be responsible for paying that fine.

Trash, Weeds, Grass: Code enforcement will fine properties that are not being maintained. The yard must be kept clean of trash that blows around the city. Even if it is not trash that you put there, you are required to pick it up. If you are responsible for mowing the yard, then you are required to keep it mowed; the grass must be kept shorter than 10 inches in length. If it gets longer, the city will mow it themselves and will send a bill for a few hundred dollars.

Outdoor Storage: The city puts fines on properties that have outdoor storage: items that are left outside and aren't being used on a regular basis. Things like porch chairs and tables etc are acceptable. They will give fines for items such as coolers being kept on the porch or a dresser or TV being stored out there until trash day. You need to keep these items inside your house until the day you throw it away or you will end up responsible for the fine.

Inoperable Vehicles: The city does not allow vehicles with expired tags or no tags or flat tires etc to be parked on the property. They call that an inoperable vehicle. If the landlord gets a fine for an inoperable vehicle on the property, you will be responsible for paying that fine. If the landlord gets a notice that there is an inoperable vehicle, landlord will begin to take the steps required to have the vehicle towed off the property and held in impound.

Locked Out: Please make sure that you give a copy of the key to your home to someone you can trust, so if you get locked out, you can get in and avoid the costs of calling maintenance to let you in.

Defective Appliances: As stated in your lease, appliances are not guaranteed to work. You are more than welcome to use any appliances that were in the property when it was rented to you. If any of your appliances become defective, you can either have the appliance repaired by a qualified appliance repair shop or you may be able to finance an appliance from your landlord. Contact your landlord to see if that is an option.

If any of these requirements are not followed, you will be charged the cost of the violation or maintenance call when maintenance arrives at your home.

I UNDERSTAND THE TERMS AND CONDITIONS OF RENTING THIS PROPERTY AND ENTERING INTO A LEASE, WITH EITHER "MACHER PROPERTIES LLC" OR "RLPJ PROPERTIES LLC." IT IS IMPORTANT THAT WE WORK TOGETHER IN A PARTNERSHIP BASED ON COMMUNCATION AND MAINTAINING THE PROPERTIE'S INTEGRITY. THANK YOU.

_____   _____
Management   Date

_____   _____
Tenant   Date

I. Lead Disclosure Statement For Leasing of Residential Property

Lead Warning Statement: Housing built before 1978 may contain lead-based paint. Lead from paint, paint chips, and dust can pose health hazards if not managed properly. Lead exposure is especially harmful to young children and pregnant women. Before renting pre-1978 housing, lessors must disclose the presence of known lead-based paint and/or lead-based paint hazards in the dwelling. Lessees must also receive a federally-approved pamphlet on lead poisoning prevention.

Lessor's Disclosure (initial)
(a) Presence of lead-based paint and/or lead-based paint hazards.
    (i) _____ Known lead-based paint and/or lead-based paint hazards are present in the housing (explain).
    (ii) _____ Lessor has no knowledge of lead-based paint and/or lead-based paint hazards in the housing.
(b) Records and reports available to the lessor (check (i) or (ii) below):
    (i) _____ Lessor has provided the lessee with all available records and reports pertaining to lead-based paint and/or lead-based paint hazards in the housing (list documents below).
    (ii) _____ Lessor has no reports or records pertaining to lead-based paint and/or lead-based paint hazards in the housing.

Lessee's Acknowledgement (initial)
(c) _____ Lessee has received copies of all information listed above.
(d) _____ Lessee has received the pamphlet "Protect Your Family from Lead in Your Home."
(e) Lessee has (check (i) or (ii) below):
    (i) _____ received a 10-day opportunity (or mutually agreed upon period) to conduct a risk assessment or inspection for the presence of lead-based paint and/or lead-based paint hazards; or

(ii) _____ waived the opportunity to conduct a risk assessment or inspection for the presence of lead-based paint and/or lead-based paint hazards.

Agent's Acknowledgement (initial)

(f) _____ Agent has informed the lessor of the lessor's obligations under 42 U.S.C. 4852d and is aware of his/her responsibility to ensure compliance.

Certification of Accuracy

The following parties have reviewed the information above and certify, to the best of their knowledge, that the information they have provided is true and accurate.

   Print Name   Sign   Date

Lessor _____

Lessee _____

Agent _____

J. Mold Addendum

Mold can create serious vulnerabilities and health problems for both tenants and guests of the rental property. While some mold grows in visible areas and can be easily detected and removed, other types are often hidden under floors or behind walls and are not easily thwarted. In order to inhibit the growth of mold on the property, Tenant agrees to the following terms and conditions in regard to maintenance and upkeep of the rental unit.

Failure to comply with any of the terms listed below will be considered a violation of the Rental Agreement and will be grounds for eviction. Furthermore, Tenant will be held liable for any damages resulting from failure to comply with these terms.

1. Tenant shall promptly report any water leaks to the owner or property manager.

2. Tenant shall not allow any accumulation of moisture or standing water to remain in the rental unit and will immediately remove, to the best of his ability, any such accumulations. Any accumulation of moisture or standing water that Tenant cannot reasonably remove by his own efforts shall promptly be reported to the owner or property manager.

3. Tenant shall be responsible for keeping the humidity of the rental unit at reasonable levels. Furthermore, Tenant shall report to the owner or property manager any indication of abnormal or excess humidity. Indications of excess humidity include buckling walls or ceilings, peeling or cracking paint, peeling wallpaper, excessive condensation on windows or walls, sweating pipes, as well as the malfunction of any heating, ventilation or air-conditioning system.

4. Tenant should be vigilant for any mold growth in the rental unit and should take care to inspect high humidity areas to ensure that mold

is not present. Such areas include carpets, bathroom and kitchen areas, hot-water heaters, air-conditioning lines, appliance hoses, showers, tubs, sinks, toilets, pipes under cabinet and sinks, garbage disposal systems, caulking around windows and doors, and wallpaper.

5. Tenant shall be responsible, to the best of his ability, for the removal of any visible and accessible mold growth in the rental unit. Any mold growth that Tenant cannot reasonably remove by his own efforts shall promptly be reported to the owner or property manager.

This addendum hereby becomes part of and is incorporated into the rental Agreement.

_____   _____
Tenant   Owner/Property Manager

_____   _____
date   date

K. 30-Day-Notice Acknowledgement

Tenant: _____

Date: _____

We understand that you have turned in your 30-day notice to vacate, which was served to us on _____, and that you will be out of the premises by _____. After you have vacated the premises and have returned all keys to us, the following steps must be taken to ensure that your security deposit is returned to you in a timely manner.

HOW TO LEAVE RESIDENCE
Upon vacating the premises, be sure to leave the residence, all appliances and surfaces, clean, empty, and neat, just as you found them when you moved in.

KEYS
On or before the schedule move-out date, you must return to our office all keys that pertain to the residence (for example, doors, storage, mailbox, etc.). Any items left or abandoned on the premises after your move-out will be removed and discarded at a cost to you.

MAINTENANCE ISSUES
Please inform us of any maintenance items that you are aware of in the residence (for example, non-functioning oven, stove, lights, fans, plumbing, and so on).

PRE-INSPECTION
Under state law, you may request to have a pre-inspection walkthrough up to two weeks prior to vacating the property. The request must be in writing and will be performed at a mutually agreeable appointment time during normal business hours.

FORWARDING ADDRESS AND PHONE NUMBER

This is very important. You must inform us of your new address and telephone number so we can forward your security deposit refund and any other correspondence to you.

It has been nice having you as our tenant, and we hope that we may be of service to you again in the future. Please feel free to call us with any questions that you might have. Thank you.

_____   _____
Landlord/Agent   *Date*

L. Ten-Day Notice----Lease Violation

TO: _____

ADDRESS: _____

_____

You are hereby notified that, in consequence of your default under the provision of the lease, specifically

1. _____

2. _____

3. _____

I have elected to terminate your lease in the premises with physical address

_____

And you are hereby notified to quit and deliver up possession of the property to me within 10 days of this date. You will be responsible for any damage, court action, and possible criminal action that may be taken if you do not deliver the premises **with keys** and properly cleaned as you received it.

_____   _____
Landlord   *Date*

PROOF OF SERVICE

I do hereby swear or affirm that a copy of this notice was served upon the talent of _____ who resides at _____

BY	POSTING ON THE DOOR	_____ (DATE)
	REGULAR MAIL	_____ (DATE)
	PROCESS SERVICE	_____ (DATE)

PERSON MAKING SERVICE _____

M. Five-Day Eviction Notice For Non-Payment of Rent

To: _____

_____

_____

NOTICE IS HEREBY GIVEN that you are in default in rental payment upon the premises located at _____, and you are hereby required either to pay the FULL AMOUNT currently due or to vacate the above premises within five (5) days of the service of this notice.

Balance Due	_____
Monthly Rent	_____
Late Fees	_____
Deposit	_____
TOTAL DUE	_____

You are further notified that unless payment is received on or before the expiration of five (5) days after service of this notice your lease of the premises will terminate and an Eviction will be filed with _____Court. Only FULL PAYMENT of the rent and late charges demanded in this notice will waive the landlord's right to terminate the lease under this notice.

NOTE: You may also be required to pay all fees and court costs incurred in such lawsuit, including attorney fees.

GIVEN this _____ day of _____ 20_____.

_____
owner/agent

N. Standard Vacating Checklist

The following responsibilities must be performed by the resident before the final checkout inspection, along with the charge for any item that is omitted.

1. General: The apartment must be thoroughly cleaned.
    - 1 BR: $50
    - 2 BR: $75
    - 3 BR: $100

2. Walls must be free of dirt, grease, and fingerprints. Bad marks or chipped plaster and paint from hard use or as the result of moving will be estimated accordingly.
    - 1 BR: $300
    - 2 BR: $400
    - 3 BR: $500
    - House: $800

3. Range, burners, broiler pans, oven, and hood must be cleaned well
    - burners: $50
    - broiler pan: $25
    - drip pans: $15

4. Refrigerator must be clean.
    - cleaning: $150
    - ice tray: $10
    - butter dish: $10
    - egg bucket: $10

5. Kitchen walls and cabinets must be free of grease. $150

6. Floors must be clean. $25 per room to clean; $300 per room to repaint

7. Carpet must be shampooed and vacuumed.

CHAPTER 24: RECORDKEEPING

- ▷ 1 BR: $150
- ▷ 2 BR: $175
- ▷ 3 BR: $200

8   Bathroom(s) must be thoroughly cleaned. $75 per bathroom

9   Damage to medicine cabinet, closet doors, appliances, fixtures, screens, drapery rods and glass should be repaired. Cost of labor and materials will be estimated.

10 Patios and balconies must be cleaned. $100 per patio

11 All trash must be removed. $75 per load of trash to dump

12 Return all keys. $100 to changed locks

13 Disconnect electrical power service with provider.

14 Light bulbs (all) are to be in working condition. Replacement is $3 per bulb.

Any damage, unusual wear and tear, and necessary cleaning are figured at $50 per hour for labor plus any material expenses.

We turned the unit over to you in good shape, and we thank you for your cooperation in doing the same.

_____

TENANT

CPSIA information can be obtained
at www.ICGtesting.com
Printed in the USA
FFOW03n1356150717
37683FF